A Design-Driven Guide for Entrepreneurs

A new wave of entrepreneurs is leading a global paradigm shift toward values-driven business. This book empowers you to challenge the status quo and create value through its unique and adaptive approach to venture-building by design.

Authored by a multidisciplinary team of practicing design strategists, business leaders, academics, and entrepreneurs, this hands-on guide models strategic design as a mindset for starting up: framing problems, applying methods, identifying opportunities, and creating pathways forward through futures and systems thinking. Carefully curated case studies of young impact-driven entrepreneurs along with resources, including action-based frameworks, diagrams, and templates for founders to replicate, and a reader's checklist to enable the transformation of daily practice, will open new dimensions that amplify the global shift toward a more regenerative world and a multiverse of possibilities.

Are you ready to journey to places where ideas for products, services, and experiences transform how we live and work? Then this guide is for you: the Design-Driven Entrepreneur.

Authors and Contributors

Rhea Alexander spearheads this project. She's a designer, innovation strategist, and educator, with expertise in interdisciplinary approaches to entrepreneurship and social impact. She's a full-time faculty member at Parsons School of Design Strategies and Founder and Director of the Parsons Entrepreneurs Lab (Parsons Elab). Prior, Rhea spent 25+ years as an award-winning designer and founder of D.I.G.S. Currently she is a board member of N.Y.C. Innovation Collective, and a co-founder of MakeOurFuture.coop.

Rose Pember is a builder by design. She is a co-founder of Manifesto and Hodge. She facilitates Cornell's Entrepreneurship Department, an Affiliate Faculty at Parsons Elab, and teaches part-time at Parsons School of Design.

Dr. Joseph Press is an architect by training, committed transformer, and a Futures Architect at Institute For The Future, where he recently co-authored *Office Shock: Creating Better Futures for Working and Living* (2023). He co-founded the IDeaLs research group and co-authored *Innovation, Design, and Leadership (IDeaLs): Transformation in the Digital Era* (2021).He is a co-founder of MakeOurFuture.coop and teaches at the Politecnico di Milano, Parsons School of Design, and the Parsons Elab.

Kiely Sweatt is a coach and innovation consultant specializing in transition management through experiential learning. She is a Director of Experience and Enablement for Oracle North America Applications Sales, on the board for The Poetry Society of NY, and a co-founder of The Wild. She's Adjunct Faculty at Parsons School of Design, the College of William and Mary, and an Affiliate Faculty with Parsons Elab.

"This book is a timely and important contribution to the next generation of design entrepreneurs. Being design-led with the nuances of context, social and environmental impact is a fundamental skill, and this book provides a wealth of practical tools, methods, and advice to help today's design entrepreneur accelerate their vision to impact."

Nina Terrey, Ph.D., *Co-Author of* Design for a Better Future: A Guide to Designing in Complex Systems *and Partner and Chief Sustainability and Equity Officer of ThinkPlace Global*

A Design-Driven Guide for Entrepreneurs

Strategies for Starting up in a Multiverse

Rhea Alexander

Rose Pember

Joseph Press

Kiely Sweatt

Routledge
Taylor & Francis Group

NEW YORK AND LONDON

Designed cover image: **© Danielle Lair Ferrari and Eshita Sharma**

First published 2023
by Routledge
605 Third Avenue, New York, NY 10158

and by Routledge
4 Park Square, Milton Park, Abingdon, Oxon, OX14 4RN

Routledge is an imprint of the Taylor & Francis Group, an informa business

ISBN: 978-1-032-12993-8 (hbk)
ISBN: 978-1-032-12994-5 (pbk)
ISBN: 978-1-003-22715-1 (ebk)

DOI: 10.4324/9781003227151

Typeset in Corbel
by KnowledgeWorks Global Ltd.

To the past, present, and future entrepreneurs of the world: may this book inspire you to evolve entrepreneurship with the discipline of design in the pursuit of a collective future.

To our families, we dedicate this work to our collective future.

Contents

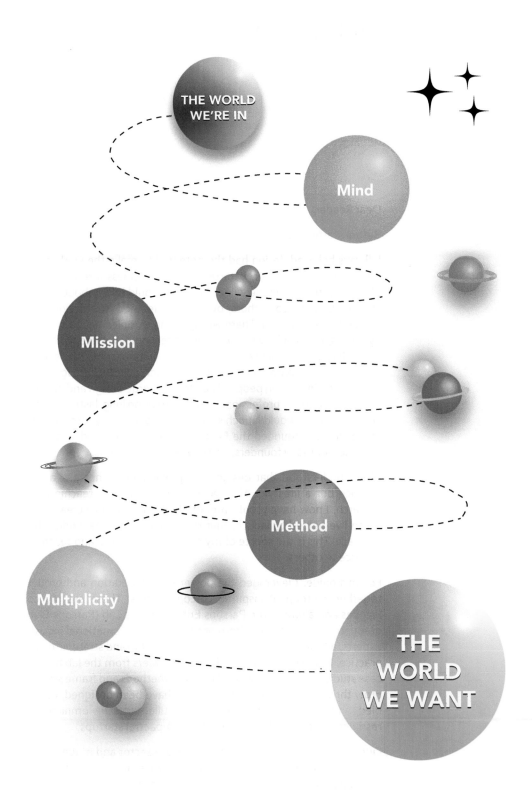

THE WORLD
WE'RE IN

Mind

Mission

Method

Multiplicity

THE
WORLD
WE WANT

Author's Note

Dear Reader,

Before starting, let me say welcome. I'm so happy you are here.

I always believed design had the potential to make the world a better place. As a designer, I started my first business a few years out of college, testing all the values I thought could bring about positive change. Like my co-authors, over time, I learned that design alone couldn't fix everything. There was growing complexity and systemic dynamics, especially with the onset of technology. I needed to better understand the new economic forces, cultural shifts, the societal realities of the context I was working in, and new technologies connecting and informing people. I needed to merge design and business innovation into my professional practice to bring long-lasting positive change. Later, I would launch several off-shoots of my first company and eventually founded the Parsons Elab, then cofound a cooperative, mentor many founders, and advise many startups.

I have understood that design entrepreneurship is not just a daily practice but a lifestyle. After 30+ years of practice, teaching, and research, I now have proof, through the businesses I've created and those I've helped to launch, that design can make the world a better place. This is the source of my motivation; to work and teach this practice to others.

For this guide, I leveraged the power of collaboration and brought together a group of inspiring co-conspirators. These are my colleagues and alumni from Parsons Entrepreneurs Lab (Parsons Elab), graduates and professors from programs, and international industry experts, all connected through entrepreneurship and strategic design practice. Inside this guide, you'll meet founders from the lab through case studies who also have applied these methods and frameworks to grow thriving businesses. The contents have been designed, assembled, and tested over the years and distilled into this omnichannel resource to help you build resilient and impactful startups.

Our values are simple yet powerful: we are sector and model agnostic; we accept the inevitability of change; we embrace inclusivity and diversity; and we passionately pursue the shared value of preferred futures. Our ethos stems from what the 21st century teaches us as the means to thrive in our volatile, uncertain, complex, and ambiguous (VUCA) world. A hyper-connected world through travel, technology, economies, environment, climate, commerce, communications, and disease. Whether it's epidemics, economic unrest, unforeseen technological impacts, human-initiated environmental disaster, social injustices, or their aftermath, it's important to think deeper and ask ourselves, *why*?

We think it's time to solve the world's most complex problems in an inclusive, systemic, and holistic way.

This guide and accompanying website have cases and tools to be used as a reference through each stage of your entrepreneurial journey and career. With an objective to design better businesses and communities, we look forward to continuing to learn with you and evolve our materials with growing feedback.

I look forward to hearing from you and sharing your contributions with our community.

Rhea

About the Authors and Contributors

Professor Rhea Alexander spearheads this book. She is an innovation strategist, educator, author, and entrepreneur with expertise in interdisciplinary design approaches to entrepreneurship and social impact. Rhea is a full-time professor who has served in leadership capacities for the graduate (M.S.) and undergraduate (B.B.A.) programs in Strategic Design and Management at Parsons School of Design. In addition, she is the founder and Director of the Parsons Entrepreneurs Lab (Parsons Elab). Prof. Alexander has taught and developed curricula and programs for graduate and undergraduate programs for 10+ years. In addition, she is a coach, investor, advisor, and mentor. Before Academia, Prof. Alexander spent over 25+ years as an international entrepreneur and consultant in the lifestyle and economic development sectors. She founded D.I.G.S. in 1991, a sustainable global lifestyle brand, won several design awards, sold to top international retailers, and was included in many international publications. Currently, Rhea sits on the working board of N.Y.C. Innovation Collective, a community of over 215 incubators and accelerators. She is also a co-founder of MakeOurFuture.coop, a global cooperative mobilizing a network of seasoned practitioners and academics empowering leaders in organizations to accelerate the transformation into more sustainable and meaningful futures.

Rose W. Pember is a designer and an educator authoring the future breadth of design impact. Rose co-founded a strategic design studio that designs + incubates ventures alongside consulting with organizational leaders looking to transform or innovate their offerings. Rose has worked on the ground in entrepreneurship her entire career. Including working as a Venture Associate guiding a portfolio of companies at the Parsons Elab, and teaching design thinking workshops for students, business workshops, and Hackathons for Cornell's entrepreneurship department. She's facilitated the launch of over 20+ funded companies through these events across industries like health tech, veterinary medicine, digital agriculture, sustainability, hospitality, and more—servicing and guiding between 500–1200 students annually. Before launching her studio, Rose worked as the third hire covering all engagement, consumer strategy, positioning, and platform design for an NSF-funded SAAS company, Comake. Rose received her M.S. in Strategic Design & Management in 2018, teaches part-time in the undergraduate B.B.A. program, and is an affiliate faculty to the Parsons Elab. In addition, Rose is the co-founder of Hodge, a commercial food waste recycling company started in 2021.

Dr. Joseph Press is an Adjunct Professor of Strategic Design at the Parsons School of Design and a Visiting Professor at Politecnico di Milano Schools of Management and Design. Joseph is also a Futures Advisor at the Institute For The Future, where he advises organizations in designing meaningful futures. His most recent book, Office Shock: Creating Better Futures for Working and Living, published in January 2023 by Berrett-Koehler Publishers. After a 10-year career as an architect, including completing his Master's in Architecture and Ph.D. in Design Technology at M.I.T., he pivoted into management consulting with Deloitte. Joseph capped his 15-year career by founding Deloitte Digital Switzerland, an interdisciplinary team focusing on the design of digital experiences for transformative innovation within cross-industry organizations. As the Global Innovator at the Center for Creative Leadership, he led programs to empower leaders to co-create solutions to challenges requiring systemic transformation. To deepen the understanding of innovation, design, and leadership, he co-founded IDeaLs at the Politecnico di Milano. The first book from this research lab, Innovation, Design and Leadership (IDeaLs): Transformation in the Digital Era was published by Emerald Publishing in 2021. The second book, Storymaking and Organizational Transformation, was published by Routledge in 2022. Joseph is currently an affiliate faculty to Parsons Elab. He is also a co-founder of MakeOurFuture.coop, a global cooperative mobilizing a network of seasoned practitioners and academics empowering leaders in organizations to accelerate the transformation into more sustainable and meaningful futures.

Kiely Sweatt has over 20+ years of experience in ed-tech, entrepreneurship, and instructional design. Her work focuses on bringing positive change to organizations through creative and innovative problem-solving methods and tools, spanning boutique agencies, startups, and numerous Fortune 100 and 500 companies. Kiely worked at Hyper Island, where she launched a founders program for designers, called 30 weeks, alongside Google Creative labs. In addition, she founded a nonprofit in Spain to support emerging artists. Her work abroad has been recognized in El Pais, El Mundo, Ryan Air, and The Guardian for her innovative approach to performance and the arts. She co-founded The Wild, an organization that facilitates connection, learning, and growth for individuals, teams, and organizations through unique experiences. She is the Director of Sales Strategy and Innovation at Oracle, North America Applications. Kiely is a part-time faculty at Parsons School of Design and an affiliate faculty with Parsons Elab and teaches Human-Centered Design part-time at the College of William and Mary.

Graphic Designers

Danielle Lair Ferrari graduated in 2022 from Parsons School of Design with a B.F.A. in Communication Design and a minor in Printmaking. Previously, she worked at Parsons Elab as a Graphic Design Research Assistant, spearheading the graphic design for this publication. Danielle is passionate about editorial, branding, and experiential graphic design. In addition, she works as a freelance designer.

Eshita Sharma was a Graphic Design Research Assistant at Parsons Elab before graduating in 2022 from Parsons School of Design, majoring in Strategic Design and Management with a minor in Communication Design.

ENTERING THE ENTREPRENEUR'S MULTIVERSE

An introduction to this guide

Welcome to the *Entrepreneur's Multiverse*! Look around: climate change, social injustice, economic inequality, pandemics, cyberterrorism, and threatening conflict. As a current or future entrepreneur, you're entering a complex world and a place of many possibilities.

Do you want to change anything? Whats driving your desire to make an impact?

After almost a decade with Parsons Elab and a lifetime of careers in design-driven innovation, we think the best way to describe the ever-evolving business environment is a *multiverse*. **Why?** Well, our lived reality is complex. Companies exist within this *multiverse* of dynamic influences, shaped by the market, customer desires and frustrations, revenue models, stakeholders, environmental conditions, and more. As a company owner or budding entrepreneur, you'll need a strong vision, resilient conviction, and a keen sense of self-awareness to navigate this galaxy and shape your opportunity. We believe with the breadth of brilliant minds, heightened desire for purpose, and collaborative interest, there is plenty of opportunity for positive impact. NASA confirmed that over 5,000 exoplanets exist beyond our solar system (Figure 0.1).

As a metaphor**, we consider *the potential for business creation as the untapped depths of the spatial systems beyond*.**

The multiverse metaphor throughout this book is grounded in cosmology, astrophysics, and world-building possibilities. We consider the potential for business creation as the untapped depths of the spatial systems beyond.

However, our current operating reality is VUCA: volatile, uncertain, complex, and ambiguous (Figure 0.2). Our environment has become as complicated as the theoretical models proposed by astrophysicists like Celia Escamilla-Rivera considering our systemic grand challenges. The social, economic, environmental, political, technological, and cultural systems collude to make problems

DOI: 10.4324/9781003227151-1

**Figure 0.1
NASA's James Webb
Space Telescope First
Deep Field (NIRCam
Image).**
Image credits: NASA,
ESA, CSA, STScI
Thousands of galaxies
flood this near-infrared
image of galaxy cluster
SMACS 0723, released
on July 12, 2022, 10:39
AM (EDT). The first deep
field image shows many
overlapping objects
at various distances,
including foreground
stars, galaxies in a galaxy
cluster, and distorted
background galaxies
behind the galaxy
cluster.

challenging, gritty, ominous, or difficult to conquer. As Horst Rittel
aptly named: just plain "wicked" (Rittel 1973, 155–169). By reframing our world through the lens of a multiverse, you, as a builder,
will be better prepared to face obstacles and use the diversity of
human lived experience (*our motivations, goals, our cultures!*) and
interdisciplinarity as tools for creating meaningful change. In addition, you'll be able to help others see the world's complexity and
dynamically locate yourself as your reality continues to evolve.

**Figure 0.2
VUCA: A military
acronym for volatile,
uncertain, complex,
and ambiguous.**

What opportunity can be born from the entrepreneur's galaxy? Technological shifts allow unprecedented reach for small businesses to compete with large organizations and have far-reaching impacts. Information distribution enables new transparency, and social platforms are amplifying new voices. These technologies, however, as democratizing as they can be, are also creating unprecedented negative impacts with lived consequences. For example, globalization has affected supply chains, climate change is eating away at infrastructure, and geopolitical problems arise from polarizing information.

We say: "out with the old, in with the imagined, the plausible, the possible and provocative!"

If anything is clear, it's that we can't face our complex world with old tools, mindsets, and methods. These are the ones that have led us to many challenges we currently face within broken and unjust systems. We need new pathways forward to provide clarity amidst the uncertainty. We must prepare for whatever lies ahead in that great frontier called the future. We are inspired by science fiction, gaming and reality-making, astrophysics, and the great beyond—because we all should be encouraged to imagine and play in many possible futures. If you feel excited by the potential, you have a guiding source of tools to shape your process and bring your ideas to this world.

But, be aware! Creating new forms of value takes time. This is the dilemma entrepreneurs face when seeking to innovate in a complex environment. Those embarking on the entrepreneurial journey now, particularly those innovators of a new generation, should know the road ahead will be uneven. While the current context may influence how you start, it does not have to define how you will get there. We encourage you to keep sight of your preferred future with resilience and perseverance. Suppose you intend to change your current situation into a preferred one. In that case, you are ready to innovate in the multiverse.

It's your world to build

Let's imagine you've entered a universe filled with planetary possibility and hope, like the one illustrated by Serwah Attafuah in Figure 0.3. Earth has evolved into a planet where the cultures are unbiased, the systems' regenerative, and net positive. In this world, there is little-to-no poverty; diversity, inclusion, and social justice awareness are universally accepted, and humans live in harmony with nature. War and disease are addressed in functioning global organizations, and the volatile adverse effects of climate change are reversing. In this preferred future, businesses naturally develop to include positive social impact and triple bottom-line values. You can envision a state of being where regulatory structures support and incentivize this value system.

In this state, people have functioning education and healthcare systems. Urban infrastructures across the globe, regardless of country,

**Figure 0.3
Creation of my
metaverse (between
this world and the
next) 2021, by Serwah
Attafuah.**

support one another. They communicate like trees, and their "wood-wide-web" is a superorganism (Giovannetti et al. 2006). Humans have evolved, living in symbiosis with nature and one another. They find harmony and stability within the systems built on open communication, deep empathy, awareness, and co-creation (Figure 0.3, An inspired vision by Serwah Attafuah).

Sounds better, right?

In real life, we're seeing the signals of an evolved world.

Although current pathways often appear to be extractive, destructive, and unbalanced, entrepreneurs imagine new ways to co-create more symbiotic worlds at the Parsons Elab Figure 0.4. In 2014, the School of Design Strategies (within Parsons School of Design, a

**Figure 0.4
Parsons Elab 2017
student administrative
and research team with
Prof. Alexander (left to
right: Victor Michud,
Adrianna Kruyt,
Rose Pember, Rhea
Alexander, and Vanya
Mittal).**

Figure 0.5
Parsons Elab 2019
team and fellows
in front of Parsons
School of Design
on Fifth Ave, NYC:
Jeff Lindor, Madison
Dailey, Rachel Doyon,
Christy Waldrop, Rhea
Alexander, Krista
Brown, Aditya Nair,
Kavitha Kothari,
and Sandeep Tupili
Andrapathy; front row:
Sasha Charlemagne,
Alexandra de Rienzo,
and Fulya Turkmenoglu.

subdivision of the New School University) partnered with the coworking community Centre for Social Innovation (CSI). In this exchange, Professor Alexander—lead author of this book—together with colleagues in and around Parsons, piloted a distributed lab with one foot in academia and the other in industry. The pilot offered a new, hybrid model of incubating startups. Rather than a "move fast and break things" pathway, the Parsons Entrepreneurial Lab (Elab) created a more holistic approach, including the time needed to cultivate community (Figures 0.4 and 0.5).

The result is a new generation of entrepreneurs who create interconnected and localized businesses across sectors that inform one another (Figure 0.5). Some of these businesses build networks that broadly share success and profits across employees, shareholders, *and* the communities they serve. Their mindsets are rooted in abundance rather than scarcity. They are nurturing their entrepreneurial spirit to co-create generative businesses with thoughtful impact. They are enabling an adjacent new economy that is more transparent and socially and environmentally conscious. Not a moment too late, the time has come for starting up in the multiverse.

Your guide to starting up in complex environments

Tested and iterated for over eight years, the Elab model has been co-creating with 77 entrepreneurs and 44 startups with over 55% female-identifying founders (as illustrated in Figure 0.6). This guide contains models and methods to help you build more holistic, adaptable, and resilient businesses. It should serve to shape your process and get real-world stories from emerging entrepreneurs, internal innovators, and seasoned transformers using design to build

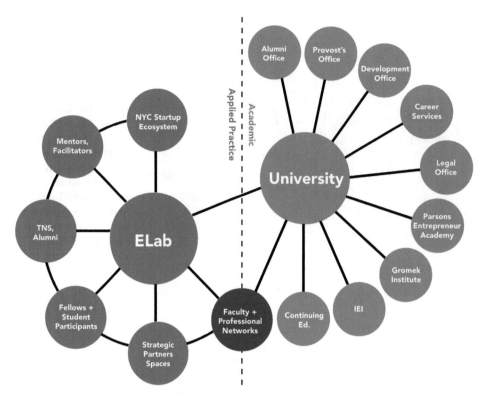

Figure 0.6 Parsons Elab ecosystem map.

companies. It's full of design-driven insights to help engage yourself and others toward co-creating more just and regeneratively inclined economies. It values humanity and the right to work with dignity. It will help you understand the types of business structures currently available to bring about the shift and introduce emerging ones that show promise. Finally, it offers suggestions to accelerate or decelerate, adjusting trajectories to drive venture creation thoughtfully, and provide entry points for cultivating communities with shared values.

The universal patterns and principles the cosmos uses to build stable, healthy, and sustainable systems throughout the real world can and must be used as a model for economic-system design.
- John Fullerton (Fullerton 2022)

Understanding the power of design to transform, our goal is to help you imagine new worlds, create, and grow new startups for generative value and beyond. To manifest change in a scalable and sustainable way, **we've broken this guide and the design-driven entrepreneurial process into four dimensions curating the design-entrepreneur's path to company longevity:**

MIND: Changing our mental models

The Mind sets the scene for design. This section outlines the design-driven approach and how to engage people (and yourself) to develop an openness to change, agility and flexibility, consciousness about bias, and a deep commitment to transition to a preferred future.

MISSION: Charting your course

A mission guides your launch. Here you clarify and chart your intention to change an existing situation into a preferred one. Begin with your values and mission to build a compelling trajectory into a future team and community culture.

METHOD: Practicing design as a path forward

Methods form the structure of the launch journey. This dimension provides design frameworks and tools with a guided process to kick-start your concept, engaging stakeholders to build your startup success long-term.

MULTIPLICITY: Cultivating collaboration for future-building

Multiplicity creates space for expansion into our preferred future. Here, you'll explore the engagement of a broader community with your initial vision through value creation, looking toward scenario planning, future-thinking, and organizational development.

We've designed this to be interactive and help you hone design-driven entrepreneurial skills. Each chapter describes methods and techniques used by designers with valuable insights and concrete lessons from seasoned entrepreneurs, practitioners, and academics. Insights are brought to life through their stories of entrepreneurialism from some of our Elab Fellows and community, which demonstrate the mindset when applying design strategies. This guide also contains bullet-point takeaways to help you use the content to your needs. The resources accompanying it are action-based, so you integrate these tools into your daily practices of building, creating, and growing your businesses.

A guided tour: The four dimensions of design-driven entrepreneurship

Let's take a tour of each dimension to map out your journey through the entrepreneur's multiverse as illustrated in:

Dimension A: Mind (*Who?*)

What areas of focus are the top priorities for you? How might you imagine them aligning across a team and community?

If you're an entrepreneur, you should lean into your role as a designer. The new generation of entrepreneurialism occurs in networks of social connections in real and virtual life. To innovate in this ever-evolving environment, you'll need to identify your old mental models and design preferred ones. Entrepreneurs must place their minds at the table and unpack the mind-body connection as a tool for building their company. Like a gamer or a virtual character, starting up in the multiverse requires an attentive, possibility-seeking mindset because there are many worlds to juggle and directions to be conscious of in the multiverse.

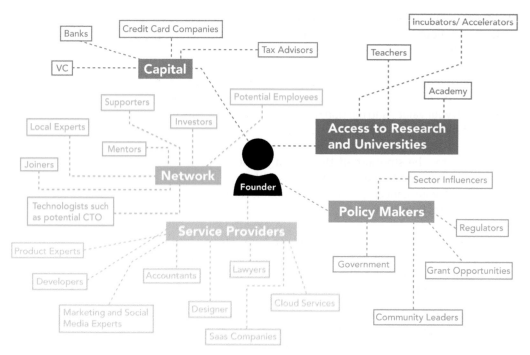

Figure 0.7 Good startup ecosystem.

The Mind Dimension shapes you as an actor equipped with a primer in strategy and Design to guide your startup journey with a strong mind and a ready approach. It's all about the individual, team, and community mindsets needed to grow a successful business in a VUCA world. It aims to help you find *where you are* by helping you discover *who you are* when starting up and sets the stage for you to clarify your mission. In the game of innovating in the multiverse, the designerly mindset accepts complex adaptive systems. It is responsive to the evolving challenges we face as the amplifier of design-led entrepreneurship. Embodying behaviors of gamers with an abundance-driven mindset enables the necessary type of exploration and creates the atmosphere for innovation to thrive.

Dimension B: **Mission** (*Why?*)

Write to yourself in the future about why you think your startup idea is good. What impact will you have? Where do you see yourself and your startup in 3, 5, or 10 years?

Why this, and why now? Because the call for innovation—to change our existing situations into preferred ones—is more critical than ever before. For many years, academics and practitioners alike have espoused the need for a shared view of the direction of change. For anyone involved in transformation, we know that initially, more ambiguity is better. Ambiguity allows for designing the details, and co-creation catalyzes collective change.

We consider this part of the *purpose* organizations must-have. Therefore, we encourage shifting away from exploitative mental models when corporations were expected to be siloed fortresses working in isolation, exploiting, and extracting limitlessly from nature for efficiency and shareholder primacy. The New School was founded to create a better world. At the Parsons Elab, we live by that ethos, imagining businesses as complex adaptive systems. Together with our greater community, partners, funders, and stakeholders we contribute to the transition toward more sustainable and equitable futures for communities and our planet.

Since its inception, Elab's mission has been business model-agnostic. We aspire to be the place that allows new value creators and creations to be born. Likewise, we've refrained from focusing on a single specific sector to encourage and inspire the integration of new technologies into the concepts developed at the lab.

Our Parsons Elab Fellows all have one thing in common: a clear mission. They're purpose-driven, design-led entrepreneurs seeking to contribute to many of the United Nations Sustainable Development Goals (SDGs) with their products and services. SDGs are like navigational stars, visible yet undefined. Indeed, the broad nature of an SDG is the perfect place to stake out your intentions to contribute to a better future. **The Mission Dimension** encourages developing a mission to guide your purpose-driven startup with core principles of social, economic, and environmental justice. We will share more about missions and how to use them as navigational stars for your startup. With a meaningful mission you've set out time to articulate and map, your company will stand with endurance and resilience. Here you can shape your world and the rules we all play by, making for more informed, bottom-up decisions that require multi-stakeholder consideration.

Dimension C: Method (*How?*)

Where might design guide you to? How might design methods shape your effective, viable, and desirable offering?

Over many years of experience, we have witnessed that where innovation is distributed and democratic, rather than centralized, hidden, and controlled—Design becomes, and is, the catalyst for change. Design enables innovation, sparking the new modalities the world desperately needs. Working collaboratively, we can step into these emerging states by *strategically designing* new futures, one business at a time. Potential entrepreneurs, game-changers, and disruptors are mobilizing to create preferred futures characterized by good ideas and technology, with inclusion, equity, trust, justice, and systemic impact. This is where you will want to join in and play, connect, and gain insight.

Design is more than a tool: it is your raison d'etre—the reason for existing—in an entrepreneur's universe. It powers the entrepreneur's energy to maintain resilience while innovating in an ever-evolving world. While your conditions may never remain (or ever be!) ideal, Design accentuates attentive and intentional ingenuity. Design empowers the creation of new, adaptive, resilient systems that respond to incessant shifts and changes. Design thrives on inclusion because creative conflict is the only way to overcome the shortcomings of shareholder primacy on the road to shared value. **The Method Dimension** shares the tools and practices of design strategies. This section shares the ways to cultivate change rather than impose it as a social process of change. It will create guardrails for systematic creativity and enable your concept validation before you launch.

Dimension D: Multiplicity (*What?*)

Imagine five years out, your business is thriving, your team is in the double digits, and your community is in the six digits; what empowerment tools do you think might help create that positive atmosphere?

According to astrophysicist Neil deGrasse Tyson, three elements make up the universe: Normal Matter (5%), what we see, Dark Matter (27%), what we can't see, and Dark Energy (68%), something we can't see that's keeping everything together by accelerating the expansion of space. He describes this counterintuitive notion of dark energy as a "placeholder term" to describe the mysterious pressure in space that acts opposite the force of gravity and causes the universe to expand.

As illustrated in Figure 0.7, startup ecosystems are growing worldwide, in almost every country, on academic campuses, inside organizations, and in many developing societies. This growth occurs through organizations and includes incubators, accelerators, coworking communities, tech alleys and valleys, refugee camps, government business development and trade commissions, venture capital associations, and more.

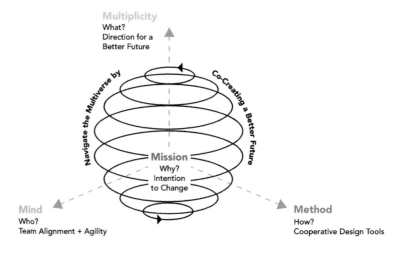

Figure 0.8 Design-driven transformation.

What is keeping all these relationships together? Our placeholder term is Design, a social process of imagining, making, and evolving an existing situation into a preferred one. Multiplicity is what holds us together as a growing organization in the future.

We learn in the Dimension of the *Mind* that entrepreneurial Design requires noticing relationships between players and within markets. Within the *Mission dimension*, a clear shared vision, sharpening culture, and the *Method* dimension, we're sewing these observations into a new system: a beautiful new venture authentically servicing these players and enacting a goal together. Design asks for thinking *across multiple dimensions*. Using strategic foresight and speculative Design, entrepreneurs build companies as living-breathing organizations that will endure with resilience. **The Multiplicity Dimension** leverages design methods to develop your business and its ecosystem into the future. Next-generation entrepreneurs are building a movement through understanding their relationship to needs in the present and into the future.

Entering the entrepreneur's universe and embarking on a design-driven transformation *(Figure 0.8) Design-driven transformation* can be lonely and overwhelming. You will want partners along the way to help overcome your blind spots and keep you seeing the light through the darker times. Partners will be there to celebrate after the conflicts are resolved and co-create new worlds in ways, we can't envision by ourselves. Along the journey to a better future, we will need to break down the barrier between public and private. Mariana Mazzucato (Mazzucato 2021) describes the backstory of Silicon Valley as a story of public/private collaboration. Contrary to the common myth of innovation as the output of private individuals, she shows that it results from the entrepreneurs' ecosystem.

Indeed, working together has never been more urgent. Innovating in the multiverse requires us to do what R. Buckminster Fuller asked us all to do in his classic *Operating Manual for Spaceship Earth:* "Go to work, and above all cooperate." (Fuller and Snyder 1969) Design-Driven Transformation, helps guide your success as it depends on others' success through organizational leadership charting various future scenarios.

Inspiring the next manual

We want to share what's worked for us because we believe it can help others create value across their ecosystems (human and non-human) and the environment. Some challenges are complex but well understood, and the path forward is clear. Others are unclear and mystifyingly complex. Our world is no longer one of the simple problems. Even small changes ripple throughout larger physical, psychological, social, cultural, technological, and economic systems. When the past is a poor predictor of the future, you will need tools that help discover the unforeseen. A successful startup will need to respond flexibly to change and disruption. They must also be creative, resilient, and collaborative to entertain multiple novel and conflicting viewpoints.

In the business innovation process, the designer is a facilitator, not just a creator. Emphasis is on building agreement across diverse team members and stakeholders rather than controlling decision-making. Creating the conditions for authentic user experiences in this technology-driven world requires working *with* rather than *for* people. Under these conditions, planning, facilitation, and research take on greater significance as essential design skills. Practicing interdisciplinary collaboration will cultivate mutual benefit for all members of the multiverse.

As authors, we are constantly inspired and informed by the many brilliant people working across various disciplines. The collective intelligence we are privileged to be immersed in includes Donella Meadows's thought leadership on systems thinking; Peter Senge's work around learning organizations; Harold G. Nelson and Erik Stolterman's exploration of what the design way means; Katrin Kaufer and Otto Scharmer's expansive theories about Presencing and ecosystem economies; Kate Raworth's Doughnut Economics; Florian Lüdeke-Freund and the folks over at sustainablebusinessmodel.org; Futurist Ray Kurzweil; Anand Giridharadas's societal provocations as a writer, journalist, and thought leader; Darren Walker, reimagining philanthropy; Kat Holmes sending signal flares up about bias in the Design; Tristan Harris on ethics in technology; Mabel O. Wilson's studies of racism and exclusion in constructed environments; Christina Figueres's impassioned work on diplomacy around climate change and policy; Robert Reich's economic provocations; Pierre Teilhard de Chardin and Vernadsky's theories on the Noosphere; Paul Hawken, Amory and Hunter Lovins' work around Natural Capitalism; Dr. Wolfgang Leidholdt's work on the Next Experiential Turn; Cosmologists and Astrophysicists like Neil deGrasse Tyson Steven Hawkings, Brian Greene, Natalie Batalha and Lisa Randall's work about Dark Matter and Extra Dimensions; Jill Tarter's work on SETI; Maria Popova, the author and multi-disciplinarian; sci-fi authors like Ray Bradbury, Isaac Asimov, Octavia E. Butler, Joanna Russ, Ursula K. LeGuin, and Phillip K. Dick; illustrators like Sid Mead, and many others who have contemplated similar, yet from different points of view. All have helped to inspire and inform our work to develop new forms of value in design entrepreneurship and business innovation.

In 1966, Barbara Ward wrote *Spaceship Earth* (Ward 1966), which prompted the United Nations to integrate social and environmental issues. Three years later, Buckminster Fuller wrote the Operating *Manual for Spaceship Earth*. He strengthened the metaphor for a new ideal of planetary management. Although Earth did not come with instructions, our spaceship's built-in safety features kept us going. However, our pilot errors were catching up with us. He called on designers to make the best use of our incredible ingenuity to rediscover how our spaceship worked. If we succeed, we might become "comprehensively and sustainably successful" (Fuller and Snyder 1969, 138).

Your Operating Manual

We recommend you use this book like a logbook to document your journey. Take this moment to share with yourself and others on your journey:

- *What destination do you want to arrive at?*
- *What do you need to know to arrive at your destination?*
- *What's the future you envision with your company concept?*
- *What does success look like for you?*
- *What design practices can help you accelerate your trajectory?*
- *What mindset do you need to maintain clarity while avoiding certainty?*

With these reflections, you will acclimate to *working* with and applying the practical tools in this guide and kick off your learning process. It should also remind you why you've landed here, how you will journal your learning, what impact you hope to have, and how your mission will create a better future.

Although there is an implied sequence describing the entrepreneur's journey, never forget that it is more iterative and cyclical than any description you may see. Expect to revisit each Dimension's content as needed to gain more confidence in your capabilities and strengthen your mindset. Both are essential to staying on pace with the rapid changes we now face in the global networked economy.

Every aspect of our lives is mediated by science and technology. Our most significant threats, from climate change to nuclear war to the unintentional effects of AI and automation, all stem from science and technology. Our greatest expressions of hope, from medical advances to space exploration to green technologies, also arise from science. Today, science can't be separated from culture: for better or for worse, their symbiotic relationship drives forward the frontiers of arts and politics. Threats and opportunities abound in the multiverse. Be sure to keep your radical optimism—always look for the good in every part of life and every interaction. With reason and evidence, this most important mindset will empower you to do as the authors of the 2015 Paris Climate Accords encouraged us all, to "embrace a strong vision of a better future" from Christiana Figueres, Tom Rivett-Carnac *The Future We Choose the Stubborn Optimist's Guide to the Climate Crisis*. (Figueres et al. 2021, 101).

Our ultimate goal is for this book to be a catalyst for cultivating a community of like-minded people. People who seek a better future see Design as a vehicle. We want to contribute to the conversation and accelerate the collective leadership required to navigate the multiverse toward a better future for all.

So if you're ready, fasten your seatbelt. This endeavor is going to be a great ride.

Dimension A

Mind

Design-driven change for mindset shift

Everything starts with the mindset. Our minds—as founders, leaders, and team members—define how we see and interact with the world around us. In this section, we outline the design-driven approach and what strategic design looks like for entrepreneurship. We'll name and practice what a designerly mind requires by reflecting on what you know (and where you are) and then practicing getting comfortable with ambiguity to change mental models for a preferred future. This sets the scene for effectively launching your company with culture from day 1 (mission and vision) and how to carry this influence with your stakeholders into your greater ecosystem (journey).

DOI: 10.4324/9781003227151-2

1

INSPIRATION FOR THE NEXT-GEN ENTREPRENEUR

Why design-driven, here and now?

Objectives

* Understand what strategic design (and design-driven approach!) entails
* Lead with the mind to build for a volatile, uncertain, complex, and ambiguous (VUCA) world
* Understand how design strategies positively contribute to starting up

We realize you may be at different points in your entrepreneurial journey, you may be new to joining this space, or you may be a life-long entrepreneur. Regardless of your position, we welcome you to the launchpad grounding this design-driven book: strategy and design. A primer on the two provides the groundwork for design-driven strategies geared to help striving entrepreneurs build effectively and with impact. **At core, the design-driven entrepreneurial process is the mind.** It allows for ways to engage people (and yourself) to develop an openness to change, agility/flexibility, consciousness about bias, and a deep level of commitment to transition to a preferred future. To grow a business in a VUCA world, we introduce design and strategy as integral parts of cultivating our minds.

Why strategy, why design, why mind

Whether you're a leader in a company or a blossoming entrepreneur in the field, your objective to create businesses, products, or services will benefit from a systemic and long-term perspective. This is the basis of *strategic* decision-making: a consideration (and awareness!) of a future that's identifiable but beyond our current time horizon. The origins of strategy came from battles where maps of battlefields and actual little lead pieces, often on large boards, were used to plot out maneuvers and plan ahead. Using these simulated prototypes, individuals were able to play out future scenarios and plot out the next steps for their armies.

DOI: 10.4324/9781003227151-3

We talk about strategy throughout this book because it's crucial to the *intentional* impact portion of innovation and how to make decisions to arrive there. Today, the challenges we're facing have reached a new level of complexity and uncertainty. People who can recognize these problems as part of complex environments—and lean into complexity—can exercise more influence on how solutions perform. Thinking strategically about solving complex problems involves setting the problem within its scope of influences and intervening to then influence how that situation should be changed.

A primer on design (*plus futures!*)

Here, strategy meets design. Designers create things within systems: service touch points within the healthcare system, products for the transportation system, graphics that communicate information or concepts, spaces for workplace systems, and even ergonomic chairs for the human body system. Designers have a broad range of mechanisms to trigger change by creating diverse products, services, experiences, or offerings.

Richard Buchanan's seminal paper *Wicked Problems in Design Thinking* proposes four orders, or "orbits," of design (Buchanan 1992)—and we build on his early appointed orbits with the more macro, strategic extension into the future to call out the prospective impact of today's scope of challenges (Figure 1.1).

Your understanding of design is likely rooted within the first three orbits. The first orbit is rooted in Data and Communication, primarily *words* and *images—traditional, 2-dimensional elements of appearance, perception, and sight—like color and spacing.* The second orbit contains Objects, Artifacts, and Products, where design is concerned with the 3-dimensional form and feel of everyday objects. In a digital world, this appearance is significantly informed by its first orbit, data. The third orbit encompasses Technologies, Interaction, and Experiences—informing not just the visual appearance of these but the experience of them. The fourth orbit is Systems and Environments; design in this orbit focuses on "sustaining, developing, and integrating human beings into broader ecological and cultural environments, shaping these environments when desirable and possible or adapting to them when necessary" (Buchanan 1992, 5–21). As we move from the first ring outward, we're zooming out: expanding the scope of designerly impact. Because each level has increasing degrees of abstraction and complexity, we see decreasing degrees of shared meaning. The power of the future to bring people together is due to the high level of abstraction and complexity. Abstraction gives space for stakeholders to create their own meaning, and complexity provides an extensive palette.

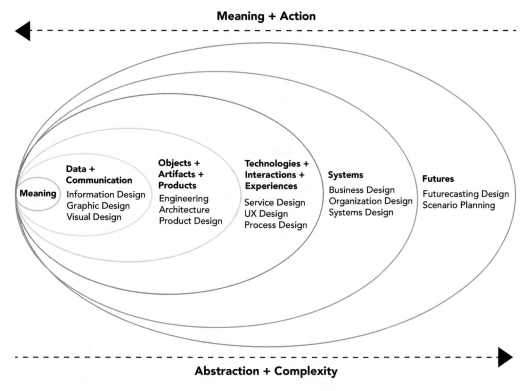

Meaning + Action

Meaning

Data + Communication
Information Design
Graphic Design
Visual Design

Objects + Artifacts + Products
Engineering
Architecture
Product Design

Technologies + Interactions + Experiences
Service Design
UX Design
Process Design

Systems
Business Design
Organization Design
Systems Design

Futures
Futurecasting Design
Scenario Planning

Abstraction + Complexity

Figure 1.1 Design orbits: Inspired by Buchanan, this graphic shows the different layers of design and different design disciplines within each orbit encompassing design strategies.

We add *Futures* as a fifth orbit because images of the future can set the mental model that influences all other design activities: that we are in fact intending to design impact in a future state that may not yet exist. This is our multiverse—leaning into the complexity of what could be with eager optimism to create it.

Strategic thinking + design making = Strategic design

Remixing methods and tools for impact is an essential catalyst of strategic design to empower the entrepreneur in a multiverse-like environment. For design methods to empower you to create positive outcomes for people, organizations, and the environment, thinking strategically is not enough. You will also want to act strategically. Applied appropriately, strategic design can influence strategic decision-making in organizations, define a business model, shape a corporate vision, identify new business opportunities, and create interventions (through strategy, products, services, or policies).

Traditional definitions of design remain focused on creating discrete solutions—a product, a building, or a service (within the second, third, or fourth orbit). In these practices, designers are often relegated to siloed positions with discrete tasks that revolve around these products and services, shaping color, form, and spacing. Although those roles still exist within design disciplines today, the scope of design has expanded to become more holistic, and organizations are implementing design principles in their corporate philosophy that guides their entire organization.

Design at large offers a practice and mindset to empower people to work across a variety of disciplines and to integrate the different worldviews of those people co-creating closely as a team. When designing strategically—across all five orbits—the practices of traditional design offer a more holistic approach to how problems are defined. The opportunities for solving the problems are inherently broader than discrete solutions—be it a product, a building, or a service. Strategic design often builds systems through which others can create their own experiences. The interventions should also be catalysts for changing the existing situation into a better one. With strategic design, you can confidently allow new ways of being, operating, systems, and services to flourish because you and those you work with (and serve) have a broader paradigm to work within over time. It's a creative and adaptive approach to problem-setting (identification) and problem-solving (lasting solutions) in order to create something useful and meaningful.

Good design can turn curiosity into ideas and eventually into actions for change. Echoing the proposition of Donald Schön that design is a reflective conversation with materials (Schön and Rein 1994), we see the nuclear core of strategic design as iterating with stakeholders between intentions and research.

The strategic design viewfinder (Figure 1.2) is framed by a dialogue between problems and ongoing solutions. We see the different strategies of design, and different design disciplines, as part of an iterative process for creating sustainable businesses. Each informs the other, as the interplay between knowledge from design research and design aspirations informs *design iteration*.

Figure 1.2
Designing strategically is leveraging perspective.

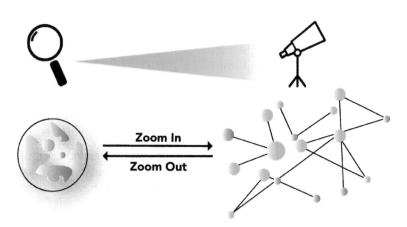

Zoom In

Zoom Out

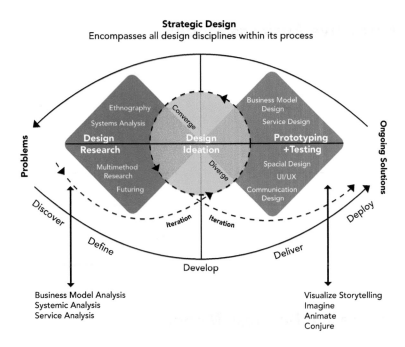

Figure 1.3
Design in the mind's eye.

The design of business: Creating new business models

Good design (*thus, good iteration on our creation*) is centered in the person, a union of mind, heart, and body (figure 1.3). Curating design as a practitioner means building mental acuity for empathy, strategy, logic, rationalization, and creativity. When we allow an understanding of design to settle from top-level "grasping"—of the methods, of the practice, and of the customs—to a more internal level of "intuiting," we expand the scope of what can be designed.

This is the distinction we notice between design as a specification of aesthetics and construction and the designer as the yielding, high-potential creative. Strategic designers partake in creating new forms of value. We can see that this holistic value creation can take many forms; one of the implicit ways is through creating new business models that better align with and represent current and future societal needs. Leveraging design methods and mindsets combined with innovations in technology and science allow us to effectively meet societal needs. This convergence within innovation in business has been led by designers for over a decade. Design-entrepreneurship capitalizes on these practices to bring about company building oriented around outcomes.

We purport this transition from extractive linear entrepreneurship—which benefits a limited number of shareholders often at a cost—to generative, circular, regenerative, or expansive entrepreneurship that will holistically benefit stakeholders and take into consideration the impact its direction will have (Figure 1.4). Many thinkers across disciplines have contemplated more heightened awareness and compassionate

Extractive Business Models

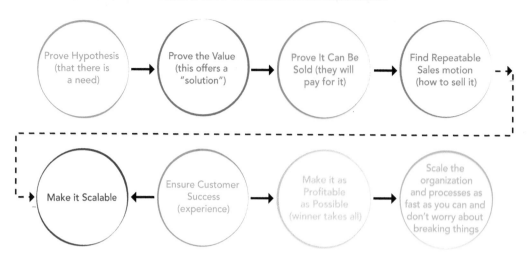

Generative Business Models

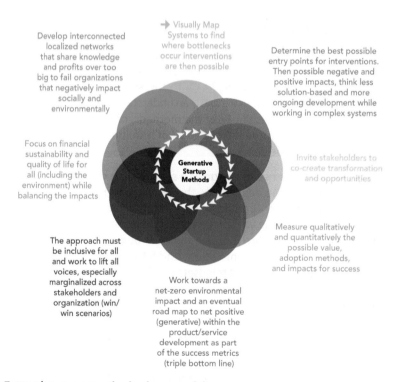

Figure 1.4 Extractive vs. generative business models.

systems: of empathetic and just societies, collaboration instead of competition, and what all of this might look like in capitalistic democracies. We are observing that the exploitative business practices of the past are not serving us universally or we're bystanders to detrimental impact. This has created space for new models built with generative values that are flourishing and growing literature around why shareholder primacy is being replaced with stakeholder equity. Today's consumers seek out brands that align with their values and adopt a new way of being. When companies are purpose-driven and have a clear mission that authentically represents their ethos and culture, they outperform older models. We see an example of this in Sarah Jones, ELab Fellow and founder, whose mindset led her to seek out a new way of doing as a design-informed company.

The designerly mind: Infusing generative company building from the core

Meet Sarah! Sarah founded Parkinson & Movement Disorder Alliance—PMD Alliance (PMDA)—in 2012. PMDA is a design-informed nonprofit organization in the healthcare space that offers opportunities for people impacted by Parkinson's and other movement disorders to learn, live more fully, and connect to a support community by including the often-neglected spouse or loved one that is the primary caregiver, support group leaders, and adult children. Through an inclusive and human-centered design approach, PMDA fills a gap in the American healthcare system by addressing the needs of caregivers and providing critical opportunities for connection, support, and community.

Their business model is a nonprofit service *and network.* With a clear mission from the get-go recognizing the detrimental effects of Parkinson's not just impacting the diagnosed, but the various stakeholders around them, Sarah's holistic vision of impact was inclusive and required an approach distinct from standard trajectory of healthcare and nonprofits. Facilitating workshops and meetups for the groups they serve, PMDA offers not only an opportunity to connect with others in similar situations but also an opportunity to learn management tools and coping mechanisms to help them better manage their responsibilities and quality of life. They also offer emotional support opportunities for self-care for caregivers, an often neglected group that suffers alongside the afflicted.

How does a nonprofit service symptoms that are hyperlocal, and create hyper-individual impact, yet adopt expansive growth? PMDA's staff is distributed, with team members operating from different parts of the country who travel to other parts of the United States to help support what PMDA calls activation hubs (Figure 1.5). They also offer virtual workshops because members have difficulty commuting, and accessibility is core to their success. Building and maintaining a shared mindset together as a whole were essential for the success of Sarah's vision. Her design work cultivating an open and learning

**Figure 1.5
PMDA in-person
event: Core
programming.**

mindset—by means of a design-driven approach—was essential to launching PMDA that could cultivate a community of caregivers.

Mental models for accomplishing a mission

The approach of PMDA and its focus on the underlying mental models and emotional competencies exemplify utilizing mindset to embed and affect the driving mission. With staff all trained *outside* the design field in backgrounds like healthcare, team members enter with high comfort around rules, and familiarity with approaches grounded in didactic, *nonhuman-centered* methods—typically framed in the language of "best practices."

On the ground, her team members need to be adaptive, quick-footed, and emotionally available to hear unmet needs. For Sarah's driving metric to create community and value for all stakeholders, her iterative approach is distinct from the expected operating model. Her employees in turn must be able to operate within uncertainty and ambiguity as they continually test, learn, assess the impact, and try again to improve. This is a design-driven approach to homing in on her distinctive value created, and she embeds this required mindset into her hiring process (and culture!).

PMDA's onboarding process inoculates members with a designerly mindset to achieve the goal of facilitating a conference, with the goal of having new team members able to facilitate a conference within 4–6 months of joining. Through this hiring and onboarding process (Figure 1.6), they help facilitate the development of designerly competencies and establish scaffolding to build comfort around the design process in order to embed design-driven innovation throughout their organization.

Pre-Hire
Three interviews & mindsetting exercise

Hire & Onboarding
Values assignment and position specific exercise

Immersive Learning
Learning design research skills and tools
Learning empathy exercises
Analogous research exercise

Assessment & Research Log
Systems understanding of the interdependencies

Facilitate Conference
First conference facilitation

Figure 1.6
PMDA's road map for onboarding.

Potential employees are screened and interviewed. They are also assessed on their ability to complete values-based and position-based exercises in the second round and an interactive project brief in the third round. These tests are not just about *competency* but more as a way of assessing potential employees' openness to risk-taking, capacity to engage in vulnerable work, and emphatically engage with PMDA members. An example project brief could be positioning a new artifact to help support a member or simulated communications with members. These soft skill assessments are PMDA's way of understanding if there is a good culture fit and also if there is potential to develop a designerly approach of incremental creation and testing within non-trained designers to satisfy PMDA's distributed network model.

Individual minds as part of growing an ecosystem

PMDA's approach points to the integral power of acknowledging individual mind as critical to successful community building and culture. An artifact utilized in their onboarding process is their ecosystem map (Figure 1.7), which offers a systems-level understanding of the interdependencies within the lives of those impacted by Parkinson's within the broader medical system. This map is used as an anchor for staff and members as a means of "knowledge transfer during the onboarding process." Formally, the map learning takes place over a 2-week process, with once-per-day lessons and introductions to the variety of tools and operational practices of the organization (Alexander 2019, 1552).

The ecosystem supports everyone at PMDA to be responsible for their own development, their learning mindset, and the development of those around them, the learning culture. As a startup and ever-growing organization, how they scale this practice and impart the mindset development is the key to their success.

Figure 1.7 PMDA support ecosystem map.

The mindset to grow a successful business in a VUCA world

This profound shift in mindset to purport (and demonstrate) *a different way to build* is about renewal, regeneration, and rebirth. Mental models, frameworks, and images define who we are and where we go. In this world of constant surprises from unforeseen volatility, we tend to focus on what we can grasp onto. We hold onto it for dear life, like a lifeboat in a sea of turbulence. Scarcity becomes the dominant mindset to survive. It's no wonder that when resources are limited, managers hoard information, micromanagement abounds, and, generally, short-term thinking is the norm. A scarcity mentality is what keeps many of us from achieving our goals, while an abundance mindset refers to the acceptance of creation (Figure 1.8): "An abundance mindset means taking a risk ... [it's] positive, optimistic—you believe there are enough resources out there for everyone" (Swart 2019).

Scarcity   Abundance

 Goals are just to fix problems. They require hard work, take a long time and motivation quickly wanes.

 Goals are simply add-ons to an already fortunate life. The possibilities are endless, and motivation is effortless.

 There is only so much to 'go around' mindset; leading to greed, jealousy and skepticism.

 There is more than enough resources to 'go around'; leading to sharing, openness and encouraging others.

 Focuses on what is lacking in their life and get stuck there.

 Looks at their life through a lens of gratitude, positively impacting everything they think, feel, say and do.

 Focus on things outside of their control, leading to worry, fear, stress and inaction.

 Focus on what is within their control, leading to inspired action, calm and confidence.

 Focuses on the limitations of a situation, quick to point out the negatives.

 Focuses on the opportunities of a situation, seeing the potential for growth and improvement.

Figure 1.8 Scarcity mindset vs. abundance mindset.

As Dr. Tara Swart, a neuroscientist at MIT, explains, "there's a balance, or you could even say a struggle, in our brains between abundance and scarcity all the time." An abundance mindset doesn't come easy for anyone and takes work. Nor should you feel like negative life circumstances are somehow your fault or the inevitable result of you not thinking positively enough: "Because of the evolutionary wiring throughout the ages for the survival of the species, it's natural for the scarcity mindset to prevail," she explains, adding, "We're 2.5 times as likely to want not to lose anything as we are to want to gain something" (Swart 2019).

When you expand your perspective and develop an abundance mindset, you can open your life up to limitless opportunities. Designing your abundant mindset is the birth of new models and is essential to creating abundant business opportunities.

Here are a few ways that transition can materialize:

- Focus on what you have ("I'm grateful to have …")
- Cultivate and communicate your passions ("I care a lot about …")
- Think like a beginner ("Why does …?")
- Build into a growth mindset ("I get to" vs. "I have to")
- Believe the sky's the limit ("I wonder if …")

On an individual level, strategic design can be deployed from an abundance mindset and one committed to routine reflection of current, past, and future. It opens the opportunity to encompass many design research and synthesis methods that can be deployed when necessary.

As teachers, we've introduced strategic design much like any mindfulness practice. Building small, but impactful practices of the mind also concurrently reflect the ability to build and improve design methods. Take this example informed by traditional mind-body yoga practice, that we've used to warm up design in the classroom.

Design by Mind(fulness)

Cultivate observation of individual body parts and sensations within the body to home in on the mind's eye and practice noticing signals around you.

Internal: Begin with the individual and internal mind's eye.
1. Lie on the floor in a place that feels comfortable. Relax your body into the ground, releasing the jaw, neck, feet, and hands.
2. Set a gentle timer for 10 minutes, with the goal to direct attention and breathe toward each part of your body. During those 10 minutes, you don't need to silence the mind but observe what you notice.

In Group: Design requires teams. If you have a team, do this with your group (even two people!)
1. After completing the individual 10 minutes, stand and begin to move slowly at your own pace around the room or area you're in.
2. Set a gentle timer for 5 minutes. Observe the natural patterns of how people circumnavigate and space around you.

Reflect: What did you notice? How did you feel after each session?

Doing this as a daily practice helps us become more present and aware of ourselves as part of the matter that makes up space. Over time, this practice helps us become more observant and better listeners—abilities that we emphasize in the next chapter as the designer's superpowers and what will inform your strategic design methods.

Entrepreneurial building with design: The methods in hand

A living strategy is one that permeates the organization's psyche and structure. Conceiving a brilliant idea for a business is often the easy part. Most of the work comes from understanding how to go about developing a blueprint for how you will research, test, and produce the envisioned outcome. Strategic design for entrepreneurs is an applied design practice used in business and social innovation that gets stakeholders onboard. It works well for entrepreneurs to test and build better products, services, and solutions because it weaves both *depth* and *breadth*.

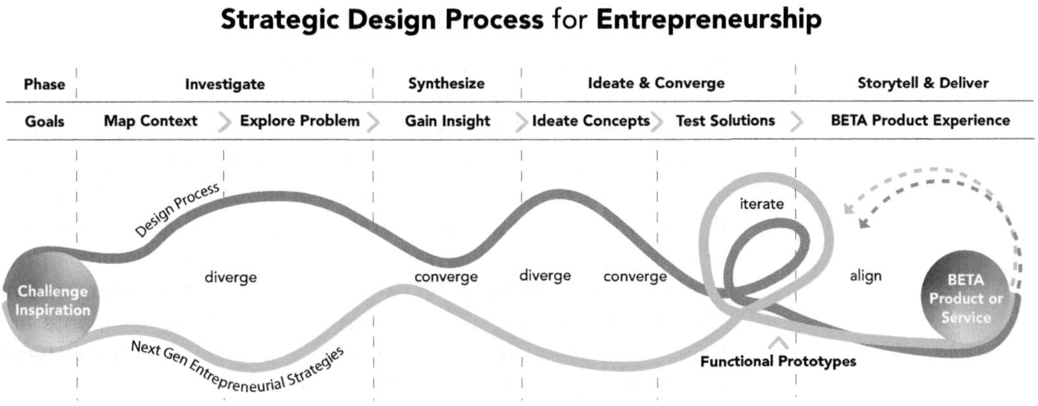

Strategic Design Process for Entrepreneurship

Phase	Investigate		Synthesize	Ideate & Converge		Storytell & Deliver
Goals	Map Context	Explore Problem	Gain Insight	Ideate Concepts	Test Solutions	BETA Product Experience

Design Process

Challenge Inspiration

diverge   converge   diverge   converge   iterate   align

Next Gen Entrepreneurial Strategies

Functional Prototypes

BETA Product or Service

Figure 1.9 Design-driven methods for entrepreneurship.

As illustrated in Figure 1.9, the process is often broken down into a series of six phases, outlining material that will be covered in the Methods Dimension in this guide. The diagram communicates each phase in a linear fashion, but we want to stress that it's anything but a linear approach. The following diagram details the strategic design approach entrepreneurs can use and later we'll show the tools and methods both use within each phase.

In the first phase of *Investigate*, we are mapping the context with systems thinking, followed by field research to explore the problem at hand. These are very divergent phases, defined by open inquiry and a deeply exploratory approach. In the third phase *Synthesize*, we converge on key insights with problem statements to locate substantiated areas of opportunity. In *Ideate and Converge*, we divergently brainstorm solution concepts to converge on the right direction and value proposition to test through prototyping value. In the last phase, *Storytell and Deliver*, we move into storytelling through launching, pitching, and futures-thinking. This process can help you frame problems, identify opportunities, apply methods, and develop ongoing solutions to transition your early-stage company into a formative, effective, and value-prioritizing outcome.

"Our prototypes are our programs."—Design Process as Company Action

We're lucky to learn from PMDA as a holistic approach to design-informed entrepreneurship. Merging hyper-individual (mind) influence in order to cultivate hyper-communal (ecosystem) strength, PMDA at core engages in all six phases of the strategic design process and utilizes these design-driven methods as a regular practice. By regularly attending to the needs of its constituents, PMDA continues to innovate and prototype new approaches. Let's look at what these strategic design methods can feel like *in situ*.

Explore problems, listen for insights

PMDA includes design research into their day-to-day work. Typically taking the form of fly-on-the-wall observations and design ethnography, new members are instructed to undertake their own process of discovery. This research is a facilitated learning experience. After observation of a support group, PMDA will debrief with the new team member, discussing observations and understanding key takeaways. This reflection also begins a practice of deep listening, as they guide new hires into understanding the underlying pain points being expressed by participants and helping to build intuition and skill to identify design hypotheses around the needs of PMDA's constituents.

Synthesize, storytell

If a particular challenge is emerging, Sarah and the team may use other design research methods to help new members. One example was a new hire struggling with the lack of clear directives and operating procedures for each conference and event. PMDA needs to be nimble and reactive to the needs of its constituents, but this member, a former healthcare (Director of Surgical Services) professional, continued to express deep discomfort with this approach. Using analogous research to surgery department operations, wherein the best-laid plans of the morning are scuttled within minutes, their team member had an "aha!" moment. The use of analogous research, this time in a context more familiar to the team member, facilitated the discovery and development of competency and capacity within the new hire and helped bring them along this journey of becoming a more design-driven practitioner in PMDA's work.

Prototype to test

For PMDA, testing is an existential necessity. Prototyping involves being able to identify unmet needs, combining the observation skills of design research with the emotional attunement to meet their constituents with offerings. It also involves a belief in one's own skills and comfort with discomfort and uncertainty, as not all prototypes can succeed. In a caregiving environment and context, there is much discomfort with possibly failing, and prototyping necessitates both an emotional and practical element of facilitation. As a continual commitment to open-ended testing, prototyping is how PMDA builds and develops programs. PMDA relies on this model to ensure that they consistently deliver value to members nimbly and with low overhead. In the words of their founder, Sarah Jones: "Our prototypes are our programs."

Navigational Log + Takeaways

- Ready to use design? *We hope so!*
- Grasp the design field and why strategic design is relevant to business
- Sample a shift in mental models
- Learn from a design-informed organization
- Place yourself (and your mind) at center to build toward your mission

2

START WITH YOUR MINDSET

Practicing ingenuity, awareness, and learning

Objectives

- Learn about the neuroscience of creativity
- Use superpowers to become aware of biases
- Illustrate how to cultivate a designer's mindset
- Implement reflective practices and teach a (future) team how to do it, too

Design turns curiosity into ideas and eventually into actions for change. As design-informed entrepreneurs, we want to be in the right frame of mind because there are many spheres of influence (Figure 2.1). An entrepreneur can influence—and will be influenced by—a variety of domains.

Despite the many attempts (including our own) to name and reproduce a formula for design, it is hard to do. The only constant is the designer's mind and the minds of those they design with, as we see in Sarah's case with PMD Alliance. This ongoing balancing act demands many cognitive functions: empathy, strategy, logic, rationalization, and creativity, to name a few. Because mindset is central to design, let's investigate the mind.

Startups can incorporate self-reflection (looking at your own character, actions, and motives) and other methods into their practice and services. Starting with yourself as a leader and founder provides an advantage for any effective company launch because it demonstrates *who you are*. Without authentically knowing ourselves, our strengths, weaknesses, and our spheres of influence (Figure 2.1), we won't be unable to create authentic value with our company.

To know yourself, know your neuroscience

At the beginning of 2021, a team of Google and Harvard scientists created the most detailed 3-dimensional map of the human brain (Figure 2.2). Merely one-millionth of the cerebral cortex, the browsable map includes tens of thousands of neurons and 130 million synapses (the connections between neurons). Your ability to build and rewire

DOI: 10.4324/9781003227151-4

Figure 2.1
The mindset's spheres
of influence.

synapses (also known as neuroplasticity) across your brain—and others'—will help you to navigate the multiverse of entrepreneurship.

Creativity opens the door to how frequently talk of mindset shows up in the designer's practice today—not as a study of creativity but acknowledged as the foundation of successful design practice. The Stanford d.schools' advocacy for the mindset at the center of creative problem solving is integral to their successful proliferation of design thinking as a method. Stanford d.school Executive Director Sarah Stein Greenberg, in her notable book *Creative Acts for Curious People*, talks about the creative approach and mindset "Approaching the unknown with the spirit and tools of inquiry will help you uncover bigger and better opportunities

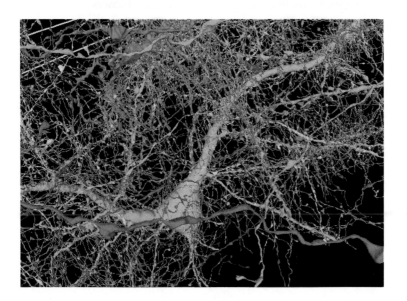

Figure 2.2
Visualizing
neuroscience: A
3-dimensional map
of the human brain
with permissions from
Google and Harvard's
Lichtman Lab (Avery
2021).

than you could have imagined beforehand. That's how design works—it can take you on a journey to learn not just how to solve a problem but how to identify what problem might be so worth solving that you rearrange your life around the endeavor" (Greenberg 2021, 8).

In today's complex and volatile world, this space requires an attitude that must be developed like a muscle strong enough to resist the gravitational pull of *the known*. Inspired by creativity and informed by a "growth mindset" (Dweck 2016), we see that a designer's mindset *can* be cultivated. Designers put themselves in situations where their brains work with diverse inputs and people (Figure 2.3).

To strengthen your brain's design muscles, here are four exercises that should be part of your daily routine:

- **Catalyze *new* synapses:** Try putting yourself in unfamiliar situations with a good dose of discomfort. This triggers new synapses (which most people call learning).
- **Collect *new* knowledge and skills:** Always look for the unknown, or something you cannot do, to grow your understanding and capabilities. By starting a company, you might already be inclined toward this.
- **Create something *new*:** Represent something imagined in some tangible, sharable way because this will spark a conversation and feedback from others.
- **Connect to anything and anyone *new*:** Reach beyond your mental models and your current understanding by looking for new associations between things and people.

Figure 2.3
The designer mindset: With permissions, depictions of the high- and low-creative networks. Circle plots (A) and glass brains (B) were thresholded to show the highest degree (k) nodes in the networks (high-creative k = 10, low-creative k = 18). Colors within the circle plots correspond to lobes of the brain (L, left hemisphere; R, right hemisphere).

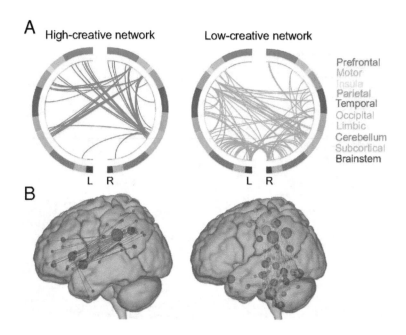

To be clear: while creative activity is the basis for design, design takes creativity to new heights. Designing is a social process, whereas creativity is an individual process. Art is a creative process because it does not necessarily require the engagement of others in the making. On the other hand, design is creating something with shared meaning, either functional or cultural. It requires a recipient to the outcome, and this achieves a result.

Being intentional about stimulating these four brain-based exercises in collaboration with others, you can access what we call the Designer's *Superpowers.*

A Designer's Superpowers

The Designer's Superpowers (Figure 2.4) are what we purport as the key to practicing a designerly mindset that will lend itself to your entrepreneurial journey. In the spider diagram (Figure 2.4), we detail eight sources to supercharge applied skills to chart where you are today compared to your growth as you build the startup. Continuous reflection is best broken down into concrete, routine structure. Like meditation, going for a walk, taking moments for observational pause, applied reflection creates scaffolding to build the leadership for operating a company.

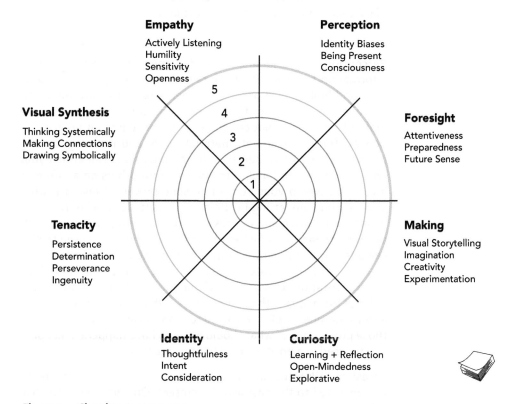

Empathy
Actively Listening
Humility
Sensitivity
Openness

Perception
Identity Biases
Being Present
Consciousness

Visual Synthesis
Thinking Systemically
Making Connections
Drawing Symbolically

Foresight
Attentiveness
Preparedness
Future Sense

Tenacity
Persistence
Determination
Perseverance
Ingenuity

Making
Visual Storytelling
Imagination
Creativity
Experimentation

Identity
Thoughtfulness
Intent
Consideration

Curiosity
Learning + Reflection
Open-Mindedness
Explorative

Figure 2.4 Charting superpowers.

Charting Superpowers

This template helps chart your strengths across the design capacities required to help you consciously develop your designerly mindset as an entrepreneur. Chart your strengths across the design capacities to direct current and future self-development energy.

1. Read each description of the seven superpowers and reflect on each potential rating: In what moments do you excel at _____? Which area prompts discomfort and which area prompts confidence?
2. Plot your level from 1 to 5. 5 is "I'm excellent," and 1 is "I need to work on this." Put a dot on the ring representing the level you feel you're at *now* to see where you can improve and what you can work on.
3. After you plot the dots for each, connect them into what looks like a spider's web. Notice any patterns that arise.
4. Do this every couple of months to grow focus and see how the web develops, where change occurs, and where transformation is missing.

Add Your Team: You can use this with more people. For example, chart several team members' strengths together as an activity, or compile the ratings to provide an idea of where the team might lack energy and illuminate an opportunity.

Perception—As designers, we need to open all our senses to allow information to enter. When we talk about senses, there are low-level and higher-level ones. The lower-level senses are the physical ones: sight, sound, taste, smell, and touch. Designers have higher-level senses that combine the lower senses into rich experiences: form, movement, material, tone, and meaning, among others. Being able to perceive these dimensions will enrich your creative palette and ability to connect with others on a different level. To develop your perceptual superpower, always ask what information I am letting in? Being curious is a powerful trigger to expand perception and increase the data coming into your mindset. Being conscious of what you sense and the lenses used to perceive is another superpower in the utility belt. Awareness means you can go meta—watch yourself, listen to yourself, and allow experimentation. Designers with heightened levels of *awareness* balance the needs of their co-creators with the things they are creating. Awareness helps you avoid rumination and second-guessing those projections of what should or could have happened, keeping you focused in a positive, constructive manner.

Foresight—With the ability to predict future needs, one needs to be connected to the past and the present. One also needs to have a keen imagination and an ability to sense. Couple that with an understanding of how technologies and innovation might influence or impact our behavior, economy, culture, and so forth to extrapolate where it might go.

Combined with our superpowers is our ability to observe and reflect deeply on our past, present, and future states, enabling perceptive growth. Schön described designing as Reflection-in-Action (Schön 1995). His view of reflection directly resulted from the design dialogue: the creative conversation with materials and the often conflictual conversation with co-creators. This is the dark matter of designing and expanding the hearts and minds of everyone involved. It's where nuclear fission can occur; powering new levels of shared understanding that can lead communities into hyperspace toward new galaxies. Cultivating the reflective superpower will make your mindset transition from stagnation to growth. It will enable you to regenerate yourself, your community, and your world. With all your other superpowers, reflection may lead to new spiritual practices and a oneness with nature. You may find a force connecting all life forms, a spiritual string theory for our multiverse.

Making—Regardless of what design specialty you practice, you want to create something that doesn't yet exist. Creation imbues all your superpowers with spiritual force. Giving life to inanimate things drives the designer, bringing out the form from a block of marble or a world from a standard Minecraft template. Unfortunately, we know overproduction and built-in obsolescence have left our planet in a terrible state. Over 50 years ago, in *Design for the Real World: Human Ecology and Social Change* (Papanek 1971), Papanek warned that this would happen if we did not change our behaviors and mindsets. So, we have fallen victim to the rampant consumption of capitalism. However, if we can reinvigorate creativity, we may find a new spirit to guide our souls toward more meaningful contributions to humanity.

Visual Synthesis—This is the act of visually thinking through a problem or graphically making sense of analyzing and explaining with few words or numbers. The goal is to highlight the key takeaways or learnings in diagram form from across your experience and various research methods as part of its outputs. We often deal with complex systems and their intersections. Visual synthesis helps make sense of the relationships between elements. For example, theater, dance, music, and visual expression offer a combination of information processed with more speed and nuance because they engage different parts of the brain. Images and illustrations help us make sense of the big picture. We use four main communication types daily: verbal, nonverbal, written, and visual.

As designers, we leverage the power of visual synthesis to help us make sense of all the disparate data points in our development and research. As design entrepreneurs, we use this skill to align the team and align with stakeholders, such as investors, partners, and your consumer: the community you are building.

How we transmit information is very different from how we process it. How we translate inputs into actions depends on how well we understand the given inputs and their context. Helping us see the links between things helps us retain information and better understand narratives. For example, think about superheroes in the Marvel® Multiverse. When told through a graphic novel, the story can quickly come to life in one's mind. With fewer pages and just from the images, we can understand the storyline, in part because it taps into our unconscious inference.

Visualizing through maps allows us to create hierarchies and diagram interdependencies, revealing disconnects and opportunities we can't see otherwise. They help us recognize, organize, and interpret information framing our perception. The famous ecological psychologist James Gibson discerned that how organisms perceive content informs how they respond to it and how they act. He made scientific advances in understanding visual perception. His wife, Eleanor Gibson, was established in her own right through her research on childhood cognition and how we learn. Together they helped us better understand how we process and perceive our world. As designers and now design entrepreneurs, we will leverage visual synthesis as a processing and communication (learning > understanding > conclusions > action) superpower.

Curiosity—This is the most common explanation for intentionally wanting to collaborate, learn, create, and connect. It provides the spark for neuroplasticity—creating new synapses—which most people call learning. This desire to learn or know more about something or someone can be uncomfortable. Don't be afraid; part of curiosity is looking for something unusual and different from what we are accustomed to. Designers are always looking for the unknown or seeking opportunities to grow.

Identity—Our memories define who we are and our dreams define who we want to be. This is not just some empty statement from a weekly horoscope but neurological facts—also called biases. Memories include the language used to describe our world, the groups we associate with, and who we see when we look in the mirror. Designers have strong identities because they have fought to see their creations come to life. This is a real superpower, particularly in facing the nonbelievers and naysayers. However, identity can quickly become a weakness, like Kryptonite. Designers become obsessive, even compulsive, when they fall in love with their creations. This unwillingness to adapt can result in alienating your team. At worst, it can lead to solutions without buy-in, thrown on the garbage heap of great ideas. Don't let memories be your cage—as a designer, make conscious choices of who you are and want to be. Allow for collaboration and criticism, and test and iterate your ideas.

Tenacity—All the Designer's Superpowers are worthless without an aspiration to make a better world. A preferred future beckons not only the designer but also her co-creators in a shared journey to shape the world as it should be. Our ultimate source of strength is the desire to connect with others in co-creating more meaningful, equitable experiences. Without aspiration, designers don't reach their total capacity. With aspiration, we can rise above our selfish interests—personal and professional—to guide what could be. Aspiration begs us to come back to our source, what we perceive and how we identify ourselves. It enables us to regenerate our minds, hearts, and bodies as we navigate the complexities and contractions of our world.

Empathy—Can you perceive the connections between things and between people? Do you place yourself in the center of your multiverse or in orbit swirling around a wicked problem? Designers build on their ability to see systems to position themselves in a larger context and develop agency to shape them. Making such connections is empowering; otherwise, can be a minefield. Mapping connections reveal allies and detractors. Mastering empathy connects all things. Connectivity includes connecting with nature—a potent rejuvenator of superpowers. Empathy helps relate to others, enabling interaction design, exploring how users (including fringe users) might interact with and perceive the new products, environments, systems, and services you develop.

Beware of biases

Our brains are firing on all cylinders when engaging our minds to create, share, learn, and iterate. The only problem is that our neurons are firing, building new synapses of love for the designed object, our creation, our idea, and our vision. This can form a cognitive bias called the IKEA Effect (Norton et al. 2011) in which people place a disproportionately high value on their products. Once formed, becomes a physiological hurdle designer-entrepreneurs must overcome to co-create effectively and build authentic, tested value.

Our cognitive biases can cause us to become stagnant or rigid in our thinking. Building a learning mindset involves maintaining a healthy innovation culture, starting one mind at a time. In addition, a growth mindset as a leader is critical to inspiring those who join your founding team: investors, partners, and users.

We all have biases, which become the boundaries of our worldviews. Bias is nature's way of trying to lessen the cognitive loads of daily interactions. For example, categorizing the people we see helps us to predict whether they are friends or foes. Cataloging experiences help us know whether we should do it again or avoid it. Over time, we accumulate biases because they enable us to navigate the world's complexities. Nature hardwires biases to adapt. Unfortunately, it is not so simple. Moreover, situations are continually changing, so biases from one experience may or may not be insightful for a new one.

Biases with significant influence on design include:

- **Framing Effect**—How we ask a question is just as important as who we choose to ask and can influence responses. Open questions are more likely to invite conversation from members, customers, or users than closed questions.
- **Confirmation Bias**—Humans only look for evidence confirming their hypotheses or assumptions. They can coax people to agree with how they pose a question or whom they ask. Ensure a diverse range of people from socioeconomic, race, sex, and age when conducting design research.
- **Hindsight Bias**—Given the opportunity to reflect on past actions, people will always find good reasons to explain their actions. So be conscious of this when assessing results.
- **Social Desirability Bias**—We tend to speak in a way that makes us look good because we care about how we look to others. Understanding what, how, and to whom we say things matter to everyone. So be aware of how narrative is and what impact it has.
- **Sunk Cost Fallacy**—This is a crucial bias for entrepreneurs to know. We tend to hang on longer than we should if we have spent much time and money, even when the data and evidence say pivot.
- **Serial-Position Effect**—When writing a survey or deciding the order of questions, we tend to value or pay more attention to items at the beginning or end of lists, so order matters.
- **The Illusion of Transparency**—As humans, we tend to overestimate how others know what we are thinking and make assumptions. Be explicit with your directions, expectations, and methods of operation.
- **Clustering Bias**—As designers, we love to cluster our data and look for patterns. Sometimes, this is done amidst randomness, and there are no patterns. So keep this in mind when trying to find meaning in your data, and don't rush to conclusions.
- **Implicit Bias**—Humans can't help creating unconscious and conscious associations between living and nonliving things or making meaning from behaviors that might not be true. Be mindful and keep these opinions in check.
- **Fundamental Attribution Error**—Humans tend to attribute mistakes to internal characteristics even when they are situational, meaning they may be caused by external forces. Knowing this, we need to check and dive deeper to unearth the root cause of an error before making assumptions.
- **Ability Bias**—We naturally bring our own experiences and abilities to the products and services we create without considering others might not be able to reach as high, see as well, or hear as us.

As a design entrepreneur, you must keep preferences in check. As we pointed out earlier, the *Designer's Superpowers* help inform and keep us conscious of natural tendencies to create biases. In a cultural climate awakening to its own meta-biases and broken systems that perpetuate inequities, it is imperative to acknowledge and work toward more inclusive, equitable, and environmentally sustainable practices for the betterment, balance, and success of your organization, community, and our planet. To achieve this, you need to understand how you form opinions and how to be open to change.

There are biases designers try to remain aware of when navigating our world, specifically when conducting research, listening to stakeholders, or designing products and services. No matter how small, these biases can negatively impact your internal culture, product receptiveness, and, ultimately, your business's overall impact and financial success. Thinking about who is at the table and who is not is a way of checking oneself on the fly. This is often endemic to broader systemic flaws and correcting them can advance beyond the current focus, circle of influence, or control for long-term success.

Sparking creative tension

The good news is that the inherent tension between intentions and the interpretations of others is a powerful catalyst for breaking biases. Riel and Martin write, "the ability to constructively face the tension of opposing ideas and instead of choosing one at the expense of the other generates a creative resolution of the tension in the form of a new idea that contains elements of the opposing ideas but is superior to each" (Riel and Martin 2017).

We can call this creative tension the simultaneous sense of clarity and ambiguity. It's the space between our intentions and interpretations. A designer's mind in action reveals the tension between what the designer creates and how others perceive that creation (Figure 2.5).

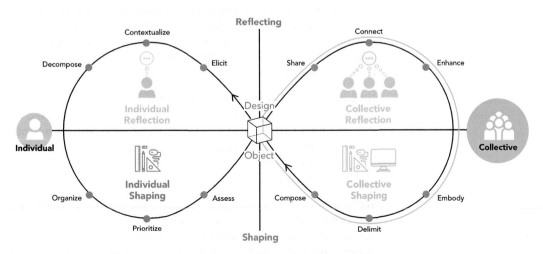

Figure 2.5 A designer's mindset in action from IDeals (Innovation and Design as Leadership): Transformation in the Digital Era, by Joseph Press et al. reprinted with permission

This creative tension is experienced by designers and entrepreneurs alike to an extreme degree because these roles bring something new into existence without a promise of how it will land. As a result, they're both driven by instinctual clarity and must navigate an unavoidable degree of uncertainty. The compass rings clear, but the map's route might be unknown, up for debate, or frequently in flux.

Design and entrepreneurship rely in many ways on the same mindset. Designers feel creative tension constantly and live in a state of flux. What designers are granted, however, is ownership of this ambiguous space of noticing and perceiving. Designers culturally rely on uncertainty as a variable in the equation and craft their scope with the new variable of change as power fueling their creation.

However, entrepreneurship and the expected runway of a founder are not hospitable to "I don't know" in the equation; there's enormous pressure to name, quantify, and plan. The work of bringing a company to life for a target audience—*which is, by nature, creation*—and the expected measurable route can feel very dissonant for entrepreneurs. We are, after all, supposed to provide the plan and answer the questions, right? *Creative tension* exists at full throttle, but we push our brains into identifying the root cause when our perception may not lend that clarity. What design grants us is not the need to clarify but to accept this process as the clarity desired. It is not a resolution in the answer but the resolve in our capacity to solve, and that understanding evolves. Design allows the mind peace in recognizing that detail will come into and out of focus by nature of creation.

How to build a designer's mindset

Part of becoming an entrepreneur is enhanced by the superpowers of the designer. Becoming a design entrepreneur involves a lifelong personal growth practice, informed by having both a reflective and open mindset (head), creating and testing new tools for change (hands), and showing empathy (heart). These combine into exercises that help foster innovation.

How quickly can one bounce back from adversity? How responsive are we to change? In a reflective mindset, we are focused on stepping back to understand and interpret events, actions, and our impact on them. This is part of personal growth work that helps you get to your personal *why* we learned about prior and leads to self-actualization.

We're going to use a metaphor someone shared with us years ago, and that's to think of reflection as a well of knowledge. The deeper you go, the greater the insights. However, reflection isn't part of many of our daily practices. To be genuinely open to it, we need to practice the art of letting go and letting come.

Doing this on the team and company level is more complex but just as important. We will discuss this in the following chapters. First, make sense of events or create meaning from occurrences at the different systems levels. Then, ask yourself what this might mean for you, your team, or your business on a temporal level (short-, medium-, and long-term). This practice builds a reflective and resilient cultural mindset. But this can't happen at the macro level without it first happening on individual levels for each team member—it is part of the building blocks of the culture.

The Ladder of Inference was first developed by organizational psychologist Chris Argyris and used by Peter Senge in *The Fifth Discipline: The Art and Practice of the Learning Organization* (Senge 2006).

It covers the steps humans generally take when making decisions. The ladder describes the thinking process we go through, often without realizing it, to get from a decision to action. It starts with experiencing and observing, and then moves up the ladder to selecting data. From there, it adds meaning, and then moves into assumptions and conclusions, followed by adopting beliefs and then taking action.

We've adapted the step-by-step breakdown of inferences in *the design-driven entrepreneur's decision-making process* (Figure 2.6) to stress the need to keep one's biases in check. This will create a more self-aware thought process for the next generation of design entrepreneurs to build complex adaptive systems.

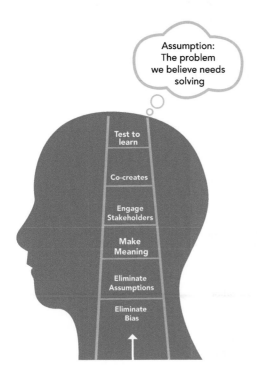

**Figure 2.6
The design entrepreneur's decision-making process.**

Surrounding a designer's decision-making process is a heightened sense of embodied cognition—an acute awareness of how the environment and its surroundings contribute to sensations in the mind and body. So, when we talk about head, hand, and heart, we are referring to how all our activities play a part in the designer's mindset. This mental state helps adapt, be agile, and be responsive while developing a concept, pitching ideas, or testing products within rapidly changing environmental, cultural, and economic systems.

This helps to process with all our senses the problem at hand, be it the meta-problem your business is trying to solve or a subset problem to get you there.

Maintaining balance: Awareness and actualization

Present in every person is the need for fulfillment of one's talents and potentialities. This self-actualization process can often be found when we achieve flow states, those moments we are "in the zone." This is the heightened time when we are at peak performance, fully immersed and balanced between mind and body, or action and awareness (Figure 2.7). At any organization's individual and cultural levels, these states of being are in the collective pursuit of a goal or ideal. At a personal level, this leads to overall well-being and happiness, which leads to better individual performance and health. At a cultural level for your company, this can impact growth and success, ensuring that the organization stays on its North Star course.

Research suggests certain practices lead to flow states and thus should be imbued into your culture as valued practices. They should

Figure 2.7
Transcending from
individual to system.

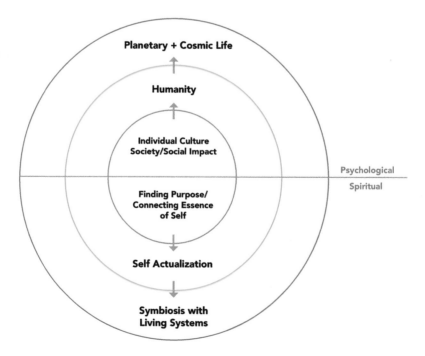

be taught, encouraged, and maintained at the individual, team, and company levels.

Reaching self-actualization at these levels helps further the alignment needed at a planetary level (Figure 2.7). We can reflect upon the alignment and coexistence with other living systems in a mutually beneficial, symbiotic relationship. The design entrepreneur's spiritual and psychological coexistence uses holistic design principles to create and balance society's and nature's needs.

> *The one journey that ultimately matters is the journey into the place of stillness deep within one's self. To reach that place is to be at home; to fail to reach it is to be forever restless.*
> N. Gordon Cosby (O'Connor 1972)

Becoming aware of how we process information and create mental models is part of your creative practice as an individual and an organizational leader. The mind + body connection is part of developing self-awareness. Just like mapping your superpowers, the attributes of a self-aware person help us understand ourselves, our weaknesses, and our strengths. In turn, how we learn and what experiences have helped to shape us. Finally, it is a conscious ability to stand outside oneself and observe the self. Below we illustrate the foundational elements that make up self-awareness akin to the three elements of nature: fire, earth, and water (Figure 2.8).

- **Benefits of Self-awareness:**
  - Helps self-control, creativity, pridefulness, and self-esteem
  - Facilitates decision-making
  - Leads to more accurate self-reports
  - Can help to predict your self-development around acceptance and proactivity

- **Things to Consider:**
  - Keep an open mind
  - Stay attuned to your emotions
  - Be mindful of strengths and weaknesses

 Raw Experience of Self

 Sub-Skills of Self-Awareness

 Self-Awareness Practices

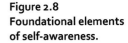
Figure 2.8
Foundational elements of self-awareness.

- ○ Know your biases
- ○ Know your emotional triggers
- ○ Embrace your intuition

- **Helpful Tools and Practices:**
  - ○ Meditate
  - ○ Strategize and track your progress
  - ○ Talk to trusted friends and advisors
  - ○ Practice reflection and feedback (use our navigational logs and chapter takeaways)

As you center yourself, you will learn to let go of any assumptions you carry. This will allow you to be more conscious of the bias and patterns around you and be ready for the future. In addition, this state of awareness can cultivate a shared mindset with those with whom we collaborate. When we are fully aware, can we practice letting go, becoming a design-enabled leader, and engaging others in a journey of co-creating a better future.

Building leadership skills

Building leadership skills is part of the self-awareness and discovery work needed to attract and keep the right team for the long haul. So, building off the list above, here are some reflective questions you can ask yourself:

- What type of leader do you see yourself being?
- How do you inspire others?
- How does your behavior enable others to model your lead?
- Are you compassionate?
- Are you being authentic, and can people see these qualities in you?

To embody these character traits, be in tune with who you are and your passion for living, and let those values come through, so others can align and join you in your mission.

Start with your mind to prepare your team's mind

A solid mental foundation will be responsive, adaptable, and resilient to regenerate a planet in balance and harmony. Like gasses and dust elements collapsing to form stars, we will unite teams to create systems. We now move from the individual to the team level. Here we need to lead and motivate exploration to co-create the future together.

Navigational Log + Takeaways

Grab your notebook or just take a moment to pause and answer these questions.

- What feels alive for you now, where you are on your journey?
- When do you think both clear and uncertain?

- Where do you resist your mind? Where do you lean in?
- What obstacle stands in the way of building your mind's muscles of awareness and openness?
- What type of leader would you like to be?
- What qualities do you exhibit to fulfill that vision of yourself?
- How are you setting an intention to check your biases as you navigate?

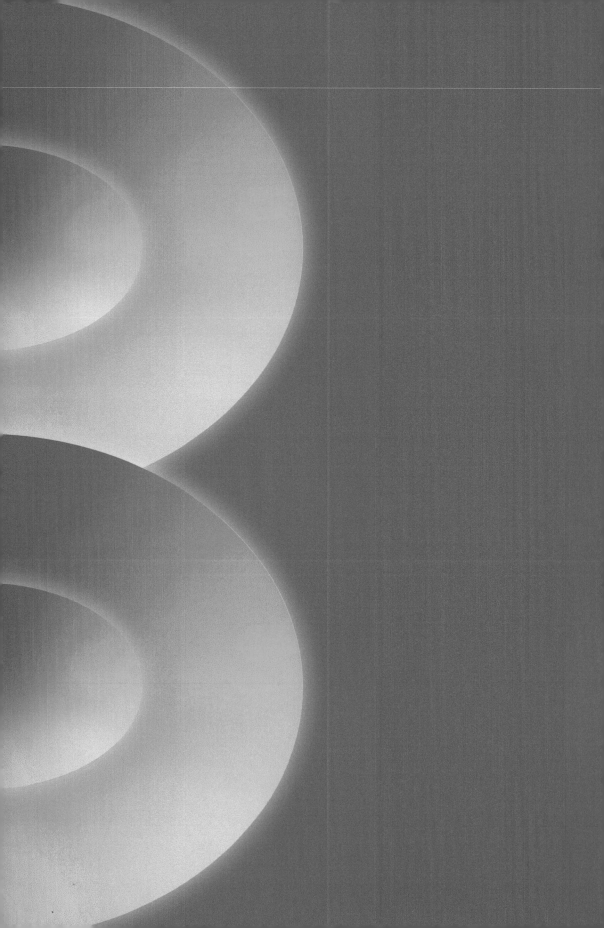

Dimension B

Mission

Charting purpose for value creation

With the mindset focused, we look at the context, the driving why: why you, why now, and why this? With these answers, we build a bold vision for the future, articulating the mission and the values that will define our purpose and unite people. A clear mission helps craft and instills a culture within companies as a world within the more extensive ecosystem we are part of and helping to shape. These values are carried forward through the offering we deliver, how we make an impact, and bring people together.

DOI: 10.4324/9781003227151-5

3
YOUR MISSION TO BUILD A BETTER WORLD

Moving from self to company

Objectives

- Reflect on your passion, purpose, and reason for being
- Leverage your values for impact, and ultimately value creation
- Learn how to create a mission statement as a call to action
- Develop mission-driven principles that lead to preferred futures

We are all motivated to do things for different reasons and yet, there are intrinsic similarities at a basic human level. This concept is the basis for Maslow's theory, first published as *A Theory of Human Motivation* in 1943 (Maslow, 1943, 370–396). Maslow's *Hierarchy of Needs* created a pyramid-shaped diagram to explain how humans can attain self-actualization and fulfillment once their basic human needs, like psychological and physical safety, love, belonging, and esteem, are met. In 2020, the psychologist Scott Barry Kaufman reconceptualized the popular pyramid as a sailboat to de-prioritize the sequential nature of pyramid steps, stating that what really should be represented by Maslow is the process and experience of life, gesturing toward a thriving state of growth.

The difference between just having a job vs. building a self-actualized path is the motivation and the drivers behind the decisions made. The driving motivation behind one's personal fulfillment is what will ultimately drive the success of your startup: to root your drive forward in anything but your core motivating values will make the difficult founder's journey all that much harder. It's important that you spend dedicated time understanding your personal motivations for starting up a business; this will lead others to join you, believe in you, and allow you to persevere (Figure 3.1).

Centering

To drive forward outcomes, we need to lose the distinction between right and wrong, instead, grapple with spectrums and gradients of perception. The attitude that produces ingenuity is a hard one to grasp and takes

DOI: 10.4324/9781003227151-6

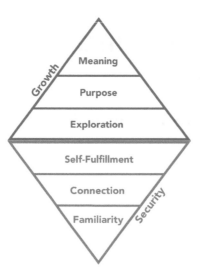

Figure 3.1 Beyond Maslow's law of self-actualization.

practice to develop. Turning the *Designer's Superpowers* into a consistent mindset (and approach) requires active self-reflection leading us into the "soft" space of qualitative growth and nonbinary reflection.

This type of self-awareness and alignment is part of the next turn in human development, moving us away from extractive behaviors to more generative practices as individuals, companies, and societies. At the core, is one's *Reason for Being*.

Mind, body, and heart are centered by a *reason for being*. Many cultures exemplify this core concept: Anglo cultures refer to a *personal why* or what gets you up in the morning. In French, the same concept is *raison d'etre*, and in Japanese, it is *Ikigai*—your life and worth. (Figure 3.2) Surfacing this is the foundation for your well-being and happiness as well as for the well-being of your future endeavors and startup.

We orient a design-entrepreneur's founding center around the understood business value proposition exercise. This alignment—value of self and value of business—will shape not only the startup trajectory with storytelling but allow you to return to a foundation when you're presented with tough decisions in the future. This will help you stay focused on what you'd like to accomplish on a macro scale with your journey, tracking toward self-actualization and happiness without being absorbed into influences you'll interact with while building.

Using IKIGAI to Be Your Own Value Proposition Coach

Determine your sense of purpose

It's good practice to check in with yourself and reflect upon your "personal why." Ikigai in Japanese means "your reason for being." It helps you reflect upon your purpose in life. Use this exercise to reflect on and draft a value proposition. This will help you stay focused on what you'd like to accomplish and stay aligned toward self-actualization and individual happiness. Take time out to reflect upon your ambitions, goals, needs, and desires to make sure they align with your day-to-day actions and trajectory.

Do this exercise and revisit it!

1. **Starting from the outside in, answer with bullet points the four prompts:**
    ◦ What do you love?
    ◦ What are you good at?
    ◦ What does the world need?
    ◦ What can you be paid for?

2. **Move into the second inner level:** Here, these four intersect to help you define what passions, missions, vocations, and professions resonate with you based on the answers from the outer ring.

3. **At the center:** Take 10 minutes to draft two to three distinct value propositions. Use your bullet points above to summarize your *Reason for Being* or what gives you purpose. These statements can be edited and adjusted but seek clarity in the exercise!

Figure 3.2 Ikigai: Determine your sense of purpose.

Mission: The starting point toward a better future

A mission-driven company has a sense of purpose. Rooted in your *Reason for Being* are your business-concept goals and your personal *why*. You have a reason for starting up, which when clarified and articulated, will create scaffolding for your startup mission. This, in turn, will help you articulate the values of your company and help you align with potential joiners, partners, and communities. A company with a clear mission has a founder that can answer "Why this, why now, and why are you the perfect person to achieve this?"—because the call for innovation, to change our existing situations into preferred ones, is more critical than ever before. The mission sets the scene and explains the reason for being, and the business model will explain *how and what* you deliver value around that mission.

Creating shared value is how to bring about preferred futures in business innovation. For many years, academics and practitioners alike have been espousing the need for a shared view of the direction of change. Michael Porter conceptualized shared value to propel forward an attitude that solving root problems experienced by stakeholders will in fact serve shareholder value more (Porter 2011). While more difficult to do, mission-driven companies build for efficacy of outcomes. For anyone who has been involved in change, we know that initially, more ambiguity is better. This allows for codesigning solutions as a catalyst for collective change.

We emphasize the time is now: accelerated by the interconnectedness and transparency of technology, citizens across the globe are exposed

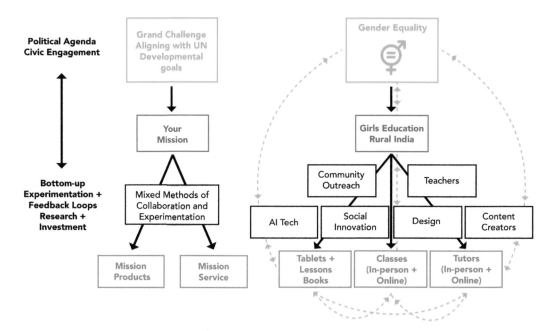

Figure 3.3 Mission-oriented innovation framework.

to the inequalities in cultural systems, political polarization by misinformation, and the economic instability of disrupted supply chains due to climate change and pandemic. This literal and figurative burning landscape inspires many of us to make a change. A change for ourselves, for the communities we are a part of, for our friends and family. We find opportunities to impact the systems we are a part of, and that motivates many of us to go out there and try something different.

In Mariana Mazzucato's *Mission Economy: A Moonshot Guide to Changing Capitalism*, the United Nations Sustainable Development Goals (SDGs) play the role of a North Star we can aspire to reach. She recommends that we navigate these by breaking them down into practical steps or targets into subsections or *mission maps* (Mazzucato 2021*)*.

The mission-map journey represents a profound shift in navigation toward renewal, regeneration, and rebirth. It is a fundamental move away from the "explore and exploit" commonly known in the startup industry designed for shareholder primacy. Changing our mental models, frameworks, and images defines who we are and where we go and is essential when defining your own mission (Figure 3.3).

Alignment of focus

In his book, *The 7 Habits of Highly Effective People*, Steven Covey popularized the framework of The Circles of Concern and Influence (Covey 1998). We build upon this framework to point out the value of using your mission to align your personal, team, and community areas of focus, to create a holistic and authentic vision of purpose. *What doesn't concern us when launching a company? What should concern us, and what shouldn't? What can we actually influence?*

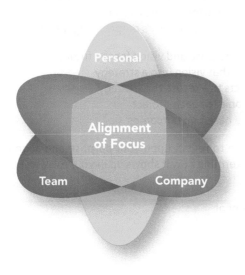

Figure 3.4
Aligning focus across levels.

Mapping what does concern us and what we can influence helps sort out signal from noise (Figure 3.4).

At the personal level: *What's within your influence and control?* Your worldview matters a great deal to the success of your vision. The lens through which you see why this is important, what story you tell of this preferred state, how your business gets there, and what it offers. But it starts with your *personal why?* What you believe in, your ethos. This work is integral to the authenticity of the mission and vision. Cultivating this is your first step. It will help you develop a personal North Star (goal) that will guide your future business metrics.

At the team level: *What's within your team's influence and control?* Once you have your *personal why* you will be able to connect with others who share similar personal why's and enroll them to co-create with you the preferred system. In this phase, you'll be developing tools that work to create alignment and clarify expectations aloud with early-stage contributors. This will forge a shared purpose and milestones.

At a community level: *What's within your community's influence and control?* Once you've completed this work at both the individual and founding team level, you'll be confident and prepared for revisiting these values and ways of living into them by co-creating your community—initially with your first few stakeholders, followed by customers, hires, and partners.

Align on purpose

Despite the need for alignment on priorities, many organizations struggle to identify and pursue their most important goals. Our purpose pyramid is inspired by Maslow's hierarchy and Antonio Nieto-Rodriguez's creation of the Hierarchy of Purpose (Nieto-Rodriguez 2016) but places purpose at the base of the pyramid implying that it is the foundation mission-driven businesses are built. It demonstrates that the effective long-term performance of a startup hinges on aligning your own purpose with your company's purpose (Figure 3.5).

- Identify your startup's purpose and vision for the future
- Set priorities based on that vision into a strategy
- Outline specific projects to execute the strategy
- Assemble aligned people for each project
- Measure performance based on outcomes

Once you've had a chance to reflect upon your purpose and align it to your startup's, let's determine how it shows up in your mission and vision of the company.

- Define Mission Statement
- Define Ethos
- Vision Statement

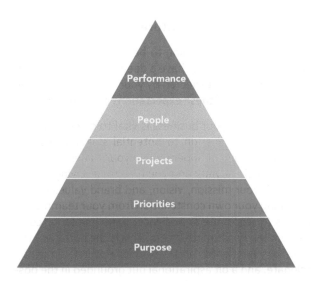

Figure 3.5
Purpose is a startup foundation.

What sets you apart

Value creation is the bedrock of business. It's what sets you apart from your competition, secures long-term customers, and brings distinct meaning to your brand and your solution. Without creating value for your business, your unique offering will be seen as just another commodity in the eyes of your target market.

In the world of an entrepreneur, value creation and values are the lifeblood of the thing we make, so it's critical to be conscious of them, adapting them to include the many perspectives of our stakeholders and the people we serve. A positive, productive culture has the power to make prospective employees and customers want to partner with you and—just as important—stay with you for the long term, through all the uncertainties that can and will arise.

But as we know, even from a young age, we don't follow anyone who can't show us they believe in what they stand for. So, as design-led entrepreneurs, we need a basic understanding of our own values. This ensures that everyone knows what we're talking about and what we are trying to accomplish.

We've seen values broken down in three ways:

1. **Core values:** these are the deeply ingrained principles that guide the actions of an organization/company.
2. **Aspirational values:** values we aspire to but might be a far stretch for us to achieve. But heck, we can try, can't we?
3. **Accidental values:** arise spontaneously without being cultivated by leadership and take hold over time.

Your ethos, your values, your culture

Much of your company culture is going to be oriented around your values. You're required as a leader to have a deep and intuitive understanding of your values and are expected by your company to uphold and live through them—even if these expectations aren't explicit.

In fact, setting the values of your business is vital to developing and communicating your brand mission to potential stakeholders and allowing them to buy in. Buy-in happens when your values align with others around you, to build loyalty and you gain trust. Living true to your purpose through your mission, vision, and brand values is mission-critical to forming your own constellation from your teammates, partners, and users (or consumers, audience, participants, or community). Just remember words matter here. This is the narrative, the written expression of your identity and reason for existing. It must be authentic, passionate, and a bit aspirational but grounded in the possible today. Start with adjectives before drilling down to what those words mean in practice. Then you will need to write the commandments and conflict-resolution documents by which you and your team promise to work. This resolution will be your roadmap when times get tough. It's the personal commitment to one another and your stakeholders to make it work through the difficult times.

Company values might start with a list of words that get built out over time.

Examples:

1. Accountability
2. Boldness
3. Collaboration
4. Continuous improvement
5. Curiosity
6. Customer commitment
7. Diversity
8. Honesty
9. Humility
10. Inclusion
11. Innovation
12. Integrity
13. Making a difference

Springboard off the results from the previous exercises where we looked for alignment of purpose across your personal, team, and firm's *why?* to develop a mission, then your Ikigai, where you discover your personal purpose, setting yourself up for self-actualization; next, we will look at the *values star.*

A values star is a great place to start with your own values; they can be adapted and applied to both individuals in your company and the company as a whole (Figure 3.6). This exercise continues along the path of aligning your purpose to home in on your company's mission, vision, and values. These, in turn, help you orient your compass through your mindset formation, to navigate toward developing a culture you value, maintain, and protect. This may sound relatively easy, but in practice, it takes a conscious effort and small daily action to bring about and feel authentic walking the talk.

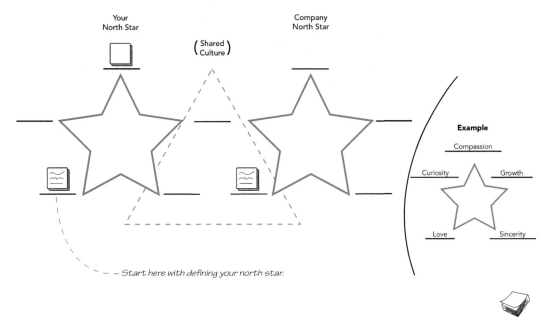

Figure 3.6
Values star, self and team.

Values Star (Self and Team): Begin with Your Values to Define the Mission and Vision of the Organization You're Building

Building on the Ikigai and alignment of focus exercises we did in the previous chapter, the Value Star helps you envision the mission for your future company/organization. While you can use our star, we encourage you to draw your own—it'll capture your character and flair.

Make your culture come to life by defining the behaviors that act out your values. Creating shared values within your mission and vision statements helps define your culture at a high level and attract people to your organization.

This exercise helps develop your company's North Star or mission statement through aligning with your own as the founding individual(s).

1. Brainstorm. Write out a comprehensive list—take a moment to flesh out a list of every value that comes to mind and resonates with you.
2. Now, sort this list by what are behaviors vs. values. Behaviors are words that are operationalized values—separating "Kindness" from "Compassion."
3. Map out the shared and different identities you wish for yourself vs. your company.
4. Identify the overlapping values that will help to articulate the mission you and your company share.

Exercises are meant to be repeated as you evolve and refine your purpose and align it to the impact your products or services can have.

Embedding your values into your company mission and vision is critical in helping to frame the direction you will take your company, the priorities you determine, who is attracted to your idea and who joins your organization, and of course, who buys into your product or service and joins your community at large.

Navigational Log + Takeaways

- Draft a clear sense of personal purpose
- Scope an initial business mission, vision, and values
- Define the impact you want to have
- Explain it to others for feedback

4
DEVELOP CULTURE THROUGH MISSION

Creating team values to grow community

Objectives

- Understand how to build your culture from day one
- Instruct design-driven practice in startup culture at the team level
- Develop an ethos of conscious inclusion and behaviors that foster diversity
- Practice designerly behaviors in team culture
- Embed systems awareness and continuous integrated feedback loops
- Build and maintain a diverse culture

We all contribute to culture in our own way, to the dynamics within our environments and the energy around us. As founders and leaders of communities, brands, and businesses, we must be attuned to the daily endeavor of consciously creating the environment and culture of our startups. There is much awareness of diversity, equity, inclusion (DEI), and belonging—all facets of company culture today, with research showing this impact on a company's bottom line. Who's attracted is based on your mission, vision, values, *AND* how they build your culture.

Culture is as important as your vision and passion because it either strengthens or undermines your objectives. A strong organizational culture can also turn employees into advocates. It encourages people—be they future employees or customers— to buy into your mission and vision because it holds accountable *in action* the reputation and values of an organization. It sounds easy and straightforward, but in practice, this can be more complex than initially thought. Retroactively creating a culture of design and inclusivity or copying-and-pasting diversity into your company mission, will ultimately prove more costly, less efficient, and less effective than proactively assessing your internal ecosystem.

DOI: 10.4324/9781003227151-7

The success of the founder's mindset

In the last few years, the failure rate of startups has been very high—and, according to the U.S. Bureau of Labor Statistics (2022), more than 20% of startups fail in the first year, 30% in the second year, 50% in the fifth year, and 70% in their tenth year. Rarely is a business so in tune with its niche that it can float along with minimal effort, and many investors, founders, and mentors reflect on this, like Paul Graham's famous "Startup Journey" curve naming the arduous rollercoaster with "the trough of sorrow." But, why *do* so many businesses fail, even if there is an initial commitment to vision? Tenacity to persist through difficulty underlines all. The success of the founder's mindset, how it informs their partnership, and the endurance of culture have strong hands in shaping continuity. Coincidentally, the most popular piece of advice we've seen from founders to aspiring entrepreneurs was the need to understand failure as a part of learning and to see mistakes as an opportunity, because mistakes are not the problem. The problem is leaving mistakes uncorrected.

We've all heard of or experienced a "toxic culture" with low morale, high turnover, lack of vision and alignment, harassment, and entrenched hierarchies building fearful employees. We have a pretty good idea of what we don't want to be part of, but often we are not aware there are microaggressions or unconscious biases that penetrate even the best-laid plans. Designing your culture from day one is critical to your success because it sets the tone for your company's health: how you lead your team, your and your cofounders' productivity, the culture for your first hires, and the workflow, values, and lifestyle that will evolve as your product, service, or offering scale. It may be easy to maintain because you are hands-on in the beginning, but as you hire more, you'll lose the day-to-day ability to manage and oversee all moving parts, and you'll need to delegate. This is where clear descriptions of behaviors, mindsets, and attitudes will be critical. Oftentimes, startups develop these documents after the fact, after something potentially damaging happens.

You may have worked in organizations or companies before starting up or heard of toxic cultures of bad environments, but have you ever thought of how they got that way? It isn't just one trait or individual. There are many factors, and over time it becomes difficult to pinpoint where a culture started to "go off the rails." Often, we see this shift when an organization stops uniting around core human values as people *first*. They stopped maintaining these values and backing them up with transparent, measurable, and attainable actions.

Design-led learning culture by feedback

Failure is just feedback

Billie Jean King (Schnall 2018)

A design-led learning culture helps to co-create the values that will guide your team culture. With learning as a commitment to growth

Design-led Learning Culture

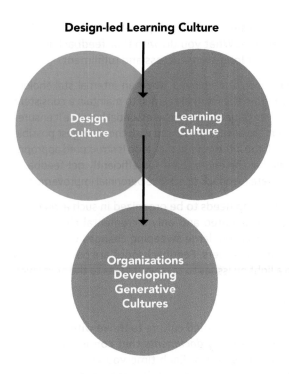

Figure 4.1
Generative
organizations.

and design as an adaptable practice centering humans, a design-led learning culture (Figure 4.1) infuses growth-forward development. How does this happen? With informed, structured feedback loops at the core.

A feedback loop is simply put, data that is returned. In practice, the data is leveraged for change (Figure 4.2). Feedback loops can be ongoing conversations where feedback and opinions are used to shape new changes and improvements on a project (or company!). This creates the *loop*: where the intent is an adjustment, for more feedback. The world's largest companies use feedback loops:

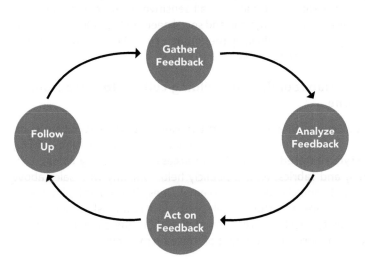

Figure 4.2
Feedback loop.

constant dialogue with users, for example, to effectively refine their platforms and/or services. What you do with that feedback is what makes the difference for long-term success and fulfillment.

An internal feedback loop is employed when an internal stakeholder collects the feedback from the internal team(s) to maintain a consistent level of quality on a given project. This loop is essential because it ensures that clients/customers are always presented with the strongest possible iteration of a project. If the internal feedback loop is structured appropriately, it also ensures that the entire team can efficiently get feedback. The goal is to incorporate feedback to achieve perennial improvement.

The internal feedback loop needs to be organized in such a way that the entire team is kept updated and only incremental changes are ever made. This helps to avoid large sweeping changes which affect the work of other team members. Feedback loops are powerful tools capable of shining a light on issues to take your ideas to the next level.

Living documents

To pave the way for your design-led culture to thrive with feedback, entrepreneurs can create *living documents* that continually evolve and grow as your business grows. Each time you view it, it is like a snapshot in time. These, often shared documents, are meant to build consensus, alignment, and trust. These living documents will eventually reflect your organization's mission, vision, values, and conflict resolution that you are asking your team members and partners to commit to, defend, and maintain. The values document should have behaviors within it, explaining how to behave in and around the company. They should align with their personal values.

As you scale, you will not be able to be in every room or every conversation. You will need to trust your team members to represent you and your brand online and in-person properly. To do so will require clear documents with bullet points, periodic listening sessions, check-ins, and performance metrics—all sensitive to the human, environmental, emotional, physical, and social needs of the individuals within the organization, making up the culture of your business beyond sales performance and business goals.

Three Elab founders on building culture-forward from day one

Meet Shawn! Shawn founded Lovesac in 1995, a furniture company that launched with bean bags and now offers high-quality, lifestyle-centered sectionals and accessories in many colors, patterns, and fabrics. Now a publicly held company with sales above $600MM annually and over 400 employees, Shawn has built Lovesac to operate like a startup at scale, with close relationships and weekly community check-ins. They invest heavily in the company's culture and the mindset development of the team members.

"I was 18 years old sitting on my parents' couch watching *The Price is Right*, eating a bowl of Captain Crunch, and I had this dumb idea: *How funny would it be to have a beanbag that was huge?*" So began Shawn's journey: one that is the epitome of flowing between learning and practice, idea and execution. Lovesac and its operational success as a thoroughly design-infused company come at the hands of Shawn's commitment, not only to the company but also to a deep understanding that the company is only as strong as his ability to weave culture: create a functional, flowing system in which the life and purpose of each player are acknowledged and independent, yet executing the same goal with the same ethos on all touchpoints.

For culture building, Shawn developed a strategic guide to Lovesac that answers questions like: *Why do we exist? What do we believe?* His approach places company as a living system. It's these values and mission that drive his company forward—and has for nearly 20 years.

Capri is a Financial Education Platform by Women for Women, founded by Nicole Hartwig Landau in 2020. Meet Nicole! Capri is pacing its growth and financial needs by first closing a seed round and before launching the first version of its subscription-based application. Nicole is creating a culture of diversity learning, a living lab of check-ins with structural sexism/racism/prejudice conversations built into their core. These values align with their mission of improving the financial literacy of female-identifying people.

Nicole placed a high value on knowing and trusting the people at the core of her company. In January 2020, she started courting individuals from her first-degree network. COVID-19 delayed the entire buildout, but she and her team persevered and managed to lay a foundation.

Creating a culture from scratch was a unique opportunity to start with a clean slate. Nicole prides herself on being a highly communicative leader. Though it was challenging for her to establish open communication when her team worked remotely, and she was the only one working full-time, they all hopped onto Zoom together for biweekly "all-hands meetings." This was a cherished time for them to be a team, where everyone could share things about themselves and their lives.

The team at Capri doesn't have a project management tool that they use across their team yet; they manage things over Slack and email. They decided to launch a "culture camp," an internal initiative for everybody to work together. Meeting biweekly for an hour, they learn about the social justice issues they value, keeping in dialogue about them with each other. Carving out a time for discussions outside of business was one of the biggest inflection points for team building. It was a great bonding experience because they had to create a place for uncomfortable and sometimes difficult conversations. It was crucial for them to schedule programming outside the normal realms of the business, to know what was working, and field the feedback from the team—aligning around the mission and core values.

Figure 4.3
Shawn Nelson, founder
of Lovesac, celebrating
with team members.
Photo credit: Lovesac.

Generative, regenerative, and self-enabling cultures

Culture can encourage extractive or regenerative practices. A regenerative culture consciously builds capacity for everyone in the community to continuously maintain balance with nature. Regenerative cultures reflect the people and geography of a given bioregion because they are built with the participation of all the local elements (Wahl 2016). By embracing coexistence within a symbiotic relationship, a regenerative culture can add value to the system by extending the health of the global community. Entrepreneurs who work with such holistic awareness are driven by the knowledge that human thriving can only happen in a healthy ecosystem with a life-supporting biosphere. We believe that generative is a pathway toward regenerative behaviors and can open opportunities for startups to embrace regenerative principles.

Hire the right team to amplify culture

Your company culture is a combination of organizational factors such as your mission statement, goals, workplace environment, management styles, employee expectations, and behaviors. Your company

Healthy Employees

- Financial Well Being
- Physical Well Being
- Burnout Level
- Stress Level
- Exertion Level
- Work-Life Balance

Healthy Relationships

- Trust in Team
- Trust in Leadership
- Collaboration
- Employee-Manager Relationship Quality
- Psychological Safety

Healthy Work Environment

- Inclusion
- Innovation
- Responsiveness
- Change Receptivity
- Development Opportunity

culture is unique to your organization. While a company's culture can be directed by business leaders and management, the employees you hire will also have an impact. When it is done strategically, you can create a great company culture that attracts the type of workers you want to employ. It's also crucial to ensure that the people who help drive your culture feel understood and valued, which will be derived from an alignment of values, allowing each person to flourish (Figure 4.4).

Figure 4.4
Healthy employees with healthy relationships create healthy work environments.

Bringing people on board is a huge and vital leap for a startup's success—and a major milestone. Solopreneurs, or individuals who build a company alone, tend to burn out much faster, grow at a slower pace and are therefore a riskier investment, and often investors will require founders to be a team. When building a team, you will not only need to look at their skills but also find people who align with your values (this is true with investors, too!). Aligning your team's core values and purpose is the key to its long-term success and sustainability during shifts in markets and crises. The faces of your brand—the people who represent you—say a lot about what you bring to the table and who has access to the table, triggering people's perceptions. Knowing this will be a key asset. One of the most important tasks is to help convey and articulate beyond actions and words as brand representatives—after all, you are all becoming role models.

Building culture at Unfold after acquisition

Meet Alfie and Andy, founders of Unfold! Unfold Stories is a toolkit for digital storytellers with minimal and elegant templates founded in 2019. Alfonso Cobo and Andy McCune cofounded Unfold, which was acquired in late 2019 by website building and e-commerce platform Squarespace. Squarespace went public via Direct Listing on the NYSE in 2021.

Cobo and McCune started to develop the app together in early 2019 after Alfie created an early version and sent a message to McCune over Instagram for feedback and advice.

When **Unfold Stories** joined Squarespace, they had to figure out how to align their values and culture to their new partners and parent company while exponentially needing to scale their team. Alfie explains how they handled that complexity and simultaneous development. They stayed on targets and timelines while developing trust and new ways of working through planned morning check-ins each day as a culture meshing strategy.

Alfie's leadership style involves being very transparent. Part of that translates into being in a mindset that they are constantly learning and that everyone should be themselves. In 2020, when COVID struck NYC, everyone was going through difficult hard times and political difficulties also. Everyone suffered and being able to work in an environment where there was an open space to have dialogues was very important. Alfie made it clear that everyone on his team should feel open to discuss their struggles with anything personal, mental health, etc., in a no-judgment zone.

Alfie's company makes sure that there is equity in how they hire, especially in the United States, with the systemic racism that exists. It's important

Figure 4.5
Unfold Stories founders Alfonso Cobo and Andy McClune.
Photo credit: Leo Chang.

to them to give, especially Black talent, the opportunity to work with Unfold Stories, knowing that they might have certain biases while hiring. Their team in New York is very diverse, and it is something they're constantly learning more about: not just about hiring but about listening to these employees and their mindsets. For example: working on stories around Black History Month and making sure their Black employees are leading that initiative. They also strive to balance their hires and look for more women: with two male founders, it's important for them to attract talent that will help in those areas where they might be lacking.

Unfold Stories ensures they are reaching the people they need to reach by attending conferences and events where they can speak one-on-one with them. Alfie is always 100% willing to offer his time to reach out to talent.

When being courted by other big tech companies, Unfold Stories doubles down on values and ethos, sometimes making hard decisions. Their rapid growth caught many investors' attention. They had big offers on the table, and it was really tempting for Alfie, as a 25-year-old, to get that money and move on. However, he knew how much potential his company had and the direction they wanted to go, and he didn't want to be dictated to do something they didn't want to do.

Alfie learned from Parsons that his company's users and their needs are paramount. Unfold Stories is a revenue-positive business, and they don't necessarily need so much money. He can still focus on the smaller positive things to grow the business, so that's how he started rejecting companies.

> It's hard to trust big companies. They always have other intentions, so we were cautious about asking questions about how they wanted to use data, privacy, etc. Squarespace really believed in our values, their products felt like part of the same family as ours, and they wanted to leave us kind of alone because we were doing it well. They trusted us, and we trusted them, and we're delighted with the decision. The merger was such a big growing experience, from a really scrappy startup to being part of a bigger company with people much more experienced than me. Now we're not just part of Unfold but a bigger user journey of Squarespace.
>
> Alfie

For Alfie, the biggest lesson early on was understanding when to tap into Squarespace's resources and when to remain scrappier and more independent. A critical part of Unfold's success was reacting quickly to trends. Squarespace, as a bigger company, moved slower, and Unfold didn't want that to affect them, so that was a learning curve: when to tap into them and when not to.

To understand how purpose and mission help align, frame, and underpin your startup culture, we introduce the Mission Board template (Figure 4.6) that helps you operationalize your company's authenticity

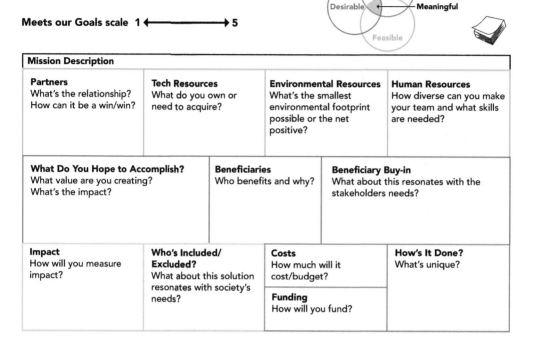

Meets our Goals scale 1 ⟵————⟶ 5

Mission Description

Partners What's the relationship? How can it be a win/win?	Tech Resources What do you own or need to acquire?	Environmental Resources What's the smallest environmental footprint possible or the net positive?	Human Resources How diverse can you make your team and what skills are needed?
What Do You Hope to Accomplish? What value are you creating? What's the impact?	**Beneficiaries** Who benefits and why?	**Beneficiary Buy-in** What about this resonates with the stakeholders needs?	
Impact How will you measure impact?	**Who's Included/** **Excluded?** What about this solution resonates with society's needs?	**Costs** How much will it cost/budget? **Funding** How will you fund?	**How's It Done?** What's unique?

Figure 4.6
Mission board.

around your mission, so you are living your intentions transparently while still aligning at the sweet spot for innovation. Using the prism of the innovation Venn diagram, which defines innovation at the convergence of viability of your concept, feasibility of your team to bring it to life, and the desirability of your audience to adopt it or need it.

This template helps you operationalize your company's mission, so you are able to live your intentions transparently. Then asks you to rate the mission's goals on a scale of 1–5 through the prism of the Innovation Venn diagram, which defines the sweet spot of innovation being at the convergence of viability of your concept, feasibility of your team to bring it to life, and the desirability of your audience to adopt it. Each area is color-coded to align with one part of the Venn.

Mission Board: Building Business Ops

Building off your North Star exercise and inspired by the hierarchy of purpose diagram, here we will work on operationalizing the mission and vision for your organization. Articulating and reflecting in this way helps to define the culture you intend to create.

1. Start at the top left, answering all the prompts.
2. Step back to assess the responses on a scale from 1 to 5. Ask yourself if all these answers align with my values and aspirations for the company's mission and vision.

As you start to think about how you will operationalize to meet your mission, make sure you are testing out the best ways to pursue your goals that still align with your purpose and values by asking questions like:

- What type of product/service/work/projects best/least align with the purpose, vision, and priorities?
- Who are the best people to recruit?
- Ways to measure performance and value creation?

Envisioning your culture > product > market fit

Eventually, your idea's alignment with your values shapes your culture. By threading through your values across all touchpoints of your (future) company, you are creating clarity and authenticity from the start, thus building a culture on solid ground.

You might love them all but you need to create hierarchies that resonate across your team and the community you are working for to make a true and authentic connection between the products or services you're creating and the people you serve.

This exercise will help you manage and message your values and vision across all your channels to shape your culture with intention.

Road mapping as cultural artifact: Cascading passion throughout your culture

We moved from understanding *the why?* Your passion for starting up, to creating the documents and processes needed to back that up and bring it to life. The goal here is to create the *how-to?* part of the business to align the team and other stakeholders with your plans to bring those values to life and make them a reality that people can get behind, celebrate, measure, and build upon. To do that, create a roadmap, explaining your vision, strategy, processes, and assessments to foster and maintain a positive learning culture ripe for innovation and action while bringing about successful products and services. If you think this is a lot, it is! The exhilarating experience of an entrepreneur and founding team experience is filled with ups and downs as they must juggle a lot until they are able to generate enough income to onboard more team members.

Preparing these roadmaps in advance will be the key, then iterating upon them in feedback loops over time will become a vital part of both your culture and its success. Not having a roadmap can lead to a confusing atmosphere that can often erode trust from teammates and partners. While charting a course, start by explaining goals to gain consensus. Then, co-create and course-correct when needed. These build trust and create a positive culture.

Asking people to put their careers, hard work, and trust into your vision is a gift to treasure and should not take lightly. How one honors this is by being honest and clear in return. There are no guarantees but practicing the superpowers with active listening and good strategy informed by design research has a proven track record for success. Pulling together a clear roadmap that aligns vision > culture > product > to market fit is the goal. Tools like this help develop roadmaps for alignment across all these important factors that make a winning combination for success.

Start building your team culture to build a flourishing community

Communities can feel magical, but they don't appear out of nowhere. In the past years, the main driver of good business has entered the market: creating community both internally and externally. For many modern companies, building a community with little distinction of internal or external (transparency) hangs on the culture of products or services to mission alignment. This is the modern way of creating a successful and sustainable business. We've learned that this kind of positive community feeling grows because of the interplay between the mindsets of the people within the organization, that is, your team, the synchronicity with the purpose and values defined by the mission, and the behaviors that shape it to form the culture. In the next chapter, we move on to understand the alchemy behind this magic within the ecosystem.

Navigational Log + Takeaways

Grab your notebook or just take a moment to pause and answer these questions:

- How do you manage conflict?
- What is the purpose of your organization? How can you best pursue it?
- With your purpose and vision in mind, what matters most to your startup now, and will that need to change in the future?
- Which projects best align with the purpose, vision, and priorities? Which do not?
- Who are the best people to execute this project?
- Who needs to be included, who is left out, and why?
- What behaviors shape your culture and align with your values, mission, and vision?

5

SUCCESS: AN ETHOS FOR RESILIENCE

Shape a connected ecosystem

Objectives

- Understand the concept of adaptive systems
- Envision your company ideals and translate early-stage culture into community
- Embody awareness to shape inclusive value for social and environmental good
- Ensure identity justice with design-informed decisions
- Build the foundation of a *living* strategic plan to inform your startup journey

Living in a dynamic world

To exist as a company is inherently political: by nature of putting our creations into the world, they are impacting others. Whether that impact is an intentional result of the product itself (or how it's created or manufactured) or unintentional (how it's disposed of, for example), our offering has a cause and effect: who we offer it to, how we create it, and who we hire to help us create it requires mindful planning. Business owners, activists, advisors, mentors, and entrepreneurs alike have an obligation to bring our reflex of awareness to assess our biases, articulate our values, and build a stable, inclusive structure to achieve the desired impact.

> *Virtue, the saying goes, is in its own reward. But virtuous organizations, like virtuous people, outperform their peers over time.*
> SHRM Foundation's Report on Ethical Workplace Culture
> (SHRM 2022)

We live in a dynamic system, a world that is constantly changing. Like the human body seeking homeostasis between the outside world and the inner body, dynamic systems aim for a state of equilibrium. Let's assume, for example, that a car is a dynamic system;

DOI: 10.4324/9781003227151-8

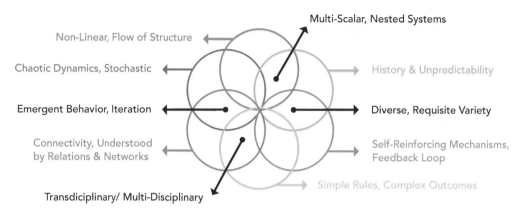

Figure 5.1 Complex adaptive systems.

it would require fuel to continue moving forward or else it would come to a stop and become static. Scientists increasingly view the Earth as a **dynamic system** that is a combination of interrelated, interdependent, or interacting parts forming a collective whole or entity. On a macro level, the Earth's systems maintain their existence and function as a whole through the interactions of their parts, called components.

Such complex environments are often referred to as **adaptive systems (or complex adaptive system, CAS, Figure 5.1)**. In short, a CAS is one that changes its behavior in response to its environment. The study of complex adaptive systems, a subset of non-linear dynamical systems, is interdisciplinary and attempts to blend insights from the natural and social sciences to develop system-level models that allow for heterogeneous agents, phase transition, and emergent behavior. Knowing this offers you a way to think about how patterns emerge from the complex interdependencies around you.

For many organizations, the way in which projects are managed is a fundamental factor in how well they can prosper in today's marketplace. Unfortunately, the current solutions available to companies for managing projects are proving to be increasingly ineffective in a world that is increasingly transparent, dynamic, and unpredictable. They also tend to leave important stakeholder voices out of the conversation, either intentionally or unintentionally. To prevent this, embedding values of social justice **rooted in systems awareness** enables your startup to be trusted by not only your team but also your community. This is an ethos to integrate from day one in the design of your startup process, instead of waiting until you're at the "organization" level.

We've discussed how having an articulated practice of inclusion builds a healthy innovation culture internally. Because the lines between internal and external are dissolving, this will reflect externally. Larger social platforms like **Unfold Stories** show us ways of

Figure 5.2
Alfonso Cobo testing product.
Photo credit:
Squarespace, Inc.

functioning like an organism that is alive and constantly changing. They needed to fully embrace the characteristics of a complex and adaptive system, with a company sitting at the crux of interdependent communities.

Alfonso (Alfie) knew early on the importance of starting with an ethos: the manifestation of his cultural beliefs that built the credibility of his company offering and allowed him to build a community that reflects transparency and is rooted in sharing creation. When building a tech product, founders also need a responsive community to test with. Done right, this can enable momentum and scale—virality as a design tool. Alfie launched Unfold by leveraging a community-centered offering with design-forward methods.

Positive feedback loops centering community

Building a positive feedback loop within a community of early adopters and trusted users is the key, Cobo explains. Being adaptive and responsive to the needs of users was crucial to their early success, as was being true to their own core values as founders. For Unfold, their ethos around social justice helped build their authenticity, which led to creating resilience within the marketplace, in turn leading to their success. Building community and building trust, both internally and externally, are inevitably part of a company's formation; a mission with social and/or environmental impact at its core is fundamental for supporting the identities within the communities you might serve. For Alfie, it was about taking a stand on lesbian, gay, bisexual, transgender, queer/questioning, plus (others) (LGBTQ+) rights.

"The social media world can be superficial and have negative impacts, especially for young people, so we wanted to try to reframe that .... We wanted our product to be linked to stories that matter and could drive potential change and connect with people ... to highlight their accomplishments." Once a week, Alfie sets out through Unfolds own Instagram account, posting pro-bono highlights about nonprofits or storytellers of the week to celebrate their accomplishments and give them a platform to create awareness.

After some success with this, they collaborated with organizations to tell their stories from a very young age as a company. One organization, All Out, is based in the United Kingdom and fights for LGBTQ+ rights globally. It's a cause personal to Alfonso, having openly discussed his homosexuality and isolation in the predominantly hetero cis-male dominant tech culture. Alfonso, in his creation of Unfold, leaned into vulnerable identities, instead of shying away from potentially polarizing views. After telling and showcasing stories to raise awareness for key causes, they transitioned also to raise money for these causes. To do this, they launched specific collections of storytelling frames within their collection, donating 100% of the proceeds to these charities like the (Red) campaign. We see tech platforms showcase values-based intent but their sincerity rooted in action began on day one. Platforms often play it safe by allowing things like LGBTQ+ stickers in countries where they're permitted but Unfold took a stand and made them available in every country, regardless of their stance on the issue—a decision that reflects honesty in ethos, even at the expense of potential users. This built trust, and transparency, and amplified their success; not hindering it.

"It's always about being real: the connection between myself and the product that I'm building.

I wanted to take part in helping because I understand how privileged I've been throughout my life, even though I'm an immigrant. Seeing stories of people who haven't had the chance I've had just breaks my heart; it's not fair. I've been sent hundreds of messages from young LGBTQ+ kids who look up to me and were inspired by me doing this product."

One key behavior in this approach is learning to help your user frame a problem as an ongoing relationship, co-solving as if you will be in an ongoing relationship as the world evolves: it's a responsive behavior and mindset that will keep you and your company relevant through impact.

Inclusion: The community-building catalyst

Mismatches are the building blocks for exclusion.

Kat Holmes

Businesses that have ethical workplace cultures outperform their competitors and peers in all the categories that matter. A good portion of workplace ethics development is about articulating and communicating values, then refining them to be actionable. Research has shown that companies making these investments outpace traditional companies that don't call these values out explicitly in their vision statements, see Figure 5.4 a systemic approach to culture.

We learn this from Kat Holmes, a UI/UX designer from Silicon Valley whose research focuses on diversity, equity, and inclusion (DEI). She wrote *Mismatch, How Inclusion Shapes Design,* a book about the disparities within the design fields, and how these deficiencies permeate the products and services designers create—from web interfaces,

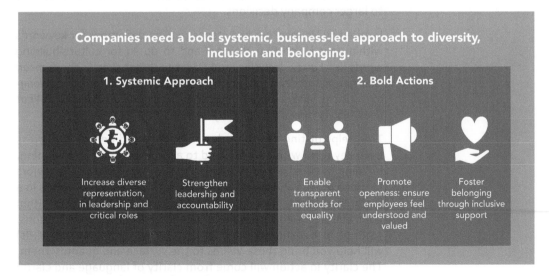

Figure 5.4 A systemic approach to culture.

mobile applications, software, physical products, and the buildings we work and live in, to the cities we inhabit. Holmes underlines that these designed creations have been thought about, strategized, planned, and designed by other humans that either *intentionally or unintentionally* left people out. The frameworks and constructs we create shape how we see the world and innovate. The language we use matters as much as the actions we take to articulate our purpose, which ultimately creates the value your business provides.

It is the "mismatches" in the meaning we give those words, our individual perceptions that can make all the difference in how they play out (Holmes 2018). What we're learning is that we bring our biases, conscious and unconscious, to our creations. This intentionally or unintentionally impacts our communities and systems, causing reverberations that can be felt like ripples in the water or space-time, impacting generations to come.

As design entrepreneurs, our job is to build upon our mission and mindset to identify personal biases from earlier chapters; we will learn how to keep biases in check, develop more inclusive "phygital" spaces (physical and digital), and hold others within our developing community accountable for their personal growth and learning mindset.

With the effective change in mind, we can build new paradigms that, from inception, take into consideration and consciously embody behaviors to invite diverse voices and perspectives into the construction of our companies, and the business's North Star. This act of early articulation puts in guardrails for exploitative behavior to translate down the line into opportunities for equity and access to content, products, services, mobility, and equal pay for equal work. A lived purpose can likewise take into consideration its impact on the environment, from micro-individual actions to larger company decisions.

Inspired by Holmes, our first step is to align definitions for keywords within your North Star diagram and to do so for culture-building words like *Equity*, *Inclusion*, and *Diversity*. *What exactly do we mean when we use abbreviations like DEI or EIB (equity, inclusion, and belonging) and the many other acronyms bantered around workplaces? What does "Equity" mean to you, as a founder?*

This helps distinguish the value from the lived behavior. Express each key term with a word cloud to align with your core meaning, building toward how you'll express this in your company behaviors to make these values real. A word cloud is a diagram of words in a hierarchy of font, size, and shape to connote the priorities within your culture. Like inspirational quotes and posting aspirations, setting up benchmarks and key performance indicators (KPIs) will help you bring those values to the surface and quantify them. The clarity in action will come from clarity of language and clarity within metrics.

Diverse companies will out-earn their industry peers. Many organizations currently focus their DEI approach on collective accountability but that doesn't produce real results in DEI outcomes. Your budding organization needs to hold early team leaders accountable, using a DEI approach that leads to meaningful accountability.

- **Inform decision-making:** Use objective criteria and integrated data to drive equitable talent decisions.
- **Customize strategies:** Support customized strategies to enable leader execution of DEI goals.
- **Require progress:** Expect and require progress on DEI goals for any leader to advance in the organization.

Informed decision–making

+

customized strategies

+

required progress reporting

=

Consequential accountability

Inherent biases impact the bottom line, but sharing collective experiences makes a company more innovative. Doing this might help you avoid blind spots, check cultural biases, and enable more diverse points of view.

Strategic (and inclusive) roadmap: The company strategy canvas, (Figure 5.5)

There is nothing wrong with strategic planning—*except when we believe that strategy unfolds as planned.* A good strategic planning process in a complex adaptive *company* is one that crystalizes your long-term intention. It is the process through which we articulate a clear vision of where we want to go, and it's how we come to a clear agreement on which direction to take.

Think of that strategic plan as the roadmap you'll be co-creating as an adaptive system to respond to the rapidly changing externalities. You might plan to go down one road but need to make a U-turn or find a new road, or forge a new path at times; it's not a failure when these changes occur—but feedback informing your system and your strategic plan.

Our objective is to help you co-create a living, breathing strategy that emphasizes a shared value with both your team and your community as a form of resilience practice. The result of designing the ecosystem is value. **Resilience practice, easily put, is how you stay relevant over time and thrive under any circumstance.**

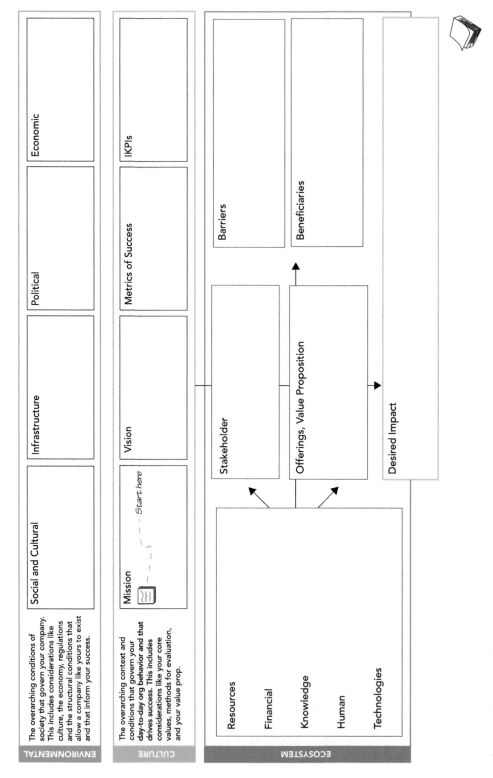

Figure 5.5 Company strategy canvas.

We reshape "planning" into cultural + systemic context shaping that's emergent—this is how change can happen. This is accomplished in part through a strategic plan and implemented through the values, purpose of the business, and its ideals. *Consider the following*:

- What is the problem that you want to solve?
- Who needs to be part of your ecosystem?
- What should be the initial governance model of your ecosystem?
- How can you relate to the value within your ecosystem?
- How can you ensure evolvability and the long-term viability of your ecosystem?

Developing a strategic plan that outlines and aligns the organization's vision and strategic priorities helps us tackle complexity and maintain a thriving community. The success of this plan will come from its "living" state: existing in a state of iteration, being updated often, and encompassing change of components across your launch process. If it doesn't meet this standard, the plan will simply gather dust and have no impact on the organizational decision-making process.

Founders using a "living" and holistic strategic planning approach view the planning process as independent yet interrelated.

Company Strategy Canvas

Articulating the desired outcome is a critical aspect of the process. This canvas is intended to help you begin articulating current views and current components of your complex adaptive company. What you achieve is born from this. You might not have all the answers but use it as a guiding light.

1. Start within the **Culture Section** by answering your mission statements, followed by your current vision, desired metrics for success, and KPIs.
2. Move on to the environmental bucket, following along and answering as best you can the prompts within this category. Think first about the overarching conditions vis-à-vis cultural and societal, within infrastructure, political, and economic.
3. Ecosystem Level: Analyze the current conditions you're working within from a resource's standpoint, financially, the knowledge base of you and your team, how many people you have vs. need, and technologically.
4. Define your stakeholders and the offerings (the value proposition you have) followed by the barriers and beneficiaries? Who stands to benefit in the current incarnation? Are there any current barriers to this working out?
5. Lastly, define the desired impact you hope to have with your intended startup; although you might not know how you will exactly create the impact, with which exact tools or services, try to define the impact you hope to have.

Assessing your potential position within the ecosystem

A company, like an individual species in a biological ecosystem, ultimately shares its fate with the network as a whole; smart firms pursue strategies that will benefit everyone. So how can you promote the health and the stability of your own ecosystem, determine your place in it, and develop a strategy to match your role, thereby helping to ensure your company's well-being? It depends on your role—current and potential—within the network.

If designing a traditional business model is like planning and building a house, designing an ecosystem is more like developing a whole neighborhood: with neighbors to coordinate, there are more layers of interaction, and the complexity often yields unintended outcomes. Such "strategic partnerships" can complement each other in different ways. It may be directly supplying products to one another or combining products or services to reach a target or larger market. A good example of an ecosystem is the smartphone business ecosystem. Network providers collaborate alongside hardware and software manufacturers that compete. However, they also complement each other by supporting a value chain that delivers a highly demanded customer experience. The result is a financial benefit for all players.

Developing ecosystem strategies has become a priority for many global companies. However, many are confused by the complexity of the ecosystem environment and daunted by the challenge of generating value from their ecosystem investments. What makes ecosystem design distinctive is that it requires a true system perspective. It is not sufficient to design the value creation and delivery model; the design must also explicitly consider value distribution among ecosystem members.

Cultivating internal team/community culture

Beyond what you consciously do to develop an ecosystem along with a positive and inclusive internal culture, the various types of business structures and legal governance will inherently impact internal behavior within your startup. We review the various structures in later chapters; however, each adds inflection points and cadences that will, in part, define and develop culture. For example, sectors that are highly regulated will have evaluative requirements, perhaps seasonal procedures required by law or built into your governance model or funder's expectations.

The diagrams following show examples of cultural checkpoints defined by the experience within those cultures. Traditional business cultures (Figure 5.6) often practice values that explore and exploit with sequential competitive growth phase prioritizing profit and signals change with financial metrics. The experience within cyclical nonprofit cultures based on analytical and achievement phases defined by discovery, deployment, and validation tend to be designated by funding cycles and necessary quantitative metrics of impact required by funders (See Figure 5.7). Compared to the experience within (re)generative business cultures (see Figure 5.8) where value is often multiplied and distributed across the system, with aspirational phases defined by exploration and redesign and transitional phases that are responsive, designed for conservation and renewal of growth signaled by the reflection of stakeholder value across the system (e.g., co-ops, circular business models, benefit models).

Exploratory Phases	Linear Phases →	**Exploitative Phases**

	Exploratory Phase	**Exploitative Phase**
Categories to Assess + Understand	**Discovery Experience**	**Growth Experience**
Mindset and Process	Iterative experimentation, learning, speed, failure, rapid adaptation, diverge to converge	linear, predictable, predatory, competitive, hierarchical
Focus	Research, Breakthroughs & Iteration	Depth, Efficiency and Growth
Strategy	Probing, analytic	Differentiation, Systematic
Goals	Discovering new opportunities. Creation of new value in new ways.	Achievement and profit-oriented. Claim of market, competition-focal.
Structure	Open, methodical, quick + iterative	Hierarchical, legal/tax-forward, thorough + detailed
Risk	High Risk	Risk Lowered
Measure of Success	Qualitative feedback, use case validation	Margins, client satisfaction, financial growth at the cost of all else
People and Skills	Can toggle between macro/micro, thrives in uncertainty, inquisitive, adaptive	Organizing, planning budgeting, consistency, timing process oriented
Financial Approach	Concept proving (traction over revenue) Investment risk-taking with little expected return	Steady revenue, dividends Returns proven, spend to make

Figure 5.6 Experience within traditional business cultures.

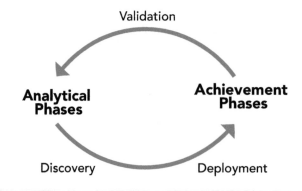

Categories to Assess + Understand	Analytical Phases	Achievement Phases	
	Discovery Experience	Deployment Experience	Validation Experience
Mindset and Process	Optimistic, mission-driven, narrative-focused on selling the idea or goal, ambitious, detailed	Energy, excitement, non-prescriptive, learning mindset, generative, iterative, data synthesis	Open, listening, and encouragement for shift made. Looking for signals
Focus	Explorative, ethnographic, data-driven, project design and proposal development, assessment	Communications, growth, mission, goals, differentiators, project management, team building, reflection and iteration, action-oriented	Impact reporting, quotes and storytelling, surfacing the unspoken positive changes
Strategy	Keyword-guided. market trends, differentiation. UVP, aligning synergistic with funders and partners missions identify synergy	Revenue, sustainment post initial funding, resource allocation, team alignment around goals, educating team about market and alignment to funder	Steady cash-flow, capture data/metrics, reassess and align resource allocation
Goals	People-focused, centering positive impact and sustainable change	Reassess, develop roadmap and blueprint to get to goals without attachment	Fulfillment around meeting goals, ethnographic alignment to goals
Structure	Data collection, divergent transdisciplinary, analytical writing and production focused, visual, expressive	Flexible, adaptive, heterogenius, non-prescriptive, confident	Evaluative, reflective, synthesizing, learning
Risk	High uncertainty. Speculative, persuasive	Moderate uncertainty, high risk, experimental	Low risk in good storytelling and learning
Measure of Success	Strong market scan, indepth, triangulation, in-depth, synthesizing research in clear alignment of funders goals	Time-based engagement, repeatable, align with funders goals and language. Education, consensus building	Qualitative feedback, use case validation, assessing alignment of goals, making intangible tangible, connecting dots for funders
People and Skills	Open, flat, inclusive. reflective, social-science mixture of quantitative, qualitative	Storytelling/pitching/selling approach, vulnerable, mutual engagement, high energy, exhausting, empathic, participatory, open-minded, compassionate, productive, action-oriented	Feedback through active listening and participation, communal and personal reflection and change
Financial Approach	Low revenue, budget-driven, projecting for iteration and learning, funder/project alignment (sponsors, foundations, govt. academic inst. grants)	Fiscally conservative achievement focused, stability, strategic, critical, activities to approved activities, communicating those effectively so funder can see connection	Exploitative: positioning for increased funding, making a case, deliberate, steady cash flow. Results meet financial goals with proof for increases

Figure 5.7 Experience within nonprofit business cultures.

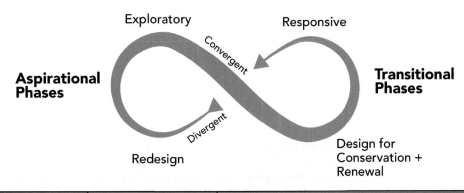

Categories to Assess + Understand	Aspirational Phases	Transitional Phases	
	Exploratory + Responsive Experience	Design for Conservation and Renewal	Redesign Experience
Mindset and Process	Divergent, iterative, flexible, human-centered, collaborative, impact-setting	Inquisitive, action-oriented, problem-solving, co-creative	Impact-assessing, iterative, inclusive, regenerative
Focus	Systemic, innovative, mindful, listening, observing, opportunities	Targeted, ideating, delivery, storymaking, production	Convergence impact reporting, reflective, contemplative
Strategy	Open-inquiry, qualitative, expansive, resource-assessment	Participatory, systemic, creative	Mindful, sustainable
Goals	Problem-setting, inspirational, documentational	Name and create, get stakeholder buy-in, prove efficacy	Margins, client satisfaction, financial growth at the cost of all else
Structure	Distributed, inclusive, ethical	Divergent, holistic, data-driven, open	Evaluative, reflective, synthesizing, learning
Risk	High uncertainty. Speculative	Moderate uncertainty, high risk, experimental	Low risk if proven methodology
Measure of Success	Opportunity definition, engaged stakeholders, buy-in	Alignment w partners/coop community values, net-positive impacts	Triple bottom line impact, community satisfaction, financial sustainability
People and Skills	Emotionally intelligent, mindful, curious, design research	Heterogeneous, creative, synthesizing, multi-disciplinary	Non-bias, non-hierarchical, adaptive
Financial Approach	Low revenue, budget-driven, projecting for iteration and learning, funder/project alignment (sponsors, foundations, govt. academic inst. grants)	Fiscally conservative achievement focused, stability, strategic, critical, activities to approved activities, communicating those effectively so funder can see connection	Deliberate, steady revenue, dividends returns proven, spend to conserve

Figure 5.8 Experience within generative business cultures.

Ecosystem design for agility and adaptability

Core values will inspire value-creating efforts as employees feel inspired to do what is right, even when the right thing is hard to do.
SHRM Foundation's Report on Ethical Workplace Culture
(SHRM 2022)

Heavily top-down organizations are often hierarchical, possibly in industries that are heavily regulated or are rooted in older societal norms from generations gone by, often still retaining legacy cultures. It is not necessarily always bad but these siloed structures can often feel confining, opaque, rigid, a hindrance to workflow, and with little upward mobility to many people who work there today in an economic climate that has been rapidly changing in societies that have seismically shifted and accelerated transitions due to cultural and economic trends, such as the advent of technology integrating into our physical everyday lives, the cultural and socioeconomic disparities exposed, new more complex and interconnected workflows, hybrid work-life, pandemic, accelerated innovation cycles, and climate crisis among other influences, have brought with them the necessity for more flat, shared leadership and accountability.

With the influence of digital design and engineering, product development methods have influenced traditional management structures, that is, traditional hierarchical structures with a rigid and often siloed company organization, and we see more often now a transformation into more networked and interdependent organization interactions (see Figure 5.9).

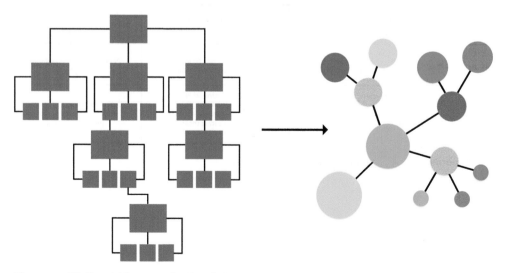

Figure 5.9 Distinguishing organizational structures.

The mind: Prepare yourself for cultivating community

What you make and the services you provide send a message that reflects your values and North Star: for you as a leader, your team, your company, and your community to rally around. As we said, to exist as a company is inherently political, and every decision creates an impact.

Ask yourself, who's at the table? Listen to your diverse team members. Listen to your community and invite other stakeholders into the process of developing your products and services. Model the behaviors of inclusion into your development process.

Having a fundamental awareness of eco-literacy, eco-design, systemic views, political will, and leadership helps inform your process.

- Share value in the name of good business
- Build and maintain a strategic plan that emphasizes shared value as a form of resilience practice at all three levels (personal, team, and community)
- Create an adaptive system within your organization to respond to the rapidly changing externalities.
- Ensure positive impact with design-informed decisions
- Stay in dialogue with your community and greater ecosystem
- Create and work within complex adaptive systems

Aligning an early form of the values and visions for you as a leader, your (potential) team, and the community helps create an authentic vision of the purpose and mission of the company that everyone can get behind and understand (see Figure 5.10). Checking in periodically throughout the lifespan of your business will be important to maintain alignment across you as a leader, your team, and the community you serve.

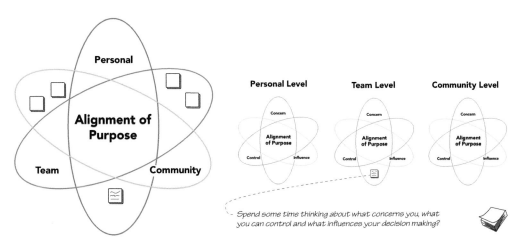

Figure 5.10 Aligning to purpose.

Aligning your Purpose

Think about your interests, your passions, and your *Why?* Like the North Star exercise, this Alignment of Focus will help articulate your mission. Include your personal interests, jotting—What fills your cup? Think about what brings you joy and inspiration and drives you to do what you do. Maybe you need to ask yourself this a few times, each time probing deeper inward. Why are you so committed to this mission, and what's your purpose?

1. Start with yourself.
   - What concerns you? What's your operating mission?
   - What do you feel you can influence?
   - What influences your decision-making?
2. Repeat for your team, followed by the ecosystem.
3. Synthesize these reflections into one clear statement for each: You Personally, Your Team, and the Community, and place the sticky note at the intersection of each.
4. Building upon these statements, craft a holistic statement that reflects all three (personal, team and community) and place that at the center of the largest diagram.

Navigational Log + Takeaways

- Consider empowerment—what does this look like for you?
- What does an honest ethos look like for you?
- Leverage and lean into your identity for your company's formation
- Embed Resilience as a founding practice
- Complex-adaptive systems: the operable success to creating a responsive company
- Try answering these questions:
  - What purposes should we pursue?
  - What rules should we uphold?
  - What choices should we make?
  - What actions should we take?
  - What should our characters be?
  - What sort of culture should we shape?

Dimension C

Method

Making, breaking, and world-building

If you can't understand other systems, your system will not operate. With a mindset and mission prepped, we shift into fundamental process and action, traveling through the phases of strategic design to shape a formative company journey. This will assess the current state of your concept and test both the business model and the business value to thrive in the face of uncertainty. We'll walk through a design-driven process with frameworks and tools to kick-start your concept, engaging stakeholders to build your startup success.

DOI: 10.4324/9781003227151-9

Strategic Design Process for Entrepreneurship

Phase	Investigate		Synthesize	Ideate & Converge		Storytell & Deliver
Goals	Map Context	Explore Problem	Gain Insight	Ideate Concepts	Test Solutions	BETA Product Experience
Entrepreneurial	• Sector signals early in company journey • Identify all stakeholders • Value prop as intervention • Evaluating market size, TAM/SAM/SOM • Assess current landscape • Analyze environmental impact (STEEP)	• Solidify customer segment • Feedback from potential customers • Forge stakeholder relationships • Source key value drivers • Build network of advisors/experts	• Define the pain points & opportunities • Elevate market insight • Identify opportunity areas • SWOT analysis	• Distinguish solution concepts vs. components • Evaluate concept against system goals • Create your initial concept/service • Environmental impact assessment • Build prototype roadmap	• Finalize universal value proposition • Roadmap product/offering launch • Finalize business model • Assess fiscal/financial structures • Fundraising plan	• Roadmap company launch • Pitch deck creation • Build business narrative, story-tell vision • Formalize customer experience • Develop brand positioning
Design	• Desk research • Identify users, experts and bystanders • Ecosystem map • Stakeholder analysis & evaluation • Causal looping • 4x4 Matrices	• Engage with stakeholders • Open inquiry, exploratory research • Analogous research • In-depth interviews • Observation • Applied ethnography • Assumption testing • Identify and explore biases	• Storytell research with visual documentation • Personas • Setting goals for outputs • Affinity maps • Empathy maps • User journeys • "How Might We" questions	• Co-create components with stakeholders • Brainstorm divergent ideas • Ideation workshops • Opportunity evaluation matrices • Prototyping strategy • Competitive landscape analysis • Low-fidelity vs. high-fidelity prototypes • Service blueprint	• Resource assessment • Test pricing and demand (with pilot) • iterate & test prototypes • Form user experience • Web testing, UI/UX • Brand development and style guides • Pivot if necessary, restart cycle	• Storytelling canvas • Narrative building blocks • Cone of plausibility • Future-back thinking, back-casting • Develop brand voice

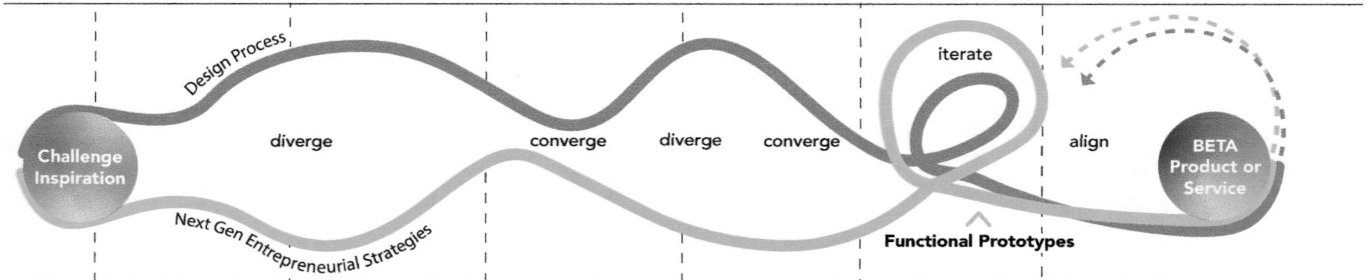

Topics, Tools, and Activities

Figure 6.1 Strategic design process for entrepreneurship.

6

INVESTIGATE TO MAP CONTEXT

Understanding systems design

Objectives

- Understand systems thinking and its entrepreneurial relevance
- See business as an intervention for change
- Map your ecosystem and chart stakeholders
- Understand the strategic design and entrepreneurship tools within phases of the business design process
- Prioritize visual processing as the medium for the strategic design process

We kick off the phases of strategic design for entrepreneurship by building systemic clarity. Very often, you need to work within systems to transform them. Effective problem solvers today need to know how to visualize the larger dynamics of the system while staying grounded in the needs of people. *Just remember, solving problems within a complex system takes time!*

The real world ((It's complex!))

The word "system" can reference machines, the human body, the economy, and something as small-scale as a light switch. By definition, a system is any group of interacting elements that together create an outcome as a unified functioning whole. Understanding a system in action means recognizing influence and adequately understanding boundaries, structure, and purpose. The term itself is straightforward, but leveraging systems thinking is challenging. It becomes more complex when you try to understand system states. The more we include human behavior, actions, and the intent of distinct players, the more complicated it becomes.

Let's run a few examples of *a system* made up of elements, interaction, and a goal:

- Your coffee machine created from mechanic parts requires your input and action to produce coffee

DOI: 10.4324/9781003227151-10

- A credit card company allows spending through a card that's paid back with interest over time
- The human immune system uses organics, cells, and proteins to protect your body from disruptive invaders
- The economy relies on individuals and businesses through a financial exchange to create value

Now, let's shift the boundaries by adjusting the purpose.

For example, if the goal is **to make coffee**, defining the system as the discrete components of the machine, plus whatever action is required, would suffice.

If the goal is **to make the best coffee**, we'd need to define what "best" means and for whom. Then, when sorted out, we might consider the type of beans, how freshly they were roasted, the water temperature, and the quantity we wish to make.

Suppose we operate with a definition of "best" as ethically produced and low intervention to produce the best taste. In that case, our goal **is to get single-origin coffee in every home**. With this goal in mind, we need to involve coffee farmers, trade law, manufacturing parties, packaging, vehicles, and workers for distribution, points of purchase, etc. We'd also have to explain to consumers why they need or want single-origin coffee.

While we can reference relatively commonplace or simplistic examples where we define the boundary, the purpose is how we shape our understanding of a system. This is the root of systems thinking that we apply to the entrepreneurial process. We weave into design-driven venture creation the thought leadership of cross-disciplinaries like environmental scientist Donella Meadows, sustainability and management leader Peter Senge, and engineer Jay Wright Forrester.

> *There are no separate systems. The world is a continuum. Where to draw a boundary around a system depends on the purpose of the discussion.*
>
> Donella Meadows

Today's world is a dynamic, interconnected, and complex environment. Your company—or the concept and soon-to-be company—is a system. It includes a set of things working together to create an outcome that would be impossible without all the parts, like making coffee. So, there's not only the complicated assemblage of the pieces but also their relationship to the goal (Figure 6.2).

Knowing that only a tiny percent of startups attempt systems-level change, starting with a coherent understanding of your systems is critical. To accomplish this perceived prosperous future state, we must chart what goes in, who's involved, and the result against our initial goals.

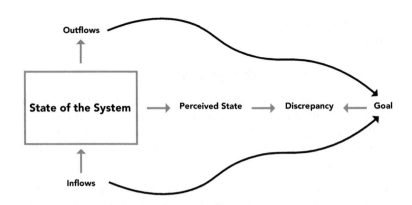

Figure 6.2
Systems function.

Understanding how influencers such as governance bodies, associations, and competition impact a sector is essential to comprehending points of entry and opportunity. Problems like world hunger or eliminating plastics are "wicked" because their systems are enormous, complex, and involve multiple and overlapping goals. In Figure 6.3, Hodgson diagrams the core components of our world systems. We argue the same hold true for an early-stage startup.

Systems incept and define the strategic design process because they allow us to journey beyond our expected scope, crafting stable expertise for our early-stage company. This includes the stakeholders we'll

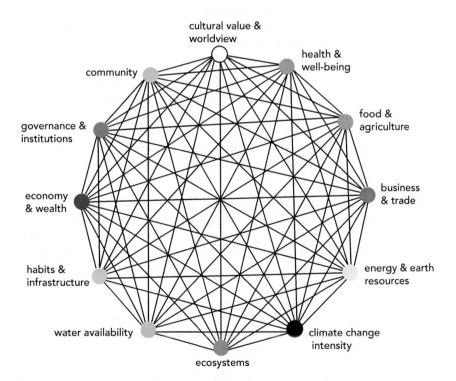

Figure 6.3 International Futures Forum World System Mode, with permissions by Anthony Hodgson (2011) connecting 12 key dimensions of a regenerative system.

rely on and what may or may not cast momentum *or obstacles* along our journey.

See your systems with superpowers

To be conscious of the whole system, we must train ourselves to let go of a singular point of view. Instead, we observe the past to build beyond our current conditions. Like a muscle—the more we train ourselves to be aware of our system elements, the easier this will become.

Recalling the designer's superpowers, applied systems require the ability to zoom in and out, encompassing a much wider angle from where we're situated. Also, an understanding of what the elements in our system are (scaffolding for enacting our ethos!).

As founders or team leads, we often find ourselves in the weeds: disconnected between the hand and heart. In the process, we find it hard to look back at what we are creating. Instead, we integrate the mind with systems tools as a developing muscle builds effectively toward the outcome we initially conceived.

Visual language + mapping

We recommend building systems-awareness muscles while developing visualization muscles. Sketching and drawing are the core of designing methods for innovation. Visuals help communicate complex systemic problems in faster, simpler, and more digestible ways to accelerate the alignment process.

Systems mapping is our first encounter to deploy core visual techniques, often the first assumption of what most understand as design. Visual processing creates another medium to align stakeholders and help show spatial and systemic relationships that are nonlinear. It allows you to *literally* step back to see patterns, intangible macroelements, and their relationship to more concrete or visible micro-ones.

Language shapes our perception and the often-linear nature of language shapes our thinking and approach to the world. When dealing with dynamic systems, we need to pay attention to the interdependent process of change, not snapshots, but feedback loops and circular systems. Graphic designers use visual representation to communicate messages to readers indirectly through cultural and visual cues. By applying a visual hierarchy, typography, pictures, logic, and layout techniques, designers optimize the reader or user's experience and allow for improved cognition and storytelling (Figure 6.4).

A good map is never static. As designers, we believe work should be iterative. We produce numerous sketches and prototypes before we arrive at a final version. We suggest making several versions of

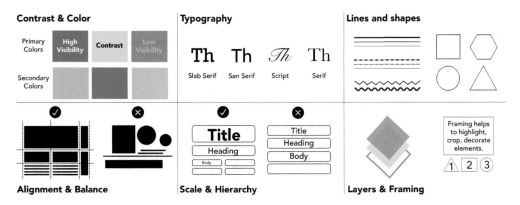

Figure 6.4 Graphic communication basics.

drawings to build them out as you collect more data from research. In mapping stakeholders and relationships, you will ask yourself and your team many questions because you need to see how everything fits together. You should come to rely on visuals as both communication and sensemaking tools. Reworking diagrams, frameworks, and maps dozens of times occur as we gain experience and information, test ideas and assumptions, and begin understanding stakeholders' influence and relationships.

Start seeing your systems and feedback loops

Strategic design, rooted in systems thinking, helps the entrepreneur uncover signals. This is, in part, where the *strategic* part of design comes in.

At the Elab, we use this sequence of activities to begin observing systems in play:

• Identify Stakeholders
• Locate Competitors and Complementors
• Map Ecosystem
• Diagram Causal Loops
• Engage the Ecosystem

The ecosystem and stakeholder maps are an opportunity to step back and see who's at play. Adopting these practices by visual mapping will allow strategizing and planning step by step. Revert back to the map, layer in new research information, step back, reassess and modify the strategy, and eventually decide how to act upon it.

Helpful Tip! Try not to fall in love with your first drawing! Strategic maps should go on the wall and be updated constantly. Use push pins or post-its or make them digitally on virtual whiteboards. Thus, allowing people to add updates or questions synchronously or asynchronously.

Figure 6.5 Mapping
feedback loops.

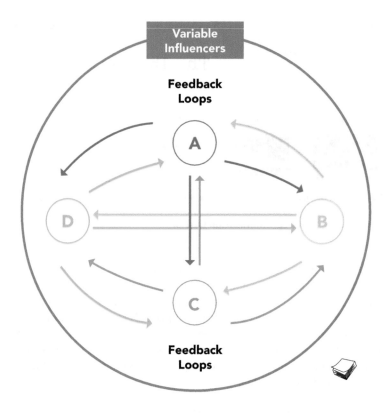

Map Your Feedback Loops

Visualizing and analyzing strategic positioning is a great exercise
to try solo or with a team. The dynamic relationship between elements crafts feedback loops we can routinely observe and use as
tools to grow, test, and shape a final offering.

This exercise aims to position yourself strategically within your
newfound ecosystem. **Each diagram will look a little different
based on your relationships; not every relationship is equal or
reciprocal.**

1. Write out key player(s). This could be other businesses,
   partners, or influencers. Add their names in place of the
   letters.
2. Think about the qualitative and quantitative feedback received
   and given. Identify what is exchanged, gifted, or requested
   between these stakeholders. Write them whether good or bad,
   financial, or energetic, abstract or concrete.
3. Analyze this feedback in the short and long-term. *What is that
   relationship like? Is it symbiotic, tense, competitive, supportive,
   or fleeting? Where might reinforcement or the need to forge new
   relationships occur?*

Systems modeling to launch a fashion brand, with Advene

Meet Yijia and Zi! Advene is an accessory brand started in 2020 and devoted to conscientious craftsmanship, responsible materials, and design, based in New York City.

Advene sees itself as a new kind of accessories brand dedicated to rethinking everyday essentials by sourcing responsible materials. Central to their ethos is co-creating products with customers while working directly with craftspeople to minimize unnecessary plastics and excess material consumption. In addition, Advene pushes against traditional product development methods by forging conscientious pathways using more environmentally conscious production methods and creating more equitable work environments (Figure 6.6).

Yijia and Zi did this with an intentionally visual approach. Conceptualizing their fashion brand, they knew they wanted sustainability to be centered. Since the industry is one of the most notably unsustainable, their tactical approach had to be different. Early in their startup journey, they created an ethos (mission, vision, and values alignment) that helped pave the way for working by building on their personal values. This would define their brand.

Yijia and Zi spent months researching their customer base to create their identity and what they value by asking representatives to weigh in on their designs before production. They investigated the best

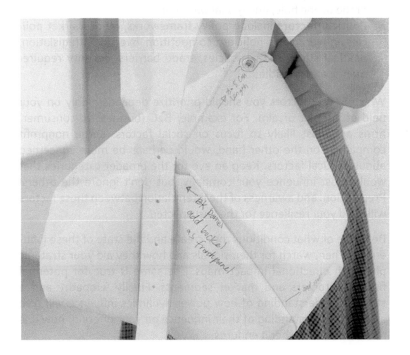

Figure 6.6 Advene's design process shows the strategic process of fewer fillers and accessories for more environmental sustainability.
Photo credit: Yijia Wang.

production locations and suppliers, and researched different channel options for the customer—from wholesale to direct, via their own e-commerce site. They researched their competition, various versions of their potential supply chain, customer analysis, price points, and potential partnerships.

Tools to think and act systemically

Using frameworks like the STEEP Diagram (Figure 6.7) will help collect the Social, Technical, Economic, Environmental, and Political factors that can potentially impact a startup. These categories shape early understanding of dynamic, interconnected, and complex environments.

STEEP Framework includes:

- **Social-cultural factors** include visual communication, art, music, fashion, media, and other cultural expressions.
- **Technological factors** include new technologies, technology effects, research, development speed, new products and processes, product life cycles, technology investments, and government research expenditure.
- **Economic factors** include economic growth, inflation, interest rates, exchange rates, taxation, unemployment, income, macroeconomics, business cycles, world trade, and resource availability.
- **Environmental factors** include material, resources, disposal, emission regulations, energy, transport routes, life cycles, effects of the ozone hole, and global warming.
- **Political factors** include policy frameworks, labor market policies, government policies, competition oversight, legislation, political stability, tax policies, trade barriers, security requirements, and subsidies.

Which STEEP factors you should prioritize depends highly on your field of interest or aim. For example, B2C (business-to-consumer) firms are most likely to focus on social factors. Large nonprofit companies, on the other hand, would perhaps be more concerned about political factors. Keep an eye for the broader categories that would most influence your company, but don't ignore the others! Preparation, and awareness of the interrelation between these factors will build your resilience for the unsuspected.

Be aware of what conditions they create and the state of these influencers. Then, watch for their signals and how they aid your strategic plan with directional impact maps. The same is true for potential future customers and market segments. Finally, empathy and a strategic understanding of how power dynamics influence will give a deeper understanding of their influence on your offering, how it is received and whether it endures.

Figure 6.7 STEEP Framework.

Try flushing out the STEEP Framework from the perspective of:

1. Single influencers, like a governance body or organization
2. Your company sector or early-stage concept

Taking inspiration from bees: Systems analogy and influence

There is so much we can learn from bees about systems: their physical shape, collaborative nature, and interconnectedness. Bees are
such a vital part of so many ecosystems our very existence depends
on them. They are a prime example of symbiosis: creating dependent, interlocking feedback loops that are mutually balancing and
beneficial. According to The Food and Agriculture Organization of the
United Nations (FAO), estimates that out of some 100 crop species
that provide 90% of food worldwide, 71 of these are bee-pollinated
(UNEP Emerging Issues Report 2010). They're part of nature's food
chain. However, due to the changing climate, bees are experiencing
colony collapse. This is a grave environmental concern for the many
species that rely on them, including humans.

**Meet Mark, a professor at Parsons! B Line is an ice cream and bee
education company founded in 2016.** Mark Randall's creation of B
Line was a way to engage with and support the symbiosis created
by bees. As pollinators, bees play an essential role in every aspect
of our ecosystem. They support the growth of trees, flowers, and
other plants, which serve as food and shelter for all earth's creatures,
large and small. In addition, bees contribute to our complex, interconnected environmental ecosystems that allow a diverse number of
different species to coexist, including humans. Mark's goal wasn't *just*
to make great ice cream, but to support local beekeepers and educate
the public on these pollinators' critical role in our lives.

Bees inspired one of Mark's long-term company goals to create a local
beekeepers cooperative, inspiring buy-in across his company system.
This reflects designerly attributes. It yields to existing systemic structures as an analogous influence for our intervention and involves deep
research of interrelated goals. How are bee colonies a metaphor for complex adaptive systems? As humans, we've developed alongside bees, but
they have millions of years of development over us. They work coopera-
tively where female bees play significant primary roles in the colony and
work together as a community, aiding and adapting to nature. This creates mutually beneficial scenarios that reflect triple-bottom-line values,
focusing on people, the planet, and profit. The trifecta from potential
mutual benefit makes regenerative value for more than one ecosystem.

Figure 6.8 Mark Randall with his bees.
Photo credit: Bibiana Heymann.

Visualizing systems shapes resilience

Back to Advene: In 2020, they were just about to launch their collection with their first handbag when COVID hit. Because of shutdowns within their supply chain, they needed to pivot and move their entire supply chain to Italy—a choice determined by assessing production influences, and having mapped possible options from the get-go. They needed to start their partnership and co-creation process over again. Even with these new design and manufacturing stakeholders, they prioritized the goal of the partnership, not simply sourcing. With their big-picture map of the flow of products across the chain of custody plotted against a timeline, more details were filled in. They could then plan, manage disruption, launch their business, and build upon it as markets reopened. Their original systems mapping was the crux of utility and their success at this point: because they had clear charts, diagrams, and spreadsheets, they were able to plug in different stakeholders to see the cause and effect these substitutions would have on their production timeline and across their system of stakeholders. Since sales rates for their kickoff collection would be uncertain during pandemic lockdowns, they had to have smaller production runs (minimum quantities to produce). They needed control and transparency over production and delivery across all suppliers and assembly.

Inviting stakeholders to the table (acknowledging interdependence)

To help Yijia and Zi, understand the complex system they were creating within their business's supply chain, they drew **ecosystem diagrams** and spreadsheets, including every stakeholder, down to the photographers and website developers. Then, all these touchpoints were charted against a timeline, crafting a **journey map** of their product and each stakeholder's role, contextualizing the steps (and buy-in!) from start to finish.

The act of investigation into the system placed change-centered efficacy over speed-center change. Prioritizing visual documentation, too, allowed for process clarity and, ultimately, a design-forward way of **co-creating** their supply chain. So, what did this look like?

First, in China, Yijia and Zi began interviewing and visiting manufacturers, determined to find like-minded partners. They interviewed "cleaner" producers of leather, searched for recycled packaging companies, designing in the most efficient ways while not compromising on style. They were also determined to "partner" rather than only hire their manufacturers in a traditional hierarchical power relationship. They understood that the shift in mentality would bring about a better communication flow and mutual respect, which is essential to managing complex systems with tight timeframes and deadlines. Understanding who their stakeholders were through diagramming, then choosing to involve them across their value chain has built a strong sense of shared ownership and collaboration. Through this approach, they create value as a company. Not only from the output but also from the buy-in their stakeholders feel in participating. This emotional investment can help organizations manage the often-disruptive flux and flow of irregular (often broken) systems and the difficulty of slotting together discrete components.

The approach to acknowledge and center the relationships is a systems-forward lens. It considers interdependence as equally important to running an effective company as the actual tangible goods produced from their supply chain.

Identify stakeholders

Design-led entrepreneurs map their systems. This occurs on all levels:

- The macro, like naming the global governmental bodies
- The mezzo, within the country

- The micro, within the city, and a map of competitors and potential partners

Laying out all the stakeholders of a project, product, or business into one drawn map. This helps get a visual representation of all the people/companies who can influence a project and how they are connected. You can layer them into your ecosystem map or create a separate one. Once all stakeholders are identified within affiliate sectors, create a Stakeholder Venn Diagram mapping intersections of alignment and departures, placing your service in the center.

Simply start by asking questions like, "who's involved?" The answers like groups, organizations, and people are your stakeholders. They can also be potential partners, team members, users, or customers, perhaps in different segments of populations, all the way to software suppliers, manufacturing partners, import/export offices, the external forces such as lobbyists and government. Ultimately everyone can benefit from these practices.

Begin clustering or grouping the various players and groups of stakeholders into sectors. For example, consider the Government or Education sectors (see ecosystem map). Using a whiteboard (digital or physical) is an excellent way to step back to look at the whole.

Figure 6.9 Charting stakeholder categories.

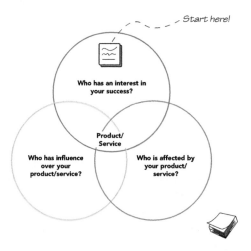

Create Stakeholder Maps or Venn Diagrams

These activities map the intersections and alignments of your stakeholders.

Working individually, think through...

1. Grab a whiteboard, 24" × 36" or large pieces of paper, and pens.
2. Reflect: Who should be in the middle of the diagram to start? Is it a customer or a business?
3. List out all stakeholders.

4. Use our diagram to help create a diagram to cluster or group them either in concentric circles from core "direct" stakeholders at the center to "indirect" stakeholders in the outer ring.

5. Using the Venn diagram with built-in clusters (stakeholder map), regroup them based on the prompts we ask in each interconnected circle.

6. Compare the two, perhaps blend them together.

7. Make a key (like on a map) and place it next to the diagram, so the readers understand what colors or line weights mean in your drawing.

8. Use lines to show relationships between stakeholders:*
   a. Dark thick lines to identify the most important relationship.
   b. Dotted lines to identify the less meaningful or perhaps more fragile. relationships.

Visual indicators help an audience understand hours of data and years of relationship building in seconds. Think about which colors symbolize what. Remember, a picture is worth a thousand words!

Team Stakeholder Mapping

1. Take the maps above and share them with the team in a facilitated workshop, asking them to build upon what's started.

2. Take the maps above and share them with stakeholders in a facilitated workshop, asking them to build upon what you and your team started to gain their feedback.

3. Ask Stakeholders to make their own version with themselves in the center. Pin it up on the wall and compare, looking for overlaps, gaps, and opportunities.

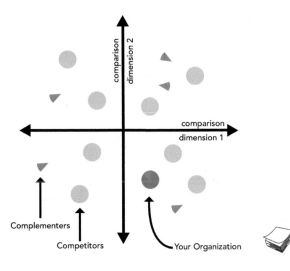

Figure 6.10 Competitors and complementors.

Create Your Own Competitors and Complementors Diagram

Use this to analyze your current market conditions.

Individual activity:

1. In the center of a canvas, create a matrix and label the X and Y with the dimensions you wish to compare.
2. Research and plot the logos of each of your competitors and complementors.
3. Then, plot your startup to assess and quickly convey your landscape.

Another variation of the stakeholder mapping (and broader system mapping) is to specifically explore stakeholders that are just like you — an organization, or company. Locate your competitors and complementors so you understand what other influencers there are for your stakeholders.

Take your systems and stakeholder mapping a step further by placing priority level, proximity or importance of stakeholders within a bullseye diagram, like Figure 6.11.

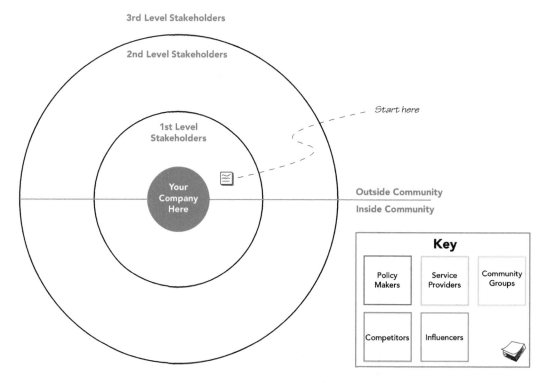

Figure 6.11 Internal and external ecosystem stakeholders.

Why, what, and how

Starting at the macro level, research the sectors at play, then identify the key actors (actor-network theory) within those sectors or within a particular network. After that, use visual hierarchy to convey who is more important than others and where opportunities may lie.

Try this activity, thinking about your ecosystem like what we mapped for the stakeholders. Remember, a good map is never static.

Create Ecosystem Maps

Individual activity

1. Grab a whiteboard or 24" × 36" paper and pens.
2. Ask who should be in the middle of the diagram to start? Try putting your startup there.
3. Ask and write down all the intersecting sectors.
4. Use our diagram to inspire a diagram to cluster or group them in circles; think about if they overlap or not and how they might impact one another and connect.
5. Make a key for the map, so the readers understand what colors or line weights mean in your drawing.
6. Use lines to show relationships between stakeholders:
   a. Dark thick lines to identify the most important relationships.
   b. Dotted lines identify the less critical or more fragile relationships.

Team activity

1. Take the abovementioned maps and share them with your team in a facilitated workshop. Ask them to build upon what you've started.
2. Do this again with your stakeholders.
3. Ask stakeholders to make their own version, with themselves at the center. Then, pin it up on the wall and compare, looking for overlaps, gaps, and opportunities.

Causal loop diagram

Building on a feedback loop diagram, this inter-relational visual diagram shows, usually with arrows, how stakeholders' relationships or behaviors are interconnected. See Figure 6.12, inspired by Peter Senge's Compassionate Systems Causal Loop diagram, which helps the entrepreneur map potential areas for growth.

Mapping the inter-relational forces and dynamics within a system often are drawn in diagrams called ecosystem and stakeholder maps.

Below, we will show some examples. After visualizing the interdependencies through drawing and sketching:

- Share them on the wall and take a step back.
- Invite the team to reflect on them.
- Iterate.

The key objective is to build it out and add layers of depth and understanding as it develops, and assumptions are tested. This unfolds as the startup and products grow. These diagrams are helpful tools in workshops with stakeholders and potential customers or clients. They can later be used in pitch decks to investors, customers, partners, proposals, etc.

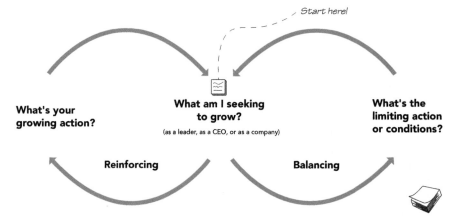

Figure 6.12 Causal loop diagram: Inspired by Peter Senge's Compassionate System's Causal Loop.

Create Your Own Causal Loop Diagram

Helps the entrepreneur map potential areas for growth.

1. In the center of a canvas, write what you aim to do.
2. To the left, write the action(s) that *reinforce* the growth of said potential achievement.
3. To the right, list what *limits or constraints* your growth to balance out or neutralize your potential.
4. To diagram compassion, try listing at the center a behavior you have, and then list what reinforces that behavior to the left and what balances it out to the right.
5. Step back and reflect.

Plan how to engage your stakeholders

This grid visually, based on the positioning and X/Y axis, shows stakeholders' interests and, therefore, the actions a business may need to take (Figure 6.13).

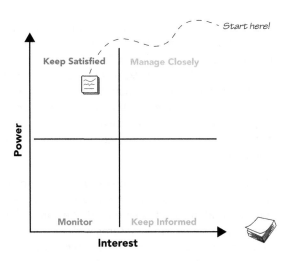

Figure 6.13 2 × 2 Stakeholder analysis framework.

Create Your Own Stakeholder Analysis Framework

Developed to analyze stakeholder positioning and priorities.

1. Draw a 2 × 2 chart, then put the description of the X and Y axis (we used an example above with Power and Interest, but you may want to diagram other relationships).
2. Label your four quadrants.
3. Plot your stakeholders to analyze your stakeholders or the competition.
4. Share with your team for feedback, insights, and analysis.

Where to enter the ecosystem

With an ecosystem mapped, one is ready to choose where to innovate. This choice is critical because where one enters can make or break a business.

The concept of a "Leverage Point" within a system was defined by Donella Meadows, the leading systems thinker and revolutionary game-changer who brought systems awareness to our attention. Understanding that the more grandiose the goal, the more difficult it will be.

The choices come from a goal, understanding system elements, and what interactions result from creating a company. We've described startups as complex adaptive systems because we see the complexity of developing a business today. It must strive to integrate the digital and the physical in potentially seamless and frictionless ways that delight users, impact behavior, and shift attitudes. Our value created may very likely have an impact we can't foresee or control. Pursuing in-depth analyses of our moving parts provides the basis to think critically about the potential impact our new endeavor could have—good, bad, or neutral.

We've seen for far too long the winner-takes-all mentality working in the short term for the few but not serving the many in the long run. The associated behaviors contribute to the planet's instability, creating a VUCA world. We live in scenarios where what a business starts offering this year may not be what it will deliver next year. Business leaders need to understand the socioeconomic dynamics, cultural signals, geopolitical currents, and accelerated environmental cycles to keep their communities and businesses thriving and safe.

We collectively see an imperative, a calling, shared awareness, and perspective from leaders and laypeople across the globe for a new paradigm shift taking hold. We can no longer do things the same way or build new systems with old ways of being and doing. Our systems are breaking; they leave entire segments of our populations out or harm the planet. We now have a deeper collective understanding and awareness, thanks partly to technology's augmenting our capacity for sharing information, knowledge, and data. This is a tabula rasa moment to shape the future. To envision and design a more just, equitable, and verdant world and bring that vision into creation. Leverage points are a powerful tool for change and critical endeavor not just bought into and played by old rules.

Keeping your eye on the big picture

Working at a systems level will help set short- and long-term goals. It will support the ability to be a trusted partner who invites critical stakeholders and customers to build community and, most importantly, sees where opportunities lie. To bridge this gap, we must activate the whole intelligence and co-create with collective sensemaking.

Just like understanding the past theoretical influences on the practice of Strategic Design, we must also look at other contemporary forces within our systems impacting business today and into the near and far future. However, what we discover in our ecosystem mapping will be foundational for our Futuring work in later chapters.

You might think you have enough to worry about, let alone take on the world's problems. But rest assured, it is good business to keep an eye on how your brand can support positive change (Figure 6.14 theory of change) and see it as ultimately good for the bottom line. We are on the cusp of a new era of experience, with an evolved sense of empathy, social justice, and purpose benefiting our shared knowledge, existence, and planet. Therefore, building a business from the ground up is both an opportunity and a privilege. Mapping the ecosystems at play enables equilibrium within your system or a recalibration of the system to be more socially and environmentally equitable.

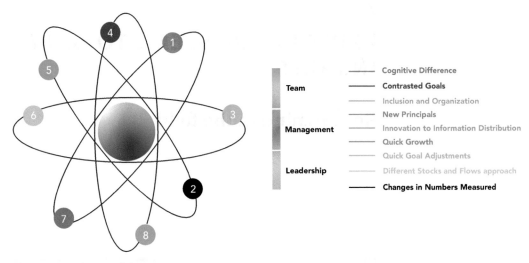

Figure 6.14 Theory of change.

The following chapters build upon these maps. The draft versions of ecosystem and stakeholder maps help gain insight into risk and possible negative impacts the startup creates. In addition, they help understand who benefits, who might need or want to partner, and the opportunities worth exploring.

Navigational Log + Takeaways

- Be thorough with landscape research for effective stakeholder mapping
- Stay open to all factors and practice active listening
- Notice and expect things to change
- Be thorough with your systems mapping
- Complete your diagrams and expect to add, change and iterate

7
EXPLORE PROBLEMS TO GAIN INSIGHT

Researching in the field

Objectives

- Understand design-led inquiry to build meaningful value
- Create a strategic-research approach to triangulate learnings
- Kick-start design-led research and embed it into your everyday workflow
- Increase research neutrality and check biases
- Debrief effectively for learnings

Previously, we introduced the essential step of mapping your systems—the placement of who, what, and where within your entrepreneurial multiverse. This helps navigate your journey forward with *mindful intent* and to make your founder-vision resilient. Below, we explore the cause and effect that could occur within and between any "node" in our system through design-driven research. Through open and honest exploration, we put ourselves in a position to discover or refine our offering (as systemic intervention!). This also increases the likelihood that our target users will love what we are doing.

Let's learn how to recognize where bias could hinder real value discovery, how to practice qualitative research, and what user-centered research methods include to drive a designerly approach to venture creation. We'll meet an Elab Fellow who launched his company, using a simple conversation with his community and a design-research approach to launch.

Inquiry as the backbone of solution-digging

For most of us, our days likely include waking up to an alarm, enjoying a coffee or tea, and opening our door (or laptop screen) to embark on the day. Rising in the morning—what we choose to do upon waking up, managing our time and priorities—can be leveraged as a "habit." **Noticing how and where inquiry shows up is how we can improve as a design-led entrepreneur.** Inquiry is inherent in being human but is also a quality distilled into practice in design. Nelson and

DOI: 10.4324/9781003227151-11

Stolterman emphasize the human instinct that creates intuition and thus shapes our approach to reason, reflection, and inquiry (Nelson and Stolterman 2012, 34). It is the underpinning of effective research, building toward *the why*. In the simple act of waking up, we might notice: *Did I rise to my alarm? How do I feel this morning?* Perhaps yesterday, you woke up feeling bright and chipper. You rose with the sun and set about your morning in a way you could look back and applaud yourself. You felt good. Today, however, you noticed feeling slow to wake up—the dread of an alarm and the onset of guilt that you had lost time. What changed between yesterday and today? What information stands out? Through this practice of inquiry, we're able to discover what the potential triggers could be and what pieces or factors—home, schedules, companies, meals, the time we went to bed—might have shifted, or combined, to cause this shift. In this example, when we rise in the morning and something feels askew—our ability to locate that cause is initiated by inquiry, applied to (and on top of) an awareness of the factors at play in our system.

Much like self-improvement, practicing effective inquiry is an iterative process and one that requires active engagement. Inquiring about a habit via research methods when engaging the ecosystem is exactly what many self-development and leadership authors like James Clear talk about when describing creating habits in *Atomic Habits* (Clear 2018): they are powerful ways to develop ourselves in whatever way we choose. The same holds for design. What we choose to do upon rising, how we manage our time, and what we prioritize can become habits to accomplish our goals for purpose with impact. The muscle of inquiry is the skeletal backbone of formal design-driven research practice. We must flex and practice this muscle to research effectively and establish a repertoire with our research participants.

Designing out bias

Our human tendencies are to generalize. However, there are negative repercussions of this. Without realizing it, biases can manifest in our design decisions (and our process of starting up!). These biases present themselves in the systems and designs being created. Unconscious bias exists in many forms, including race, gender, culture, age, and religion. As creators of living, intangible systems, we must be aware of our natural biases as we make design decisions to better connect with and design for a wider audience.

Design research helps us avoid causing impact without intent. As blooming design-driven entrepreneurs, we need to create systems that can respond to diversity and measure the impact it will have on the end user. Macro considerations like bias and systemic friction are often why we're building meaningful companies in the first place—*but how do we remove this during research while integrating our awareness of their influence and underpinnings into our learnings?* Fusing qualitative and quantitative data, we find out what's *real*, true, and *ideal* (Nelson and Stolterman 2012, 37) for our future users, consumers, or stakeholders. Our job is to listen, observe, and distill driving behaviors. Research through the lens of design acknowledges the complexity that we inhabit day-to-day and seeks to understand the social and environmental interactions, habits, and patterns of people and all life forms (all stakeholders!)—the systems we live in.

Research to reveal assumptions

Design with inquiry also leads us to our operating **assumptions before launch**. Knowing assumptions early gives a founding team the best chance of making course corrections—and not wasting time and money, no matter how much we want a solution.

Oftentimes, assumptions look like early attachment to solution functionality first. "Where should the button go," they ask before understanding the basic human, business, or societal needs for the idea to even work. Over time and through multiple waves of research (and later testing), we can begin to move toward more refined offerings. To help us define our needs, however, we need to eliminate our assumptions. Proving or disproving our key assumptions gets us closer to understanding the basic needs we are solving for—what's real to them and their ideals.

Research as a conversation: The Shape + feel

Let's begin with the basics: an inquiry into a problem context is what likely led you to startup. We're going to go out on a limb and assume you've had many colloquial conversations with people about your company. These might be conversations with a friend in your primary customer segment, stakeholders or perhaps just conversations with mentors or advisors helping shape your offering. These conversations ARE research by inquiry—and can be formalized into a practice that cements strategic design into your regular day-to-day and your startup workflow. Whether you're chatting with the person behind you in line or sitting down at a table to record an interview, your conversation should be led by the inquiry—**the social field**—between you and your stakeholders or participants but know that your intuition to converse about your company, your offering, and the learnings that naturally emerge is important.

This is part of design-led research for business: integrating multiple methods from multiple data streams (Figure 7.1). Design entrepreneurs expand and exploit our systems awareness by engaging the system directly: jumping in rather than sitting on the sidelines. What does this mean? We are going into the field, on the ground, navigating this game with all of our tactile senses in the physical world, guided through question-asking—all homing in on, building, and enabling the practice of inquiry. By opening our ears and attentively listening, we're directing our stride toward the golden center of meaningful experiences—where the good stuff happens.

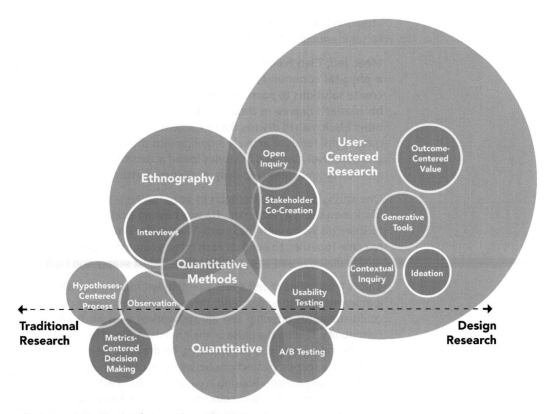

Figure 7.1 **A spectrum of research methods.**

Tim Brown and the IDEO team first diagrammed the intersections of Viable, Desirable, and Feasible to point toward innovation (see Figure 7.2)—which we take further to shape not only innovation but also meaning (Brown 2009; IDEO 2022). It's still common, however, for innovation to be perceived as just a matter of being viable for business or operating on technology advancement alone. We pay a lot of

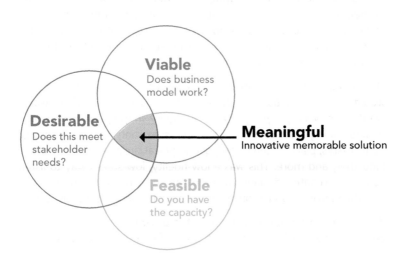

Figure 7.2 **Innovation VENN diagram.**

attention to our customers' desires because it's still something we don't factor in enough; it's what will set our products and services apart.

Meet Jeff, Elab fellow and founder of Gentlemen's Factory! GF is a phygital community for men of color, helping its members to create solutions to pursue further and achieve goals. While earning his master's degree in Urban Policy, Jeff organized gatherings with other black men to discuss their experiences. Jeff realized there was a meaningful result to actively inquiring into the frictions he'd noticed and attentively listened to stories found across the groups of men he grew up around, observed daily, and worked with.

One spring Saturday afternoon in 2019, 60 New York City resident black men sat in a restaurant. He was hosting a brunch and stood up to share his vision with the group: "I want black men to have a space to come together, to build up each other's successes, and to have the quality dialogue and opportunities that we just simply don't get."

This is a snapshot of Jeff's first event-styled focus group and partic- ipatory method to understand, through discovery research, how he could shape his offering. Jeff always worked with his hands in the community, feeling the pulse of their needs. A proud immigrant born in Haiti and raised in South Brooklyn, he grew up seeing wealth dis- parity and apparent distinctions between zip codes and even block-to- block—between gated housing areas and housing without gates. The distinction was and is skin color, due partly to generational wealth. His work experience explored this as a journey: from personal bank- ing to building stakeholder support for drug prevention programs, Jeff spent his time on the ground listening to what people walked in the door with, what his black community concerns were, and the lived experience of his community. Nationwide, we know this to be true: the message of success looks different and has a much harder, less opportune route for Americans of BIPOC (black, indigenous, and/or people of color). Jeff's passion for community-grown success drove him to launch the Gentlemen's Factory, which started under the name of Groomed Success. Ruminating on the question of where black men gather, Jeff announced a "Gentlemen's Brunch," merging fashion trends with community development. In 2014, before even incorpo- rating the company or landing on a model, he put together this first offering, charging $50 per person.

His approach was rooted in inquiry: *What would the response be? How would the conversation go? Is this offering something others would want and be willing to pay for?* And his inquiry, in turn, was rooted in an understanding of his constituents' systems: existing price comparisons, benchmarks, places often visited, geographical circles, respective career industries, and more. This was a low-fidelity, low-stakes way to listen actively in a context designed to inform an outcome—built on what he'd been hearing in personal conversations and observing his friends' lack.

If you were to ask Jeff how to drive the growth of your startup, he'd answer: "Lead with your ears." It was Jeff's intuitive and passionate

Figure 7.3 Gentlemen's Factory founder Jeff Lindor.
Photo credit: Jason Thomas.

community engagement that launched his company. His community focus underlines his offering discovery (and iteration!) through research. Before announcing the event, booking the time, and naming the purpose, he spent weeks asking colleagues and friends to assess their interest, and the response was promising. These first conversations planted the seed that affirmed his prototype was viable to launch, even if it was just testing the waters. Jeff, who was part of his initial target demographic, prioritized hearing from connections to shape the early stages of his company. He knew he wanted to explore a place for black men to gather and knew that the opportunities on the market were slim—but the topic, shape, cost, and offering detail arose from these one-to-one conversations and his experience in the community.

Action research: Ensuring research is shared cross-team, cross-company, and cross-community

We believe that the principles of action research, demonstrated in Jeff's story, are a great way to achieve shared understanding. Action research differs from other research methodologies in three fundamental ways:

1. Its primary goal is rooted in social change.
2. Participants in action research studies accept responsibility for helping solve issues around a focus of inquiry.
3. Relationships between the researcher(s) and participants are more complex and often less hierarchical.

More often, action research is an approach in which theory and practice are explored by posing questions, collecting data, and testing hypotheses through several cycles of action. The goals of social change are as unique as the participants, contexts, and areas of inquiry.

Figure 7.4 Gentlemen's Factory founder Jeff Lindor greets members of the community.
Photo credit: Jason Thomas.

Jeff's success using action research

Design-driven strategies draw from anthropology and sociology to find where users are and take an intimate look at who these groups are beyond demographic affiliations. Learning what motivates people, challenges them, and comprises them might sound intuitive or easy, but positioning them beyond product or service *users* places an important sense of intent on balance between our commercial drive and our inquiry. Putting our subjective interests aside in favor of our stakeholders' is a practice that's informed by listening to both self and user. Getting good at this is critical, especially if you have the vision to create a community of customers.

Action research, used in design-led entrepreneurship, is based on collaboration between the innovators-as-researcher and the consumer of a new product or service. Another critical aspect of action research is that it seeks to accelerate both problems solving and change initiatives through practical and actual outputs. This can be in the form of a verbal or visual representation. Accordingly, entrepreneurs should always co-create their research because this is the best way to overcome inherent biases and achieve shared meaning. Jeff is a great example of where micro-practices (methods) help uncover a path toward addressing macro goals for his company's overall vision.

Plan your research by triangulating

Consider a research plan less like a manual and more like a roadmap (a company journey). While most of the design research is iterative, the context of starting a company requires a good degree of adaptability and practicality. Building a structure, especially in the uncharted entrepreneurial territory, is helpful to drive you toward your North Star outcome.

In design, it's bad practice and nearly impossible to rely on a single method, source of data, or approach. The ideal research strategy is **Triangulation**—a combination of **approaches**—the *how*, with **types** of data to collect, such as qualitative or quantitative data, along with various **methods**—the many processes you will use to collect, analyze, and visualize your data.

This is where we introduce the Golden Triad framework (Figure 7.5) to help direct our attention to the process, guiding you as a planning tool.

Triangulation is the strategic approach to designing your research, and we do so in a way that will shed light on the internal behaviors of our stakeholders—not only whether they like and will use our product or service but also what their motivations are, what values they maintain, how their values influence their habits, what their goals are, how their relationships inform their interactions—all the way down to what times of day different actions occur. We couldn't possibly rely on a single type or method to access all of this!

Example research scenario

If my objective is to figure out whether my first wireframes for my minimum viable product (MVP) are sufficiently doing their job for my end users, how do I approach this task?

Option 1: Schedule 20 × 10-minute interview sessions with my male users' ages 24–26 because they're the first people I hope will adopt.

Option 2: Integrate some wireframes into a questionnaire and send it out to a wide range of my possible users where they can

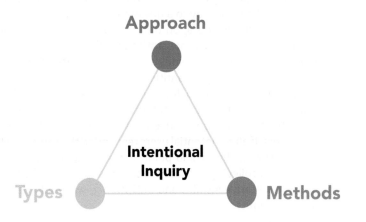

Figure 7.5 The golden triad.

answer primary multiple-choice questions with some open-ended feedback.

Option 3: Put my wireframe images onto a similar device and ask five potential users to role-play how they might imagine using this application, even though it's not functional.

If your answer was a blend of all three, you're right. Each option includes a data type and a method to get it. What they lack individually is a cohesive, holistic approach. While each option is an excellent example of research that would be beneficial, using only a single option would limit the creator's ability to see and perceive a clear picture of his MVP's efficacy. One option alone would provide insight, but our founder might be limited by either the lack of a data type or the singularity of a specific method. Use the Golden Triad to start with your approach, which will lead you to Type, followed by the Method.

Considering your research, consider questions like:

- Am I relying on one primary data type?
- Is my approach singular—Am I only approaching one group of stakeholders?
- What am I starting with, and what should my sequential method be?
- How and in what ways am I engaging my participants?

Deeper into data type

Types of data determine how we can contextualize the information and how we understand the insights derived. Quantitative data comes from numbers, counts, or measurements that we have to contextualize and frame within numerically driven parameters. Quant data is often what we think of when "research" comes to mind and is often assumed or positioned to be the most efficient way to get hardline answers.

Examples of quantitative data and metrics include the number of views per day, the total Daily Active Users (DAU), the percent growth of your paying customers over time, the portion of people who respond the same way to a question, and any physical metric or parameter. Qualitative data, on the other hand, relies on described qualities—this is data that is not statistically reliable but characterizes the qualities of a specific individual or a group. Qualitative information is often collected in large quantities, leading us to process quantitative insights derived from qualitative data. We cannot, though, derive qualitative insights from quantitative data. Going back to Option 1, we'll be able to collect qualitative data from open-ended questions with the users. If all 20 potential users responded the same way to one of your questions, that would point us toward quantitative data. In Option 2, we'd collect quantitative responses to the wireframes without much qualitative insight, and in Option 3, we would derive only qualitative insights.

Deeper into methods

Across our broad systems mapped, how do we access all possible sources? This is where we frame our methods. All research includes methods, and design research tends to mean that we have fluidity around how we position our research: Is it experimental? Is it descriptive? Is it exploratory? How you outlined your objectives sets the tone for your strategic triangulation and the type of research you're conducting. Where we are in our research process and what our objectives are will inform what methods we choose.

Because our approach must triangulate a topic, we must strategically balance our methods—like we see in a cumulative strategy, Options 1, 2, and 3 together above. In Option 1, we see a qualitative method using **short-form interviews** to better understand our primary users and home in on a specific demographic. In Option 2, we know a **questionnaire** was created to get a quantitative response from a broader range of potential users. In Option 3, we see a **participatory method in interview form** for qualitative data geared toward the behavioral underpinnings of a primary persona.

What exactly are some methods, and how do they compare? How do they differ over time from your emergent inquiry? Figure 7.6 maps the positionality of participation across active and reflective processing. We encourage and recommend high-participation levels in design, which lend to terms like "co-creation." We want our stakeholders to be as clued into our creative process as possible, which

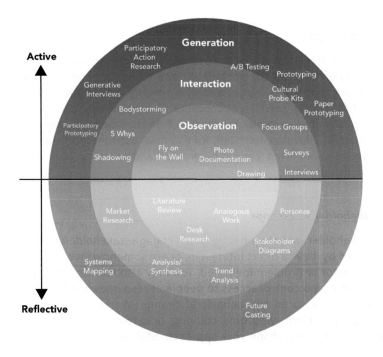

Figure 7.6 Strategic design active and reflective methods diagram with permissions from Parsons BBA Program Diagram by Elliott Montgomery.

helps build transparency into our product and culture and makes the shape of our inquiry clear to our stakeholders.

We can think of degrees of participation through Jeff's path to build The Gentlemen's Factory—and how he integrated a sense of inquiry through his early building process. If you want to understand socio-emotional motivations, build rapport with users, cover a wide range of topics or points within your scope, and try some of these practices:

Short-form or impromptu

An impromptu interview is an informal, unstructured qualitative method that tends to be more of a "spur of the moment" meeting that lasts under 30 minutes.

Long-form 1:1 in-depth interviews (IDIs)

IDIs are a qualitative data-collection method in which respondents are engaged in a one-on-one setting. In-depth interviews are most appropriate when you ask probing questions that invite a meaningful conversation/response designed to produce a depth of information from relatively few people (the opposite of a survey). They are traditionally conducted in-person, on video, or over the phone—with the researcher asking questions to an individual respondent. Depending on the subject matter and context, interviews last 60 minutes and should aim to be recorded in some way to reflect upon later.

Focus groups

The value of focus groups is the opportunity to get feedback from all walks of life and their interactions. They are used in traditional market research to gather target audience opinions and attitudes about specific products, services, or concepts. A company may use a focus group to gather customer feedback before they decide to take the concept into development. Jeff, for example, used this participatory method to both listen (early in his process) and co-create (later while building his model).

Stakeholder workshops

A stakeholder workshop is one way to engage stakeholders—those affected by, have a direct interest in, or are somehow involved with your sector or problem identified. You may also include gatekeepers, those who control access to people or resources needed when developing a social and behavioral change. Workshops could be mapping problem symptoms, coloring, or categorizing aspects, or having them help shape your approach. Stakeholder engagement can help speed up and clarify decision-making, directing you toward value quicker. These can help create sustainable change by building relationships with key persons and demonstrating your user-centered priority.

Kick-starting research practically

While Jeff has a strong intuition and listening ear as a leader, this practice is replicable—and critical. We tend to think that "user research" and "design research" must carry a lot of formality. Still, design for an early-stage startup might look a lot like these short, one-on-one, quick, and informal conversations woven together in a way that produces a strategic direction. Your strategy (and clarity) will crystallize as you build your knowledge base. Getting accustomed to having quick conversations with high frequency is a practice that helps set the stage for more formal or more structured, long-form interviews.

What's important to remember when having these short conversations is that, as a practice, we want to be ensuring we're listening actively and openly to the words of our participants, that we ask quick, open-ended follow-up questions, and that we're note-taking. While even brief conversations with someone we know *feel* memorable when we're in them, these notes (and possible quotes!) will function as the basis for your business research story, and you'll want to be able to reference these later.

Let's break down how to build capacity like Jeff's. What does this look like practically?

- Be sure to keep all your research notes (however brief!) in the same place.
- Start a folder or a running document to note take.
- Keep track of your names in a sheet, tagging and categorizing each participant as you engage. Tracking these names, phone calls, and conversations helps build your knowledge base and actively builds your network.
- Divide up roles! When you're in research mode, the best option is to have a cofounder with you in an early conversation.
- Assign a primary note-taker or use a transcription tool to focus on the interview.
- If you're alone, consider asking if you can record the conversation. *Make sure to acknowledge their consent for this!* The audio (and transcription) allows you to revisit.

Optimizing research conversations

Screen the right participants: Participant screening surveys are questionnaires that gather information about potential participants' experiences before the interview, focus group, or workshop, to quickly identify and prioritize optimal candidates' representative of your target audience.

The more targeted you are with your questions, the better the participants and data. The development of the screening doc is often best done individually, then reflected upon with the team to be sure it captures everything.

Aside from the participant's details (name, gender, occupation, employment status, age, and location):

- Add the preferred communication method (remote/in-person) and time/day.
- Questions should be topical and around their habits or perhaps uses of certain products that do similar functions to your product or service.
- A tip is to think about the assumptions you need to test and see if there can be questions framing these.

Like preparing the actual interview questions, be sure to test your questionnaire with team members and then on strangers to make sure it is screening participants effectively, to stay targeted with each group. If you didn't use a participant screener before the focus group or interviews, do a quick scan of your participants so you know who they are, what motivates them, and how they might want to be involved.

Strive for meaningful questions: While conversation can be light, the goal of qualitative research is to gather an in-depth understanding of user behavior and why they took those specific actions. (Asking a LOT of why's!) People aren't always used to diving into detail because what they know is intuitive, but it might not be for us. Ask your participants to elaborate:

I'm not sure if I'd be interested in paying for that; it's just not worth it to me.—user

Do you mind elaborating? What would make that worthwhile, enough to pay for?

Asking the right questions builds client-consultant and user-provider relationships. It provides crucial information, encourages interviewees to think of ideas they would not have, and helps them clarify their thinking. Asking the right questions and timing is both science and art.

Always debrief together: After your interviews, you are ready to debrief. The interview debrief helps align and share what has been heard and learned with your team while it's fresh in your mind. Because we all hear differently and through our prisms, it's a critical component to build into your process (Figure 7.7).

Debrief Questionnaire

Reflect upon the Production of the Interview, Focus Group or Workshop	**Reflect upon the Findings from the Interaction**
Compliments: What went well?	**Key Observations: Reinforced** What did I hear repeated more than once?
Improvements: What didn't work, was unclear, etc.?	**New Observations:** What surprised me? What did I hear that I haven't heard before?
Polish: How can we take it to the next level?	**Takeaways:** I'd like to highlight or assumptions that occurred that need testing?
Key takeaways for next time:	**Notes:**

Figure 7.7 Debrief and iteration questionnaire.

Debrief Template

Debriefing is one of the most important parts of qualitative research. Have each facilitator explain what they observed, heard, and stood out.

Part 1: Production (Container)
1. What worked well with the format? What about the place, timing, or operations worked?
2. What didn't go as planned and explain why?
3. How can you take execution to the next level? Use specific examples.

Part 2: Findings (Content)
1. What did you hear more than once? What was affirmed?
2. What surprised you? What was a new observation?
3. Reflect on assumptions or questions that come up.

Personas and applying ethnography

With research documentation, founders can begin to build personas. We, as founders, move from triangulating what's unknown to testing what we think we know. Initially, these function as hypotheses. The value of building hypotheses through initial exploratory research creates a precedent of adaptation in later-stage research. We see this in Jeff's story, as he moved from a discovery-based approach with low-fidelity and short-form methods to an embedded practice of programming (early prototypes) that informed his pricing and aligned his concept around several personae. Throughout his early-stage research and evidence-gathering, Jeff clarified how influential his initial hunch was: that black and brown men's success looks different for every individual—and mistakenly treating them as a monolith is partially to blame for low success rates and funding for other programs.

The importance of this divergence shows success meant offerings were going to vary from person to person. Who were the first community members that would be able to validate not only the offerings but an actual business model? After his first discovery research phase, Jeff spent a year with no membership model. He committed to explore and evaluate with a driving question in mind: What do black and brown men need? His research practice formalized at this point, compounding his informal and quick vetting conversations with strategized surveys and focus groups. He put together various events on various topics that, as his concept progressed, shifted from focus groups into actual early prototypes. He acknowledged early on that stereotyping this audience, even if demographics appeared similar, would be treating them as a monolith; this would ineffectively serve them as humans seeking success and growth and as constituents wanting (and paying for) value from his company.

Incorporating co-creation into his research practice was core to his success. It allowed his community members to add to the services they needed vs. what he'd launched. "The more people tell me, the more I can design for them."

Digital offerings during COVID became coaching and live events online. Jeff listened to dozens and sometimes hundreds of members talking at these live events more than four evenings a week. In many ways, the online shift gave him exposure to more voices, and he leveraged this. His leadership habit of listening to the community's pulse before his incorporation turned into business practice informing his company's development and adaptation.

Key Learnings

- Lead with your ears
- Hands-on approach to leadership is authentic
- Prototype quickly
- Focus on the problem

Key Tools/Frameworks

- Focus Groups
- Surveys
- Incoming Member Questionnaire
- Personas
- Stakeholder Map

> *Be flexible, and don't be so hard on what your product is—but always focus on the problem that you're solving. Your product will adapt if you're designing well.*
>
> Jeff Lindor

Remember, it can get chaotic, so it is essential to be organized and somewhat scientific, capturing results from tests and experiments.

Otherwise, this is an area where you can waste time and money. To be innovative and create meaning for people, one needs to be at the nexus of what is desirable for users, what is feasible for you and your team to build, and what is financially viable for you and your users.

Meeting your research goals and planting seeds for synthesis

As you research, you discover new things. Breaking the tasks down into easily achievable steps makes the process less harrowing. Expect to step back, set yourself up to process, observe, contextualize your research narrative, and ensure your team is on board with the process and any potential pivots.

Prepare for Synthesis

In-hand:
- Do you have 10+ conversations in hand?
- Do you have a research log with names, themes, and demographics listed?
- Do you have multiple methods of research in hand?

In-heart:
- Do you feel affirmed by conversations you had?
- Do you feel an urgency to speak with more people?
- Do you feel a sense of what your core problem is?

In-mind:
- Do you know who your customer segments are?
- Do you have a multitude of value proposition ideas or insights?
- Do you have trouble pinning down a clear value proposition?

Navigational Log + Takeaways

- Validate and explore assumptions through a strategic research plan
- Seek out blind spots with curiosity and deep listening
- Solidify key trends, develop insights, and understand needs
- Be encouraged by feedback, grasp main issues of concern to stakeholders
- Pay attention to initial patterns noticed

8

SYNTHESIZE TO NAME OPPORTUNITY

Framing our future outcome

Objectives

- Locate your company (and yourself!) within research data across types and methods
- Sort and identify pattenrs through visual synthesis and identify patterns through visual synthesis
- Work collaboratively to ensure research is shared across the team
- Identify opportunity areas through patterns and driving themes
- Define problem statements for ideation of business concept

Here, we will review expectations from research, assess the undercurrent themes and influences found within our system, and turn them into directions for brainstorming. Synthesizing your research insights is distilling research findings into the key observations that set the scene for successfully developing a business concept. This is when you wrap your head around the raw data behind your observations—connect the dots that reveal patterns of potential impact—all while continuing to move forward. We'll land on key insights and problem shaping with point-of-view statements and "How might we …?" questions.

Naming the opportunity space through the act of synthesizing will lead us to the design phase of ideation. We'll break this chapter into **preparing to synthesize** and **synthesis in action**. If you're unfamiliar, this may feel structured—but we learn structure as design-informed practitioners. A balancing act: space to pause and consider, with momentum to drive and progress. Step back, set yourself up with designerly guardrails, and observe your thoughts. We'll contextualize your discoveries through a research narrative to ensure your team is on board, building a path for consensus around any pivots or reshaping that might arise.

The roots of synthesis: Recognizing patterns

Children often spend time outdoors playing and sorting through found objects in nature: rocks, leaves, flowers, and so forth. Among this wild

DOI: 10.4324/9781003227151-12

ecosystem of the backyard is both a wealth of diversity—color, shape, texture, living and nonliving, moving and still, light and heavy, old, young—and still, amazing simplicity found across all these elements through what they hold in common, distinct from what they are. It's easy to forget that childhood intuition still lives within us and tapping into it can ignite a level of curiosity that aids our synthesis.

Processing research is heavily convergent, but the secret ingredient is an open mind. Though it sounds counterintuitive, childhood openness leads us to recognize alignment while our adult-cultured minds may resist. Whether it is plants and rocks, building blocks, or Legos, we are born with and spend our childhood developing and **recognizing patterns**. Synthesis is the deconstruction and reconstruction of our research data as it shapes our action-driving insights through noticed patterns. When we're younger, our pattern recognition is unfettered by the layering of societal readings we are cultured to adopt, which makes our analysis more biased and nuanced.

Synthesizing your research: Where to start

Start by collecting all individual and group diagrams, worksheets, and canvases—like a persona or any system maps. Pull out key learnings from 1:1 interviews in your debrief logs, quantitative data, and assumption charts.

You should clearly understand what your research approach was from using the **Golden Triad**, with multiple types of data, having utilized multiple methods. A company example could look like this:

1. **Approach:** Exploratory; understand effects of media across diverse people to see who/where to home in on
2. **Types:** Qualitative + quantitative data
3. **Methods and tools:**

   a. Desk research (market data on phone use), secondary research (journal on media change)
   b. Site Visits (high-use locations)
   c. Short-form Interviews (15–20-minute conversations with ten target users)
   d. Google Drive as a clear archive for data (photos, transcriptions, notes)

With our inner children in hand, let's go!

Preparing for the synthesis

You and your team have likely created a lot of assets in the form of diagrams, notes, and images. Prepare for creating key insights by using visualizations (diagrams, templates); demonstrating the connection between things you observe, hear, and see visually will make them more generative for future phases such as brainstorming and iterative reflection through prototyping, pitching, and eventual piloting.

Collectively, map patterns across the various templates to create newly synthesized visuals that capture the insights into themes for later ideation and value creation. In any given sentence or conversation with a potential stakeholder, we hear the "truth" of what they're experiencing and the perceived way it feels. Multiply this by our total number of conversations, coupled with our multiple research types, and have an enormous amount of information to overlay on our existing understanding of the ecosystem.

Research synthesis allows us to move forward with developing a business concept. It affords you as a leader or founder to converge around clear actions while also producing a user-centered roadmap and narrative that can allow your team to converge around you. Then you can align on the next action in our process: Ideation.

The actions built into research synthesis can vary and, for a founder, could look like:

- Naming two clear insights in the form of full, user-centered need sentences
- Identifying the contextual "why" of the pain points or symptoms of the problem, that your user experiences
- Producing visual diagrams that communicate patterns found in your research
- Naming and planning a new research area to build onto what you have
- Distilling down the topics to ideate around

Establish expectations: Kick-start your expectations as a group. Setting expectations is necessary to align yourself with your team and stakeholders and assess the right amount of time to review research. This activity is part of the process because it creates our designerly guardrails, shaping team cohesion as much as our future product insights. Here, identify your goals, approach, and tools, and set your intentions and goals for outputs from your research.

Planning Your Synthesis Approach

Name outcome: What outcome are you expecting from your research? What does success look like? What will that state feel like? *Jot down a few bullet points for each question. (Individual—3 minutes, followed by Team—3 minutes)*

Name output: What tangible takeaways do you expect to produce? What will the artifacts look like and where will they live? *Jot down a few bullet points for each question. (Individual—3 minutes, followed by Team—3 minutes)*

Some examples of outputs could be templates and exercises from this chapter, such as:

- Clustering diagrams from team workshops
- Affinitizing high-level insights we call "key" insights in an Affinity Chart
- Pattern recognition of things that keep occurring during your research into a grid of themes
- Developing problem statements around those themes
- Checking your work with the *Whys* exercise to be sure you've identified the root cause of your constituents' pain points

What you'll need to accomplish could look something like this:

- Elevate market insights from research
- Define the pain points and opportunities
- Identify opportunity areas for brainstorming

You should have at least **ten stakeholder interviews**, from across the categories, to effectively make sense of your system research.

Bias reminder! As entrepreneurs, we often fall in love with our ideas and tenaciously stick to our original concepts without staying open to the data and new ways of approaching problem-setting and problem-solving. Don't rush synthesis and reflect along the way. Remember, the more diversity of stakeholders you have in your synthesis process, the more clarity, sincerity, and bias-free results you'll be able to land on. Bias for entrepreneurs is like kryptonite for Superman; it weakens your plans. It's so easy to want to see what will validate our path forward but remember the childlike mind and push ourselves to see what arises. It is critical to "park" your assumptions for these exercises and then return to them only if they are validated by your research without bias.

In scientific research, it's common to have a clear understanding of the impact bias can have on data; so it is with design research as well. Check for bias in your method and approach as you pull your research together. Consider who's at the table: make sure you're not accidentally leaving anyone's point of view out or injecting your own, which can skew the results.

Ambiguity over answers. Everyone will arrive at the table with their perspective, completed research, and intuitions. The ambiguity that surfaced at the start of the session is GOOD! Allow the fluidity of the early-stage process and trust in the container you've created through your established objectives and agenda. Remember, our attentive minds should sharpen like razors but with a loose grip on our controllers. You're surveying all possible outcomes, all possible insights, and without zeroing in too soon. **The clarity of the outcome arises from the process.**

Synthesis in action

Debrief, align + affinitize: It's important that the people on your team who you're synthesizing with also participate in research themselves, whether individually or as a unit. Bring all the research outputs together to assess as a team. The goal of the session will be to sort through your various research outputs to find patterns and connect the dots within the various outputs. **How insights differ from regular research findings is that insight is something we can act upon as creative opportunity spaces.**

Preparing A Synthesis Workshop

Name possible pathways: With named outcome and output in hand, take 3 minutes to list out all the possible paths that your synthesis might produce. Where could it lead you that you might not expect? *This could be an affirmed direction, a clear target segment, or understood value pathways.*
   (3 minutes individually, 5 minutes as a team)

Name your agenda: Based on your outputs created above, create an agenda for your session around the type of information you're synthesizing or the outcomes you're seeking.

   Block no more than 2 hours, and no less than 45 minutes. The time will vary according to your team size, but your agenda should provide a buffer for each exercise. If you cut your synthesis short, you risk losing alignment and disrupting your team's flow state.

Prepare the scene: Use large walls if in-person to pin things up, gather sharpies and post-its, or use a digital whiteboard to collect all the materials. You'll use post-its or this whiteboard to cluster and group research findings visually into key insights and themes. Pinning up all the archival materials (templates, diagrams, maps, etc.) on the wall helps your team stand back and gain some literal perspective or distance to be more objective.

Note: Just as important as team alignment is taking time before, during, and after the team synthesis workshop to process and reflect.

Affinity mapping

The Affinity Chart is an organizing method for categorizing large amounts of data under themes based on their relationships. This tool helps bucket your key insights and observations under themes. See Figure 8.1 based on high-level human-centered categories. Try to respond to the prompts with your team and stakeholders over a series of workshops to deeply understand the complexity and nuances of the space you plan to intercept.

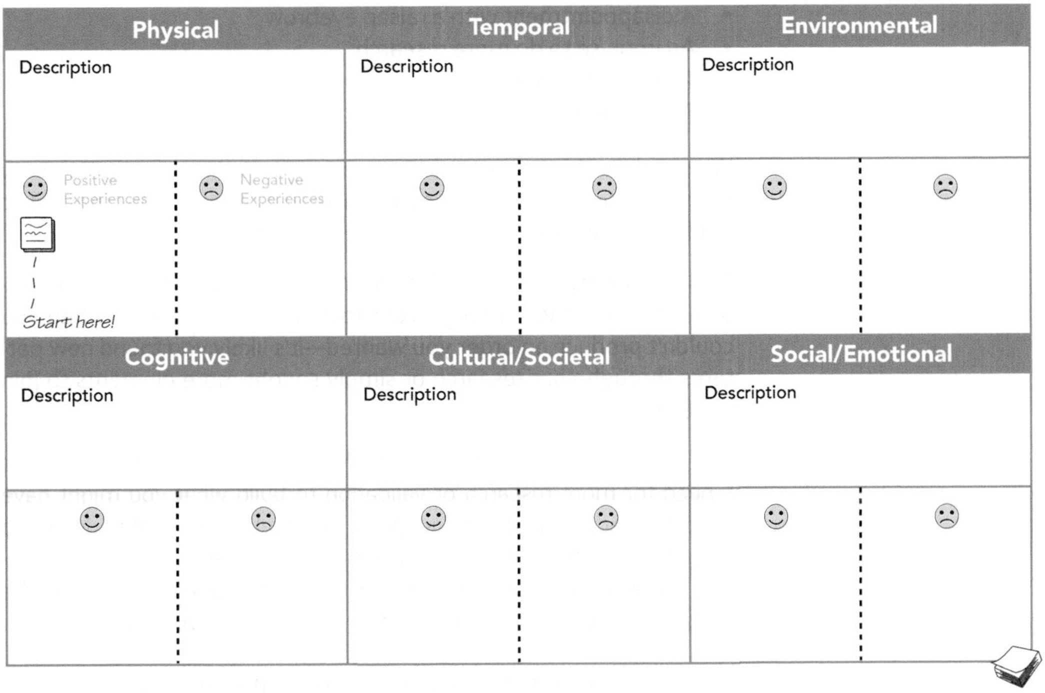

Physical		Temporal		Environmental	
Description		Description		Description	
🙂 Positive Experiences	☹ Negative Experiences	🙂	☹	🙂	☹
📝 / \ / *Start here!*					

Cognitive		Cultural/Societal		Social/Emotional	
Description		Description		Description	
🙂	☹	🙂	☹	🙂	☹

Figure 8.1 Affinity mapping for qualitative themes.

Affinity Mapping

Organize key data points across your research into affinity groups. These could include statistics from desk research, key insights from observations, and interview quotes. Use the headers as prompts, although you might not have information across them all, to understand users' needs, behaviors, and motivations.

1. Write your key observations from your stakeholder research onto individual post-it notes. Be sure to include all perspectives.
2. Organize your post-its within the categories into "positive" or "negative" areas under the high-level categories.
3. Write a description or theme for those affinity categories.
4. Reflect on themes and responses to create Insights and "problem" statements.

Framing the problem space

Through the action-reflection cycle of synthesis, a story about our research can emerge by connecting the patterns to reveal opportunities. Synthesis is a convergence where your *active reflection* produces *reflective action*. At this point, the entrepreneur's world is going to feel a lot like:

- A moment of realization, a "coming to"
- A driving excitement

- A disappointment with a raised eyebrow
- An impulse to do more research
- A deflated dead-end
- An exuberant "aha!"

We speak to this trigger point as a name for *action* because it's easy to expect our synthesis to produce favorable results—ones that affirm our hypotheses and validate the direction that we're going.

This isn't always the case, though! Your childlike wonder at the patterns that emerged through your toys was disappointing when you couldn't produce an order you wanted—it's likely you found new patterns through your research or simply sought more elements to join the collection.

This is the trigger: a requirement for further action, whether it prompts a need for more research or validation to build what you might have hypothesized. While the trigger point may feel like a deflated dead-end or tingling excitement, our job as design-led entrepreneurs is to recognize the feeling produced from our process and distinguish that from the action of what the results point us toward, thus removing our own bias.

Writing problem stories to frame opportunities

Create a few statements about the (problem space) themes your synthesis has produced. Figure 8.2 is a fill-in-the-blank activity to help you formulate your point-of-view statements and the questions.

Figure 8.2 Problem statement framework.

Problem Statement Framework

_____ needs a way to _____
(user name)   (core action)

because _____.
                    (indicating insight)

How might we design a _____,
                          (name some sort intervention)

so that _____ can _____
              (user name)   (core action)

more successfully?

Problem Statement Framework

These "point-of-view" statements, or problem statements, are the building blocks for you to construct a few **"How might we?"** questions that will prime your brainstorming in the next phase of the design process and our next chapter.

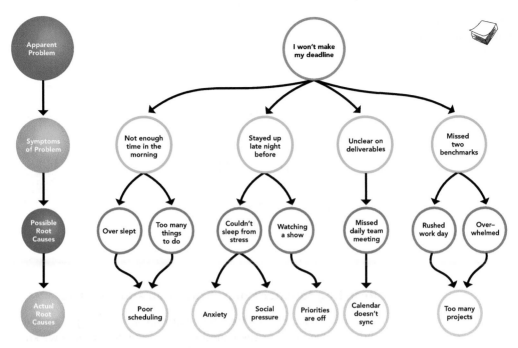

Figure 8.3 Guiding towards root cause with "why?"

Cross-checking cause and effect before defining the problem (use why)

Reflecting on the causes and effects in a scenario will help you get to the root cause of the problem to help you better understand where there is an opportunity for a new product or service. This is called First Principles. Understanding the emotions behind people's actions will be an essential part of this process, the WHY beyond a result, to get to deep-rooted behaviors and emotions. Figure 8.3 demonstrates the **Why's Prompt.**

The Why's Prompt

Working backward enables you to understand the emotion behind an action. *Why?* will get you closer to the root cause to better determine the *How?*

1. Start by naming a resulting problem that your constituents or community is struggling with, then ask why? This will spark a few answers.
2. From there, ask *why?* again, this will spark more responses. Do this for at least three to four iterations.

The more you ask this simple question, the more you get from the culturally expected, tactical, and often superficial responses drilling down to the root cause, which often is emotional, possibly fear-based feelings underlying unconscious hindrances or blocks.

Resisting founder's bias: Stay open and inclusive

As entrepreneurs, we often start with an acknowledged problem: either we've faced or seen another close to us face or one we know we need to solve. You might see what you want and have some idea of what the output will look like: a mobile app, a desktop app, a particular bag, or the style of a product. The hypothesis-testing approach to *exclusively affirm what we want to see* in our research can be problematic and, as a mindset, tough to shake.

Meet Elias and Emma! Founded in 2020, Singbird is a music-sharing mobile application. Elias Grau and Emma Wernsdorfer were both undergraduate students looking to solve the problem of sharing live music remotely through an app that authentically captured reactions during live performances. Unlike other streaming-focused platforms, they built an app to connect tight-knit musicians, performers, and DJs with music enthusiasts, enabling live streaming, reactions, and community experience.

With an early commitment to their vision, they fell into the trap many striving entrepreneurs do: they fell in love with their initial idea. Their blinders, familiar with founders, caused them to seek validation for what they thought to be true, but it was only part of the story. Reflecting on their research, synthesis, and prototyping phases over 18 months later, they realized that they had approached their synthesis with blind spots. Because they were so determined to prove their one hypothesis, they missed out on speaking with critical stakeholders like agents and nightclub owners who could have rounded out their understanding of relevant systems. This resulted in incomplete data that, when synthesized, produced a picture of what they *expected*, not what existed.

Let's give them some credit, though: researching at the height of COVID-19 in 2020, when most businesses were closed, is tough! At that time, countries were headed into lockdowns with little knowledge of the devastation soon to come in the live-entertainment space. However, with a lot of solid desk research around their target audience, ethnographic research through speaking with their perceived customer segment (young music enthusiasts and musicians), and surveying over 400 potential users, their foundation of data was directed toward understanding what features they wanted to have and why. *How did they want to be spoken to? What did they want to feel?*

Through their research synthesis, Emma and Elias narrowed their segment to creatives aged 18–34. However, they failed to look at the whole system with all its stakeholders reaching out to others in the music industry, like music managers. Looking back, they wished they had been able to learn early on about these other stakeholders' needs. Though their research produced clear insight statements around their audience, the picture of their opportunity space was too narrow. "We should have done more outreach, did more one-on-one interviews, and later testing with these other stakeholders," Elias expressed. Emma added, "We would have also benefited from doing group testing as well." Without a clear understanding of the system around the problem space, the efficacy of their initial product was diminished.

After two years invested, Elias shares his learnings and encourages pushing against default solutions: "One big lesson is to keep it simple! If you want to be an entrepreneur, you can start with something in your wheelhouse; defaulting to building an app when you're not a developer leads to many problems and complications. Wanting to make a scalable tech product is a huge undertaking!" The vision of a scalable tech product clouded their research approach and thus altered their undertaking.

What would a design-driven process from the start look like? It likely would have led them to analyze their system, approaching research with exploratory conviction with diverse stakeholders to locate pain points, resulting in more dimensions for opportunity spaces and differentiation of value proposition. Design-led entrepreneurs practice "parking their assumptions" when shaping research and seeking patterns, with attention to the *unseen* pieces of the puzzle.

Start making your business case through visual synthesis

So, you've got a good understanding of the problem space, you've been able to generate insights and you've even revealed the affinities of stakeholders in your ecosystem. Now comes when you need to communicate all the great work you've done to your collaborators, partners and even funders to help brainstorm or tell the narrative: *"why is this problem worth solving?"* Early on, we learned about the power of graphical hierarchy as a visual aid.

Here you can layer in the new key insights, pain points, and opportunities discovered by using techniques like emboldening, color coding, and enlarging data points, to elevate visual diagrams. Synthesizing visually is a critical step in telling a concise, coherent, and compelling story. It brings to life months of research to make it meaningful to others who have not spent the time and energy, to reach the same levels of understanding within minutes. Think about the storyboards from your favorite film. Those sketches create a narrative journey for the characters to come to life before the film is invested and actors are hired. Similarly, the visual narrative of your research observations conveys user experiences, the environments they inhabit, and their aspirations for a better world. They should expose narratives, patterns, and relationships across time, in ways that expose opportunities and evoke empathy and emotion in the viewer.

Why we visualize

The main goal of data visualization is to make it easier to identify patterns, trends, and outliers in large data sets. Edward Tufte, the founding father of data visualization, once remarked that data doesn't have to be boiled down and simplified; rather, "these common questions miss the point, for the quantity of detail is an issue separate from the difficulty of reading. Clutter and confusion are failures of design, not attributes of information" (Tufte 1990).

Data visualization can help tell the story and deliver the impact of data in the most efficient way possible. Data visualization takes the raw data, models it, and delivers conclusions. In advanced analytics, data scientists create machine learning algorithms to better compile essential data into visualizations. It communicates information in a manner that is easily understandable, fast, and effective. This practice can help entrepreneurs identify areas that need improvement, which factors affect customer satisfaction and dissatisfaction, and what to do with specific products (where they should go and who they should be sold to).

Data visualization can be used interchangeably with other words like information graphics, information visualization, and statistical graphics. Whatever word is chosen, empower yourself to see and convey the patterns of many data sources. Your choice of visualizing synthesized data will depend on what you are modeling, the audience's expectations (and limitations), and your intended purpose. Innovative techniques like data immersion in virtual reality change the game, and the level of impact data can have on your innovation ecosystem.

Preparing for ideation

You should have synthesized your research findings, named key insights, and clustered observations around driving themes.

- Have you elevated your visuals to help tell the deeply connected story of your research to contextualize ideation prompts?
- Have you created a few *point-of-view statements and* shaped *"How Might We?" (HMW)* questions to prompt ideation?

This will drive your coming brainstorming workshops, where stake-holders will conjure up as many ideas for solutions as possible. Elias and Emma show us the importance of reflecting on our research foundation and the implications it shapes our business opportunities. So remember to involve as many people as possible in both the research phases *and* the coming ideation. After brainstorming when you're converging on a solidly formed concept to advance, consider your capacity, personal goals, and ambitions from earlier sections about aligning your personal and company values and goals. In the next few chapters, you'll access tools to generate diverse ideas or components, align on a value prop, and begin prototyping.

Navigational Log + Takeaways

- Sincerely listen to your research data
- Suspend judgment or predetermined hypotheses
- Involve many stakeholders in problem setting process to cross-check root causes
- Craft realistic opportunity areas from bottoms-up value
- Visualize learning as a team—*see* your trends and patterns!

9

IDEATE TO CONVERGE

Generate concepts to prototype solutions

Objectives

- Understand the process and purpose of ideation
- Co-create value and decide on an informed concept and components with stakeholders
- Identity value/company experience to test with initial prototypes
- Create and deploy a testing strategy
- Assess low vs. high fidelity prototypes and effective metrics to test

Slow down, speed up: Design divergence plus convergence

We'll launch this stage of the journey of the methods with suggestions and context around ideation, followed by converging on a concept, evaluating that concept, and setting you up to test the value components of this concept. You'll also meet Shahrouz through his startup story on how Designity pivoted its model to succeed.

Strategic design creates a guiding structure for our process that shapes our direction through divergent and convergent thinking. Our accelerometer, in the beginning, reads low, turned to home in on an internal coda that will guide our process: listening inward and listening outward. Having completed research involving conversation and observation of our stakeholders and synthesis done visually outside of our minds to see patterns, we should land with key themes and critical insights that present us with areas to explore. These areas should intrigue us, prompt a desire to inquire, and make us keen to answer our questions.

Here, feedback loops get tighter: a position to directly juxtapose divergent ideation with convergent decision-making. The sequence of this feels rapid and requires structure to succeed. Ideation feels expansive, exploratory, and divergent while converging on a tactical product or offering to prototype is methodical and convergent, demonstrated in Figure 9.1.

DOI: 10.4324/9781003227151-13

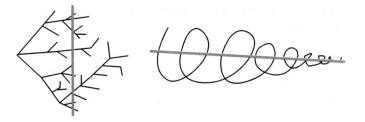

Figure 9.1
Illustrating ideation vs.
prototyping.

Ideation
(expansive and exploratory
divergent thinking)

Prototyping
(convergent, methodical
testing and iteration)

This distinction, and the back-to-back difference in thinking, is what an effective methods process should look and feel. Building your company with design-led strategies means inserting a structure that may not necessarily feel natural in the entrepreneurial process. It also means acknowledging how hard you're stepping on the accelerator. So, while the startup journey feels fast-paced and you may feel crystal clear on what you're building, pausing to document and test through design methods allows you to lay the foundation for your journey.

We've got a Mad-lib to guide this chapter and position you in the structured process—ultimately, conceiving, formulating, and evaluating your solution across this phase.

> Design-led methods take the shape of_____, in order to _____ for our startup.

Examples might look like:

1. Design-led methods take the shape of *instruction and guidance—guardrails for ideation* to *generate fresh, insight-focal ideas and aspects* for our startup.
2. Design-led methods take the shape of *value-centered convergence and opportunity identification* to *find clarity between solution concepts from our solution delivery* for our startup.
3. Design-led methods take the shape of *assessing and evaluating within matrices* to *realign our converged concept with the initial goals* for our startup.

The objective of our tight feedback loop here in method types—divergence > convergence > divergence—is to shift into focus the qualities and characteristics that shape our solution successfully. Our goal is to see if the identified problem areas *are solved* with the users we've named to serve.

Solution concept vs. solution delivery: Generate outcomes

Ideation is the generation of ideas. It describes the process of coming up with—*imagining, conceiving, putting words to, and formulating* concepts. In building businesses to effect meaningful impact, our ideas are generated to create business solutions (a concept, model, or offering) or ways to deliver value through this solution (experiences, features, characteristics, and touchpoints).

For non-designers, this part of the strategic design process likely feels and looks the most creative: the wild, the crazy, the "what could be imagined" but isn't yet real. In *The Design Way*, Stolterman and Nelson (2012) name the strategic design process's end-creation, including "the Ideal." This isn't what doesn't exist, but what exists in the minds of our potential users that haven't yet been created or articulated. To be systematically creative in the entrepreneurial landscape is to build for endurance—and observe what will create lasting value, in what order of scale, and for whom.

Our job in effective ideation is to bring opportunity to life and document our resulting efforts as a way of conceiving real value. Beginning to name aspects of our value proposition—and often, laying a foundation for what can turn into a product roadmap or future implementation plans.

You may have started this chapter (or this book) with the idea for an app in mind, a magazine concept or a services model, or a fashion product you'd like to create. On the other hand, maybe you began with a single idea, or you're referencing these design-led methods for help on your existing early-stage company.

Whatever you have in mind, the transition from research-driven insights into ideation for value-testing prototypes hinges on the clear distinction of your **solution concept vs. solution delivery.** Ideation requires that we understand that the solution we're building is not only how it's delivered to our users. When we ideate, we hinge our generative process on sentences like "An app that_____," we merge two core parts: the outcome we're designing and the actual tactical way that we plan to enact it. We can ideate broadly (not distinguish the concept from delivery), or we can ideate with clear distinctions (generate solution ideas, followed by aspects, physical components, technologies, or characteristics of these ideas). Both work but understand that the solution isn't an "app" **but what the app or software intends to accomplish for users—** *the motivation behind it.* By building our ideas around the delivery alone, we hinge on what we know is currently popular—that we use mobile smartphones daily! What if technology changes? Could it be integrated into future software? Or what if users no longer want this mobile solution?

Ideation in action

Ideation encourages creators to come up with ideas that can initially seem a bit crazy. These ideas can be crafted into original, creative solutions to a problem. In contrast, others can spark even more sequential considerations. Often great ideas are sparked from completely random or seemingly unrelated places. In design research, we call this Analogous Research, which can morph into seeking unconventional or mirrored patterns elsewhere to find inspiration within our business space. When you incorporate stakeholders into your generative process, you can invite tactical positions to collaborative name-value solutions that you might not conceive alone. Working on a solution in healthcare? Maybe invite a pastry chef or marine biologist to a workshop-style ideation session. We *encourage* pushing beyond what you think is reasonable, related, or relevant.

Brainstorming is usually ideation, but ideation isn't always brainstorming

In the proper context, brainstorming sessions can allow people to think more freely, without fear of judgment. It encourages open and ongoing collaboration to solve problems and can generate innovative ideas. The distinction is the structure of the process and who's standing around you. Ideation can be understood as an individual pursuit that covers any generation of new concept, idea, or feature, while we tend to frame brainstorming as a group activity—like the prototypical brainstorming workshops. Brainstorming belongs to the designer's category of ideation. Still, the practice's success will be contingent on your research, the qualitative insights you've generated, and the structure you afford to the process. Allowing enough time for these sessions, adding structure and spending time debriefing are the critical components of successful brainstorming sessions. The objective of these sessions is to go crazy—even to the degree that it's challenging.

The "How" of ideation: Start with structure, set your outcome

Our context may not look formal for an entrepreneur, and the container for ideation will be yours to structure and create. Ideation for entrepreneurs might also be harder than for a hired design team. Why? Well, you're inside your budding concept or rooting business! Inside the company, you have biases that you've worked on debunking. With some of your visions in mind, pulling yourself out and wiping the slate clean might be difficult for what might feel like a step backward. However, effective ideation derived from your fresh insights will contribute to the breadth of your vision, allowing you to explore beyond the original ideas you've been percolating. This breadth will come from the container in which you place your process. Brainstorming sessions are divided into two phases: first, the creative phase, and second, the critical phase. The structure is necessary to allow actual divergence—we mean going "wild." This sounds like an oxymoron but it's true. Having parameters and a clear plan helps keep everyone on track during the creative phase when it's easy to splinter off with side conversations or feel daunted by "what could be." The second critical phase is where you align verbally and push your thinking by enabling focused dialogue.

The facilitator leads and sets the structure. It's their job to set up the space for brainstorming by clearly establishing basic rules and ensuring they're mutually understood. This includes introducing the usual two phases, understanding and communicating time obligations, and following a clear agenda.

Understand that you **don't** need to ...

- Immediately get everyone involved
- Put limitations on the brainstorming session
- Shoot down ideas right away
- Focus on the quality of ideas
- Limit the ideation to one brainstorming session

And our rule-of-thumb—**DO principles** that will near-guarantee increased efficiency and efficacy of your company building divergent processes:

1. **Warm-up your brains.** Whether people know each other or don't, crafting warm-up exercises allows individuals to step into a shared social space and a shared intention. As part of our own relevant systems beyond the concept we might be building, we must acknowledge what we're arriving at. The room has an influence on how our process will run. A traditional icebreaker makes people more comfortable, builds common ground around what can feel like vulnerable participation, and aligns expectations around what participation should look, feel, and sound like. An example of a warm-up exercise is "Draw Your Neighbor as a Superhero."

2. **Adjust to "Yes, and" and "I wonder" language and approach.** Trust builds culture and allows for innovation. To this end, we need to practice a *yes and* mindset. This is not a space for critiquing others' ideas, making fun of them, or putting boundaries on them. *Instead, borrow from improvisation and comedy to build off others' ideas in a positive way. Go for quantity over quality, and wild ideas without limits.*

3. **Create a time parameter for any given exercise.** Timeboxing exercises add pressure, generate "heat," and keep the activity exciting and on pace. Ensure you have a timekeeper and stay focused on one question at a time, avoiding side conversations.

4. **Start individually before generating as a group**. It's good to arrive at the table with overflowing conversation and ideas but take the time to structure individual work into your space. Spend adequate time generating individually before generating as a group. This is critical for a brainstorming session especially!

5. **Don't delete the duplicates.** Redundancy is an essential tool. Remind yourself and your team that if you come up with a similar idea to someone else, still offer it up. That doubles the value and points to shared insight.

6. **Incorporate others**. Working as a group is integral to building upon each other's ideas. While you might be a master of your own startup space, the value of diversity is critical to divergence. Diversity fuels divergence and leads toward enduring value.

Exploratory exercises help participants go wide with divergent thinking. There are many tools to help teams **brainstorm.** We suggest starting with the most exploratory tools to the least.

We build off your work to synthesize the research for creating ideation prompts or "How Might We" questions in the previous chapter.

Take this example: *How might we maximize the treatment of wasted organic material for all the stakeholders in the supply chain?* **The Goldilocks Zone** is the perfect place when scoping a research question or an ideation question. The **"How might we" question** is not too open or closed but just enough to allow for a variable range addressing an understood outcome. You should already have several insights and HMW questions before setting up an ideation session with your stakeholders and team members.

Brainstorming session is an excellent container to start from, where the objective is to generate open dialogue around mutually understood areas of opportunity or questions. Your brainstorming session should include a clear intro (shared context and information), and all participants start on the same ground with the same information. Use a whiteboard or ample empty space to jot notes onto post-its. Ensure you divide the session into clear, digestible chunks: Creative (Phase 1) for the individual, for the team, and Critical (Phase 2) for the individual, for the team.

Franken-ideation is a mash-up exercise that aims to imagine two opposite ideas converging, like "How might Disney redesign the N.Y. Subway? Or how would NASA approach museum curation?" This functions to cross-pollinate stakeholders and influences in your space.

Mad Libs games can also help by allowing just enough control but total freedom for participants to fill in the blank. Imagine prompting a team with a consistent phrase to fill in the blank. You can ensure alignment and still generate space for dialogue.

99 ideas is an exercise that provides structure. Require 99 distinct ideas to be generated, which can take the form of concepts, characteristics of concepts, features, methods, or delivery of the idea (like desktop or mobile). In some examples of this exercise, every individual is required to generate 99 ideas—wow! We recommend generating 20 per prompt, which can be different opportunities, themes, or even more questions.

Venn diagrams are good visualizations to cluster ideas around themes and the overlapping areas where the ideas intersect. Offering necessary reflection time for participants to voice their opinions. We use these more often in the synthesis phase and will show you a few in the next section of this chapter.

The value of co-creating with stakeholders (bottom-up generation)

Who's in the room? Holding brainstorming sessions or structured value-creation with stakeholders builds trust and support. In design, we call this co-creating. Co-creating allows for your potential stakeholders to participate in the generation of value that you'll then incorporate into your key value propositions.

This approach is distinct from a traditional brainstorming or team-centric ideation activity because you intentionally integrate diverse starting knowledge. In addition, working in a bottom-up fashion allows for a more holistic response. It considers all the stakeholders' points of view and concerns—from their own minds vs. your research-derived insights. Sometimes this is a terrific way to validate some of your own assumptions or concepts. It helps gain **buy-in,** which is integral to launching any business today. The more authentically we can integrate critical stakeholders into the conception of your company, the stronger your ties are within the system you're intervening in. The complex systems our products and services will impact—shown and documented in our ecosystem maps and company strategy canvas—require acceptance of the solution to function. Even if our users buy the product or offer, it's less likely to last if it doesn't integrate into the entire user journey. Be it a neighborhood, country, or a global sector, we are all interconnected and cannot possibly understand the relationships and corresponding impacts without inviting them to the table.

Not only does meaningful integration of stakeholders into divergent ideation foundationally build value but it also adds essential elements to our roadmap, future planning, and launch timing. Keeping stakeholders and potential customers as early adopters engaged is an integral part of your strategy to bring a product/service company to market. The more momentum you can generate around your early-stage concept or the potential of what you'll get to fruition, the better. Remember, the more often different stakeholders have repeated similar ideas, the more critical these ideas become.

Figure 9.2 Rhea Alexander facilitating a brainstorming workshop (with Vanya Mittal).

Ideation Workshop

The goal is to develop many ideas so that you can converge and anonymously vote on the top ideas. Executed by individually putting a mark next to the concept(s) of choice (dotmocracy). Then have open discussions about why you landed with the top 1–3 ideas. People might vote around feasibility, impact, or other reasons, so it will be essential to understand how the decisions are made. There are a few anonymous voting techniques to use that allow for differing opinions and less bias. Below, under convergence, we'll explain more.

1. **Set the time:** Plan your workshop days. Opt for at least one formal, structured 90-minute brainstorming session with the core team and others with your stakeholders and even customer segment, expert, or unaffiliated outliers. Outliers are helpful because they bring outside perspectives and ideas from analogous sectors.
2. **Set the scene:** To help your participants situate themselves, contextualize the "How Might We" questions you've framed with relevant content and context—like any personas, synthesis matrices, 4 × 4s or sticky notes.
3. **Ensure human-centered diversity:** Include at least three conversations documenting their ideas, concepts, and features with key stakeholders.
4. **Document:** Begin the workshop with structure in place. Take photos and document your generative process. It may feel evident at the moment but returning to your thought process is difficult.
5. **Communicate:** Store your ideas, concepts, features, or characteristics in a location for easy reference.

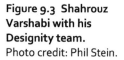

Figure 9.3 Shahrouz
Varshabi with his
Designity team.
Photo credit: Phil Stein.

Ready to converge on a concept?

Meet Shahrouz! An Elab fellow and founder of Designity, an on-demand virtual creative agency. Shahrouz Varshabi started out with one idea, but the Designity thriving today is, simply put, a different company—and for a good reason! To profile Designity's story is to watch an excellent synthesis and journey through the design process.

Shahrouz is a good example of how a concept is adjusted through various iterations and that an openness to change with persistence in the process leads to a successful outcome. So, the short story is: yes, you will likely change your offering and how it's positioned. This is both the root of valuable ideation and the result of practical concept evaluation.

Let's look at Designity's design-led value creation through ideation and iteration. Designity launch process came through this lens of the divergent-convergent process loop, where we discovered that often what we learn from research might not actually align with our initial value proposition—and the level of attentive empathy required to step back from our conceptualized offering, in favor of ideas attuned to integrating all stakeholder needs, wants, and desires.

The U.S. job market grew into an emerging gig economy between 2014 and 2018 with the launch of contractor-driven companies and skill/property-share models. During this time, Shahrouz launched Designity to improve student portfolios by creating an opportunity to add real-world work. The initial value proposed was twofold: students could build their experience with professional guidance, and companies could receive less expensive, readily accessible design work. Yet through his startup journey research process, the online agency's value proposition was transformed to focus on creating the required digital infrastructure for a reliable and collaborative outsourcing

Figure 9.4 Shahrouz Varshabi from Designity presenting at Elab.
Photo credit: Elab

model—one mutually beneficial for the U.S.-based freelancers and clients, without the focus on student-portfolio work.

Where did the shift come from? Shahrouz jumped into platform prototyping and marketing angles for the launch concept at his initial idea stage. He spent a lot of time prototyping the platform visuals. He then quickly launched a pilot as a first-round test of the software. After spending time and money prototyping this initial concept, his early launch fell flat: it didn't immediately resonate with customers or clients. Even with improvements to the UX and iterations on the platform, he was not reaching the customers he anticipated. He reflects in retrospect that he built his platform without fully understanding the behaviors and the psychology of one whole stakeholder group: the clients. He initially angled the business proposition toward designers, speaking primarily to recruiting them, assuming that if he got them, the paying clientele would come. The storytelling that was derived from his initial idea—a design marketplace for students to build their portfolios—ended up ignoring the concepts, features, and character-istics required from the clientele.

How did Shahrouz test his assumptions and iterate?

Without interviewing any stakeholders, his expectation was (espe-cially with clients) to refine his go-to-market strategy and product-market fit through the marketplace launch. Only *after* piloting, a multitude of cold calls, and ineffective sales meetings, did he gain insights that enabled him to pivot the marketing to resonate more with customers. The shift in his positioning dramatically changed his early-stage launch; once he cracked that nut, he could grow his sales revenue with less cost and effort.

Reflecting on his approach at the time, Shahrouz tells us that, in hind-sight, he feels that he didn't spend enough time early on testing his assumptions. Hence, his startup journey pivoted substantially several times, more than he admits he probably needed to. Because he worked, in part, from his lived experience, he admits it tainted his research perspective—making his research biased toward the designers. "Sometimes," Shahrouz feels, "we can be perfectionists and fall in love with our ideas, which is dangerous. We must listen to the feedback, the pain points, and needs."

A more deliberate and conscientious method is to do more upfront research, spend more time interviewing *all* the potential stakeholders, and then integrate their divergent needs into the concept-generation process. Thus, allowing a more informed convergence on the early value proposition. While we advocate for iteration and should expect it, the human-centered approach ensures that our iteration propels our timeline forward, fulfilling our evaluative metrics, as opposed to reversing or backtracking our creations. "Don't get distracted by building the product and tech," says Varshabi, "instead, focus on the customer and solving their problems first! It's a costly mistake to get a perfect product that will need to change."

Prepare for Convergence

In-hand:
- ▢ Do you have 10+ concepts in hand?
- ▢ If concept-ready, do you have 10+ value-components solving user problems?
- ▢ If components-ready, do you have 10+ characteristics or features of a solution area?

In-heart:
- ▢ Do you feel excited about the potential of what you could be building?
- ▢ Do you feel a sense of ambiguity around how and what?
- ▢ Do you feel an urge to "make it real"?

In-mind:
- ▢ Do you know your relevant stakeholders would support your direction?
- ▢ Do you feel like you've heard their voice in the generative process?
- ▢ Do you have a handful of questions to answer?

Converging on a concept: How to bring it all together

Once you have held enough brainstorming sessions with all your stakeholders, team members, and outliers, it's time to bring the results together in a final session connecting all the dots around value creation and impact.

Defining value can be a bit elusive at first. However, as you start to define what that looks like for your customer, you'll crystallize around a few concepts with a distinction between your why (outcome value) and how (how it's delivered). Identifying and then selecting the ideas that will bring your customers the most value within your feasibility and market timing is the object of these exercises, and you'll be looking to answer questions like:

- Does your selection address significant customer problems?
- Does it take advantage of ground-breaking technology?
- Does it offer a radically new experience?
- Does it leverage a unique opportunity?
- Does it create regenerative opportunities for society and the environment?

Coming off brainstorming is a high point and often one of the most rewarding parts of the process. Your enthusiasm will likely propel you and your team forward through the next phase. Authentically, pursuing value is non-negotiable in outcome-centered startups. This pursuit is also evaluated alongside our founding abilities, timeline, funding, and resources. It takes fortitude to set up a methodology for testing assumptions and assessing the results into feedback loops resistant to the "path of least resistance."

Remember, as designer entrepreneurs, strategists, and business owners, we are responsible for checking our biases and assumptions all the time. Every design decision carries some opinion or perspective about the world. Unfortunately, some decisions are solely based on the creator's assumptions. From a simple ethnicity question in a form to the way we will design a new product/service, we could be missing the opportunity to break stereotypes and misconceptions. This holds true for the way we understand our values and how they appear in our execution path. For example, we might prioritize sustainability.

Acts to converge

Converging on an idea takes time and analysis of the concepts you developed in the brainstorming sessions. You might have held several different sessions with various stakeholders, so teasing the top ideas out may take a session or two. In some sessions, you might have had time to vote on ideas, while in others, you stopped at creating solutions. Either way, remember that repeats are a good thing and important to highlight because if several stakeholders come up with the same idea, it might have traction with many other constituents in the market.

A popular voting technique is called **Dotmocracy.** This is a simple technique of independent voting on ideas for various prompts using a sticky dot or a simple mark placed next to selected items on a wall or diagram. This works well for teams of 4+ people with 4+ items to evaluate. You can also integrate stakeholders, users, or the public into this exercise to mark consistency for specific ideas, features, or concepts. The rationale is simple: the ideas with the most votes win and move to the top of the list of concepts to advance into prototyping.

The result of concept convergence

In today's fast-paced, overly automated, and digitally driven society, there is an even greater need for things to feel more human. The ideal value proposition is to-the-point and appeals to a customer's strongest decision-making drivers. It is the reason why customers turn to your company over another. To help, we've created a few templates and matrices to help evaluate and land on a concept to advance.

Concept evaluation for value creation: Opportunity evaluation matrices

If ideation is exploratory, expansive, and divergent, synthesis is the opposite. In this phase, we are trying to converge on and narrow down to the concepts and features that best address the pain points and tasks needed by your product or service users. While the previous chapter focuses on the synthesis of our research, the process and acts of synthesis occur at several stages in our design-led journey—but the shape might look different.

Our focus for convergence in the context of an entrepreneurial journey is through several Opportunity Matrices and Landscape analyses. We recommend these to guide your evaluation with the structure we introduced in ideation, all pointing toward guardrails to answer what to advance, what to prioritize, and why.

The 2 × 2 matrix

Once you master the 2 × 2 matrix, you'll be able to synthesize all sorts of data more effectively to communicate varying types of value in visually simple ways.

STEP 1: Opportunity evaluation matrix

Understanding how the ideas you generated address significant customer problems, leverage ground-breaking opportunities, or offer a radically new and valuable product experience is essential. These after-the-fact descriptors like "ground-breaking," "innovative," and "radical" are the result of practical innovation (which does not always feel like it at the time).

Map the level of reimagining you have accomplished. This exercise will give you a sense of how your concept design might provide the highest value to customers and the community. On this matrix, you can plot your top ideas into categories for the team's discussion and review to debate the various concepts intended for value creation within the context of the marketplace. Mapping these back to your core values as individuals, a team, and a company will ultimately help you select and chart a course (see Figure 9.5):

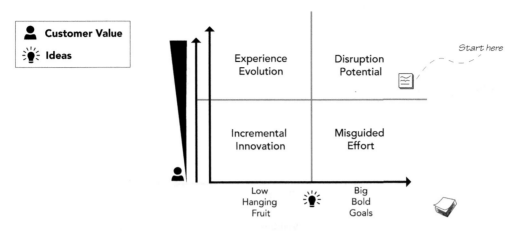

Figure 9.5 Value distinction × customer experience matrix.

STEP 2: Social and environmental impact matrix

This is your opportunity to project into the future and add to your development ways of benefiting society and the environment. We suggest you refer to the United Nations 17 Sustainable Development Goals to help think through the distinct, universally challenging goals we collectively should strive for and how to incorporate their identified targets into your concept metrics (see Figure 9.6).

STEP 3: Prototype + pilot priority opportunity evaluation matrix

Early on, you have important decisions about what to test first to get a proof of concept. First, you need to consider your runway (the amount of money you have on hand to cover development costs and the time you have before others will get to market). Next, evaluate the **feasibility:** within your startup team's capacity (technical, skill-wise, and financial) against the **viability:** what parts to test first to

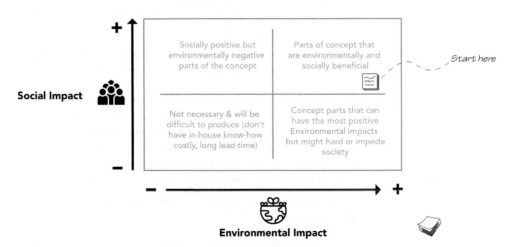

Figure 9.6 Social × environmental impact matrix.

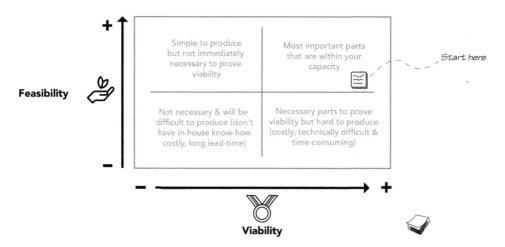

Figure 9.7 Feasibility and viability priority matrix.

get closest to a minimum viable product (MVP). Finally, you can test your product, service, and business model to gain buy-in from investors, early adopters, and founding teammates and eventually bring a return on your investment (ROI) (see Figure 9.7):

Concept Evaluation Matrices

Developed to help you evaluate which concepts to advance into prototyping.

1. **Value Horizon Evaluation (Value Distinction × Customer Experience)**
   Creating value and understanding a concept's potential impact is the first hurdle your concept needs to pass. Evaluate the various ideas for their potential to generate change by plotting them on the matrix. The two upper quadrants are ideally where the advanced concepts should be (experience evolution and disruption potential).

   Once you've determined which to advance, run them through the prompts in the following two matrices to ensure they align.

2. **Stakeholder Impact Evaluation (Social × Environmental)**
   This 2 × 2 matrix will help you plot your concepts more granularly through the lens of social and environmental impacts. Each matrix quadrant represents a value from low to high on the X/Y axis. Plot your concept's features, and then discuss with your team the potential each has and where they can improve.

   Be sure to plot the projected positive and negative impacts they might have.

   Lastly, evaluate the concept through the lens of your current team's financial and skill-wise abilities.

3. **Prototype vs. Pilot Priority Evaluation (Feasibility and Viability)**

   Prototype/Pilot Priority Matrix is part of the concept evaluation. It helps entrepreneurs and startup product development teams prioritize features, characteristics, or aspects of the primary solution concept.

   Feasibility on the Y-axis concerns the skills and finances needed from low to high.

   Viability on the X-axis involves prioritization: what part of the concept needs to be tested first to get to an MVP. What is the fastest way to test a product/service or business model to gain buy-in from early adopters and teammates and eventually lead to a return on investment (RIO)? Know that you can't test everything all at once.

   After these exercises are complete, step back to review the results. Then vote on the top concepts and features, allowing time for each participant to explain their point of view and be heard.

Landscape assessment

We recommend checking the competition around your finalized concept *before y*ou advance into prototyping (see Figure 9.8 and accompanying activity). Preliminary competition can sway our perception of value. With intense ideation and synthesis, your own driving why and your company's why are more stable to compare. *Who can be both inspiration and competition? What else exists in the market?* Consider your initial system mapping: who's in an analogous industry or a similar model in another country? What's your competitive advantage? Whatever the conditions are, it's important to jot them down and share with others because you might not know all the companies out there, and new ones pop up every day.

Once you have evaluated your concept against what's currently offered in your potential sector, local or global, and have determined it is still worth developing (because of its unique value proposition), it's time to start planning the testing phase and moving on to prototyping.

Prototyping as value testing

Prototypes bring design language to the entrepreneurial first steps of our company. The purpose of making prototypes is to get a sense of what's involved in bringing a product to market and to test if the concept you've aligned on meets user and stakeholder needs. Pacing ourselves beyond an incremental fix requires a dramatic commitment to testing. So yes, to disrupt, we require small steps.

Prototyping shifts us from researching assumptions around hypothetical directions with our constituents to testing assumptions baked into the

Why conduct this analysis?	Write your goals for this analysis			
	Your Company Concept	Competitor 1	Competitor 2	Competitor 3
Profile — Overview				
Profile — Competitive Advantage				
Marketing Profile — Target Market				
Marketing Profile — Marketing Strategies				
Product Profile — Product & Services				
Product Profile — Pricing & Costs				
Product Profile — Distribution Channels				
Swot Analysis — Strengths				
Swot Analysis — Weaknesses				
Swot Analysis — Opportunities				
Swot Analysis — Threats				

Start here

Figure 9.8 Charting competitive landscape analysis.

Competitive Landscape Analysis

You've spent a lot of time evaluating the competition (repeatedly!) as new businesses come on the scene and your core value proposition shifts and focuses. If you're doing something right, someone else will want to do something similar. Focusing on what you can gain and clarifying your distinction will lend you fortitude in your prototyping journey.

This research will help determine if *and why* this is the best concept to advance and where you might need to spend some more time understanding or testing for distinction. It will also inform a valuable competition slide you can use in your visual pitch.

1. **Starting Point**
    Jot down the top three things you want to confirm about your competition. Examples might be whether they are mobile-first, how they reach within communities, or the unique services they offer. Then use this to cross-check that you've included that research in the below buckets.
2. **Profile**
    Fill in, the Overview and Competitive Advantages of your top three competitors, and then write what you feel your offering description is and the advantages that differentiate you at this top level.

3. **Marketing**
   Within the Target Market and Marketing Strategies section, fill in and again look to differentiate yourselves and freshly position your concept. It could be through the language and brand voice or the mode of delivery as examples.
4. **Product (or offering)**
   When evaluating the Product and Services, use a simple bullet list of features, characteristics, or components. The same goes for Pricing, Cost and Distribution Channels: a simple list will do, depending on where you notice similarity or divergence.
5. **SWOT**
   Although a traditional tool, a SWOT analysis is still effective for assessing your concept's Strengths, Weaknesses, Opportunities, and Threats. This assessment tool was completed last to build on the research tools above.

future deployment of our offering. For example, are users willing to pay for this product or service? Does the value we imagine creating land the way we anticipate? What does this solution look like integrated into their current day-to-day? What key components do we need to prioritize? Prototyping helps us figure out all the features that go into bringing a brand to life around our solution and will build a roadmap for launch.

Creating an experience through our concept solution helps more than just branding. It encompasses an interconnected and balanced mix of elements that transcends the digital and physical into a sensory amalgam that leaves an imprint on people—across users and systems. We use prototyping to ascertain our creation's lived experience and access hands-on feedback. In entrepreneurship and our startup journey, these small, digestible puzzle pieces will eventually build toward the cumulative influence of our concept across spheres.

What's a prototype? Prototypes are mock-ups or simulations of reality. Making things real enough to determine if there is a promise and if it's worth moving forward creates a gradual build and validation vs. diving from the value proposition to the final concept. Determining the fidelity of the rough samples or prototypes is needed, so you don't spend too much time and money going down paths that do not yield returns on that investment. This is where data collection and feedback loops come back into the picture. This initial phase of prototyping is often called rapid prototyping for this very reason. As you refine your prototypes, their quality should improve, their representation of the future becomes more sophisticated, and the fidelity of our vision becomes closer to that of your final delivery solution (see Figure 9.9).

Most companies use large-scale market research efforts to test products with hundreds or even thousands of people; testing a prototype with just a few users is much different. Though prototype testing borrows from the methodologies of focus groups and design research, it's typically a much smaller and more informal effort.

Figure 9.9 Level of fidelity × stage of prototype: Iterating toward launch.

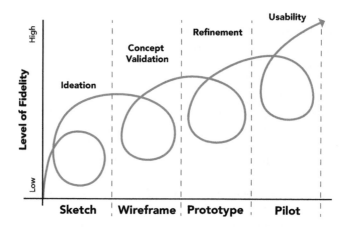

Types of prototypes: Low-fidelity vs. high-fidelity

Low-fidelity prototypes are often paper-based and allow for more imagination and minimal user interactions. They range from a series of hand-drawn mock-ups of digital interfaces. They could also involve cardboard or scrap materials to simulate a physical product. Role-playing in-person services can also help you imagine the roadblock or hurdles you will need to address along the refinement process. In theory, low-fidelity sketches are quicker to create. In addition, low-fidelity prototypes help to enable early renderings of alternative design solutions, which provoke innovation and improvement. An additional advantage to this approach is that users may feel more comfortable suggesting changes when using rough sketches.

High-fidelity prototypes usually allow more realistic user interactions. High-fidelity prototypes take you as close as possible to an accurate representation of the user interface with some functionality with the buttons (mouse-keyboard). If there is a physical component, a tangible object has some functionality that addresses the job to be done. High-fidelity prototypes are assumed to be much more effective in collecting real human performance data (e.g., time to complete a task or quality of the delivery) and in demonstrating actual products to clients, management, and others. It leaves less to the imagination and addresses the potential challenges and costs in real product development.

Remember, the purpose of making prototypes is to simulate reality, to make things real enough to see if they are adoptable and desirable at a price needed to enter the market. They help grow the company and enable the team to stabilize, fund margins, and future growth while meeting its mission.

Assessments and feedback loops will help you benchmark and meet your objectives while prototyping to keep track of the development and iterations. Because we are creating complex adaptive systems of our own within even greater systems we can't control; it is mission-critical that we capture and clearly organize the data we're collecting to enable proper assessment.

Planning your tests to get to a minimum viable solution or system (MVS)

Strategizing your prototype development involves knowing your runway (amount of time and money you have before you need to launch on the market). This can be because you have little money or your product is time-sensitive, perhaps a season, holiday experience, or product. Planning the types of prototypes needed and the cost of developing them will be necessary to keep the launch on schedule and within budget. A **prototype plan** is like a research plan: it states the objectives, assumptions, tests you will make, key performance indicators (KPIs), and several iterations along the way against a timeline with precise dates for deliverables so your team can align and collaborate to meet these goals.

A great way to prepare to test your prototype is to pick your most critical **assumption** and build a prototype around that.

Choose your prototype value

Below, we will discuss a few ways you can test your concept out in various levels of refinement or fidelity over time as you ramp up to be market ready.

Whether you're testing a physical product, a digital one, or a combination called phygital, or you are offering a service, you'll want to test it out on different customer segments.

We'll go through a few tools to develop concepts from the nascent phases to the launch.

Prototyping the whole experience

Looking at what you're creating through the lens of our six senses allows designing the whole experience. Looking at the offering through cognitive, social, emotional, physical, digital, and temporal experience assessments helps to see missing elements or enhancements over time into future iterations of your product. This exercise (Figure 9.10) starts to become speculative and can inform future work when future-proofing the company. To address all the senses, one might come up with ideas to include augmented reality tools to enhance the interaction with your audience or to leverage artificial intelligence interfaces like bots to offer additional interactive support to customers. Below we have a honeycomb framework called Framework for Sensorial-led Design Analysis (seen in Figure 9.10 and accompanying exercise) to assess and enhance the experience of your solution. See Figure 9.11 for an example of it in use.

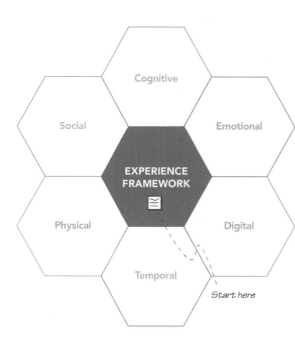

Cognitive:

Related to learning; acquiring knowledge and understanding

Social:

Related to interacting with other people; connecting with, relating to, and forming relationships with people

Emotional:

Related to emotions; intuitive, mental feelings and states of mind

Physical:

Related to the five senses; how your body physically feels

Digital:

Related to the use of digital technology; virtual interfaces, communication, and interactions

Temporal:

Related to time; including quantity, quality, and sense of time

Figure 9.10 Experience design framework for sensorial-led design analysis.
Photo credit: Rhea Alexander and Darcy Keester (2021), CC-BY-SA 4.0.

Experience Design Framework for Sensorial-Led Design Analysis

To be sure you're creating positive remote, online, or in-person experiences, use this template to prompt thought through the various senses.

1. Start by naming the experience in the center.
2. Moving clockwise through the six phases, fill in the template starting with the (positive) cognitive experience you hope participants encounter, ending with social.

Goal: By building upon the initial ideas, a honeycomb of possible enhancements such as features in a mobile application or website, or your physical space will improve the experience journey informed by design.

Many frameworks and tools for prototyping help you see the interconnections and workflow, from the big picture down to keeping track of the details, especially when it comes to digital interfaces such as websites and mobile applications. Tracking how they integrate into the brick-and-mortar experience of the brand and work culture are all key design elements essential to developing your brand and marketing strategy. These parts of the business intersect and make up the whole brand experience.

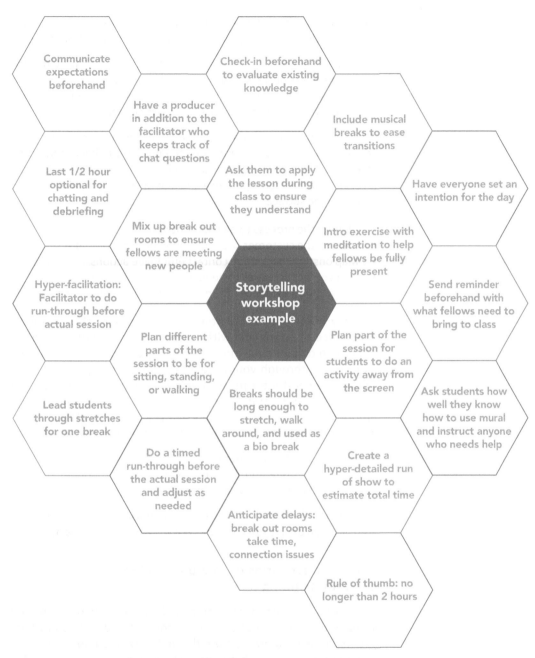

Figure 9.11 Example of an experience framework for a storytelling workshop.
Photo credit: Rhea Alexander and Darcy Keester (2021), CC-BY-SA 4.0.

Service blueprints and journey maps

Developing a service blueprint and customer journey map through
your service will be essential artifacts to reference. Like maps on
an adventure, uncovering treasure that helps shape the experience
you are offering, they help bring your user into the center of the

experiments. They also log where opportunities and pain points may lie in the customer journey through your product or service.

A **service blueprint** is an operational planning tool that guides the executing team on how a service will be provided. It specifies the physical evidence, staff actions, and support systems/web infrastructure needed to deliver the service across its channels.

A service blueprint gives a complete picture of how the service and related experience is delivered, end to end, front to back, and across channels. It is a powerful tool that simultaneously provides a high-level view of the user experience and a detailed view of what is going on below the surface:

- Identify the process to be blueprinted
- Identify the customer segment (thinking/feeling/doing)
- Map onstage/backstage contact employee actions
- Link contact activities to needed support functions
- Add physical evidence of service at each customer action step

Journey maps are experientially based and plot the emotional experience of interfacing with your brand, from perhaps the initial search online to paying the bill. They can also chart recurring experiences through your product or service, mapping the emotional rollercoaster the person might experience, from disbelief or lack of trust to frustration or exuberance. There is a whole list of emotions a person can feel. Hence, it is a vital tool when evaluating the prototype tests, you undertake with various stakeholders.

Journey maps offer a communication tool to help your team align around the positive and negative experiences throughout the customer's journey through your offering.

By mapping the activities, goals, KPIs, and users' emotions step-by-step, you can gauge what features are working and what is not.

Embodied scenarios or role-playing for empathy-building

An improv-inspired tool, this template helps you plan out a pretend scenario that will act out the service concept to understand where you might need to give it more thought, how you might build and test a prototype, and what roles each team member needs to play to deliver.

Also called bodystorming, this is simply brainstorming but done with the body. Bodystorming is used to generate and communicate progressive ideas quickly to get feedback, build empathy and understanding around delivering them, and improvise further. It is done by getting your team together to act or simulate the experience. All you need for this one is your physical bodies and perhaps no reservations about getting a little silly. For this activity, you need to act out the existing product or process. Refer to Social Presencing Theater for more information on this technique.

Plan for a simulation or role-play exercise, play-acting your service roles and customer experience, and write down how you envision setting the scene. Next, think through and jot down how you want your space to look and feel to simulate the intended concept.

Like scenes in a play, jot down what type of props you would need to procure, to enact this. Use childlike imagination, perhaps substituting Lego or paper artifacts to simulate intended products you would offer or technology you would create.

Envision how many people would be needed to enact the experience, to make it a positive. Keep in mind some people might need to play specialized roles in this simulation.

Walking through someone else's experience is the key to building empathy and a deep understanding of their needs. Still, the best way is to enact with actual constituents to be sure you're not bringing your biases into the equation since we know experiences differ from person to person.

Digityping: Prototyping mobile applications and websites

Creating quick digital tests using software-enabled products or services, like digital prototyping, can save you time and money by ensuring product development is based on data from the outset rather than untested assumptions.

Here are a few examples to get your thinking started:

- Ebooks
- Software
- Video
- Audio and music
- Photography
- Graphics
- Digital art
- PDF documents
- Social media posts and tags

Prototyping is perhaps one of the most important parts of the web design process. By building a prototype, you can test ideas with users, be wrong, learn, and, most importantly, do all the above quickly. But choosing the right tool can make or break the outcome.

- Start by asking yourself, "What do you want to learn from your prototype?"

Figure 9.12 Time × scope from concept testing through to launch.

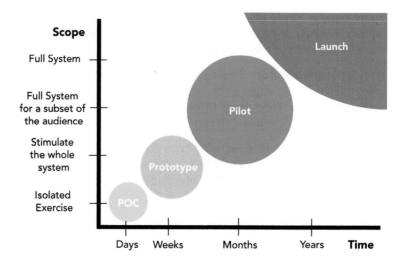

- Think about what resources you have, to build a prototype.
- Start with paper prototypes from templates.
- Test user interface using accessible digital tools and apps.

The power of pilots

Like prototyping, piloting is a later-stage way to test, iterate, and refine. But piloting requires a higher level of fidelity and a greater commitment (Figure 9.12). When piloting, an organization has developed a prototype and business model that works and is taking the next step: testing it with a small group of users over time.

Pilots work best when you are looking to understand how it works in "reality" with real users, not testing with friends, colleagues, or family, who may be biased. If prototyping aims to learn, piloting is to collect data; effective pilots are designed to gather feedback, track behaviors, and document outcomes.

Sometimes a pilot will validate a concept and prototype. However, even in this state, "failure" is still seen as informative and not a setback.

Piloting

The pilot project is an initial small-scale implementation used to prove a project idea's viability. In business innovation, it's an opportunity to run small tests of your products and services relatively inexpensively, on the market, or with a sample set before you invest heavily in it. Piloting puts your product or service to the test to help discover whether there is a market. In addition, it gives you valuable insight into the challenges you and your new business will face.

Start with clear goals and define the scope. Then establish a realistic timeline. Finally, identify the target audience, how you will measure success, and a clear communication plan.

When designing your pilot, ask simple questions like does it work? Do people want and need this? Would they be repeat customers? Is the price point scalable? What's the impact? Do you like being in this business?

Business today is like an octopus, a highly functioning, complex adaptive system that is:

- Resilient
- Adaptable
- Conscientious (environmentally and socially)
- Financially sustainable
- Pleasurable (HCD experience)
- Impactful (needed)

Delivered through products and services, it should include the digital content, the physical experiences, interaction with the physical product prototype (if there is one), and a business model form. This could be a questionnaire at the end of the simulation with price tiers to survey their perceived value at this juncture or potentially ask questions about future features to roll out.

How to validate a concept before fully developing it

We have some basic steps to help strategize and plan a quick concept test. Start by using free website tools and templates to mock-up something quick. Next, create a simple landing page to explain the concept; this also tests the brand's voice and starts you thinking about visual identity. For example, you can say it is "coming soon" in an approachable way that suits the identity. After that, create a signup page and be sure to capture the email addresses of interested parties. Finally, post the link on a Subreddit r/startup, possibly run Meta or LinkedIn ads, and maybe register on Product Hunt (if you have a live product).

Then track the number of people willing to sign up and be sure to gather comments.

In the signup, add a few survey questions to help your research and validate your value proposition. Include comments or a feedback button and create solid content on Medium, YouTube, etc., about your philosophy and value for all stakeholders and differentiators. And finally, make sure everything is posted on your landing page.

You will be conducting many product and service tests, so it will be necessary to capture the data coherently, and then act on it with your developers. Reference the feedback log template (Figure 9.13) to create your own

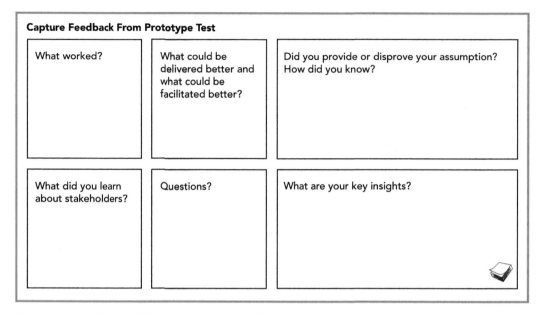

Figure 9.13 Log for debriefing a prototype workshop.

Developing a Feedback Log from Testing Prototypes and Pilots

Whether testing online, in workshops or 1:1 with users, capture the needed data to make necessary iterations to improve the interface and experience for better overall results.

1: Be sure you are asking or prompting your team with the right questions. Take inspiration from the above diagram. Start by asking "What worked?" and then make your way through the prompts.

Goal: Always step back, assess insights and learnings, and be clear with the following steps.

The never-ending continuum of feedback loops and user testing

Why do we emphasize this so much in design entrepreneurship and strategy? Feedback loops are a part of your everyday life, whether you know it or not. Understanding them can help you see their good and bad sides. Feedback loops can also help you make better decisions in your day-to-day life.

As designers, we often work hard to design the best possible solution for our users' problems, only to find that they get used way less than we thought. However, there's a way to support a feature, better yet, a specific behavior, by using reinforcing feedback loops we talked about earlier.

Feedback loops happen naturally in nature, where infinite interdependencies regulate and maintain homeostasis. However, a lack of information and feedback can make massive and often unforeseen changes to large systems. The climate, financial market, and human body are great examples of systems that rely on feedback loops.

Baking feedback loops into your company, cultivating learning mindsets for innovation, and building a learning culture are critical to keeping a business sustainable. In addition, making processes and time to capture data, assess, and track test results and next steps is vital to building your startup.

Along with developing feedback loops, one must also have time to establish "holistic" strategic planning; this is the ability to look ahead at what needs to or might happen next (speculatively) and plan for it. We say to do this "holistically" because it will be good to look at your plans from all angles and each stakeholder's perspective, not every entrepreneur does this at their peril.

How did Shahrouz test his assumptions, and what was his prototype?

First, Shahrouz tested his assumptions by developing a series of rapid tests, and then eventually digital prototypes, constantly testing along the way and continuing this methodology to remain responsive to the needs of the market and his initial customers. We know this to be the design method.

The first Designity "prototype"

The first version was paper, then moved quickly to a web-based version. At the time, Shahrouz focused on solving the pain point of students and early career designers needing to build up their portfolio and field experience. Therefore, the language and tone were directed more toward attracting them, offering potential badges and ratings to help them advance in their careers.

Metrics of success

Shahrouz went to many local NYC design schools and university career service departments to attract students and recent graduates. The onboarding of these participants happened quickly. In addition, selling the platform's functionality was relatively easy for them. It costs them nothing to join. So this part of the equation was working, but he soon realized that without many client projects to choose from, they would tire of it.

When he tested with potential clients, however, their concerns were more around vetting the designer to see that they were a fit, the management of the process, the contract management, guaranteeing a standard quality of the deliverable, and managing the timeline. There were many more pain points for these platform users than he had initially anticipated. His early research had focused more on the designer's needs; the brand's voice spoke more to them, and they were easier to reach because he was a designer. "Be careful; designers like to build things to perfection in their vision ... building a business is a different focus; it's on the end-user." Shahrouz realized his own biases impaired his objectivity. The real job to be done was not giving a voice to designers but rather managing the creative process for clients who are not adept at the creative process and sought to execute a company's need around creative services.

After rapid testing with both stakeholders over the first year, he gained more and more insights into the behaviors on both sides. That helped him develop his brand voice, understand the complexity of the needs from both sides, and address those details through some of the platform's functionality, changing his business model to target the clients' needs first. He pivoted to become an online agency that managed projects for clients by employing seasoned project managers who manage freelance design teams.

This also helped him gain his first round of investment funding. Which happened when he was able to make more and more transactions occur, receive recommendations, and ultimately repeat customers.

Long term, Shahrouz has shared some advice for entrepreneurs:

Collect user experience first-hand: There are too many tools and technologies out there, so Shahrouz feels that to stay relevant and grow, he, as a founder, needs to focus on user experience and stay connected to clients. To do this, he often listens to client and sales calls weekly to collect qualitative data and learn if end-users are happy or upset. If he hears about an issue more than three times, he addresses it immediately. To manage this data, he has a notebook, then once a month, he implements it.

Monthly team brainstorms: After brainstorming in three-hour blocks each Friday afternoon around all the features and customer journeys, Shahrouz and his team turn them into actionable plans. He uses workflow/project management software to organize tasks and implementation. He then breaks down each iteration into weekly challenges every Monday morning in a team meeting.

Transition reflection: How do we know when one "stage" ends and the next begins?

We realistically know that to name and follow explicit "stages" or "phases" in design is ... counterintuitive. So much of what we discuss is intangible: a mindset, an approach, a sense; this ambiguity is inherent to the design and implicit in sound design.

As an entrepreneur, however, we're often pushed into contexts where we must name operational costs, explicitly articulate value, and quantify the impact. How can we use design and follow a process if it shouldn't be expressly ordered? What leads us to approach the next phase of our company launch or growth without ending a chapter?

We use Shahrouz as a design example of recognizing transition and an entrepreneurial representative of this real-life picture.

Use these questions to reflect on bridging your company phases:

- *Mindset signal:* Do *you as a founder* feel caught between a rock and a hard place? An example of this might feel like a chicken and egg scenario where you're confident in what you want to prototype. Still, you think you can't effectively deliver this without funding.
- *Workflow signal:* Do your folders feel disorganized like you're creating new documents daily? Do you change your organizational structure all the time? Does your workflow feel fragmented? An example of this might be indecision or frustration around whether to use collaborative docs like a Google sheet or a live document vs. a static one. Another example is getting a GANTT organization tool like Asana off the ground.
- *Advice signal:* When you talk about your company, what's the first response? Is it a clarification question? Or is it an inquiry question? An example can be, how do you know that this concept is needed? Or, if that sounds ambitious, how much would that cost to build or buy?

Each of these signals you're in transition—and you might be feeling these all the time! There's rarely a circumstance in the early stage of building where funding is the only obstacle. This scenario is common when toggling between synthesizing your research, ideating, and prototyping/testing.

Once you have a good feel for what the first iteration of the product, service, and brand voice (look, feel, and language) might be, get ready to test the business model.

Next, we'll cover how to test a concept through prototyping the business model, strategically refine and communicate your value-add through another round of analysis and synthesis, and then eventually through a pilot of what you expect to deliver on launch day.

Navigational Log and Takeaways

- Incorporate teams and stakeholders to ideate and define core concepts and components
- Be holistic with your concept evaluations—zoom back out to impact!
- Build your first hands-on prototypes to test the value
- Get used to comments you might not want—and lean into these feedback loops!
- Acclimate to testing users' sensorial experience
- Plan for the phases between concept testing to piloting

10

PROTOTYPE TO TEST VALUE

Business Viability and Evaluation

Objectives

- Develop a business and revenue model to test
- Use your strategic plan as a live document instead of a static one
- Practice feedback loops and design-informed business strategies for long-term stability
- Understand legal structures and funding opportunities
- Test pricing, product/market fit
- Develop your value chain as a source of value creation

You future business health: prototyping models

Strategic design is about planning for the future, and we know the future is uncertain. A real strategic plan ensures we gather all the information we need to start, providing goals and milestones to track our progress. It should be a living, iterative document that can be referenced at any given time in its lifespan. While drafting, the first iteration is an essential first step, it's certainly not the last. After that, we must test, collect data, and iterate. All too often, strategic plans are drafted, and then left to gather dust. Yet, they are the heart of your business: the story of your vision made up of your research, visualizations, roadmap, journaling, and chronicling of your business.

Previously you created a plan to prototype and test the service and/or products you'd like to bring into the world. While iterating that based on feedback, you will do the same with your business model.

Before testing the business model, that is, how you plan to make money and bring your ideas to fruition, let's investigate the greater ecosystem and reference your ecosystem maps. We will be toggling from the macro systems level to the micro level, looking at your specific circumstances in time.

How we can maintain the long-term health of our business is about planning for the future. Health is usually defined as the overall human well-being of the body and mind. It is a dynamic condition resulting from the body's constant adjustment and adaptation to environmental stresses and changes.

DOI: 10.4324/9781003227151-14

The same concept of health can be applied to the overall state of your company, meaning that a healthy business is constantly adjusting and adapting to the environment in which it operates. A company's ability to adapt is impacted by its resources, which include cash-on-hand and current information on the company's performance. Without proper systems of evaluation in place, it may be hard to understand the resilience of your business when the time comes to respond to changes in the business environment.

The heart of your business—The business model

One needs to be aware that within economies, there are many different types of business models operating. Selecting or creating your model is an important step and one that will need prototyping and testing, and then piloting in conjunction with your product or service. What's important is thinking about the different ways of creating value and deriving revenue through your services, products, or a combination of the two. Some of the most apparent models you might be familiar with are subscription, bundling, freemium, leasing, and retail—but there are many more.

Before you start: Contextualize your model

Understanding the context in which you are building your startup is very important in a volatile world that is changing faster and faster. So, let's step back before we get into micro details of costs and operations, and look from a bird's-eye view to take stock. Creating a circular Context Canvas like in Figure 10.1 identifying the macro trends

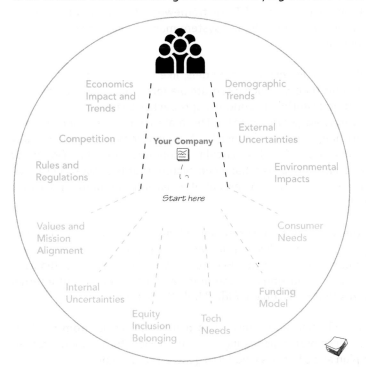

Figure 10.1 Context canvas.

Context Canvas

The goal is to survey the landscape, mapping your needs to these macro forces and trends. Then look for connections, potential implications, and impacts before you dive into your own world-building. This will remind you, immediately, of these conditions. Then, as they change, you update this map.

1. Imagine the circle cut into slices like a pie. Start in the center top (around noon) by writing a brief note about your business model value prop, service, or product to build off.
2. In the top section, jot down all the macro trends from a regulatory standpoint, economic, environmental, tech, industry, etc.
3. After you've surveyed what shifts are happening externally, start adding your needs to the bottom part of the pie. Jot down your constituents' and tech needs, the funding model, values and mission, and any uncertainties on sticky notes. Pin it up and keep building upon this graph over time.

(context) at the top, followed by your needs below, will help you plan the business models you should test. Eventually, you can make it into your "world" diagram, layering in concentric circles of information. Note: this is similar, and influence by, system mapping in Chapter 6, like the STEEP framework. Consider this development on (with more detail!) system mapping in favor of economic resilience.

Today, we have economic models, like Kate Raworth's Doughnut Economic theory, which integrate planetary and social needs, thus elevating traditional economic approaches to incorporate a holistic worldview (Raworth 2017). This makes it more regenerative and flourishing, not only financially, but environmentally and socially as well. Considered a circular economic concept, Doughnut Economics espouses a balanced system that is constantly renewing itself and addressing essential social and environmental justice needs.

In the doughnut of social and planetary boundaries diagram, Figure 10.2, you will see a similar system approach we take above for your Context Canvas. Eventually, you can make your diagram with layers and rings to communicate the external and internal factors that make up your ideal holistic system.

After reflecting upon these data points and results from product/experience prototype testing, you can consider formulating a **strategic plan** and a business model to generate your income.

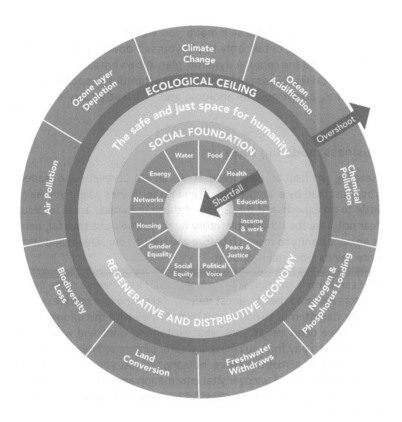

Joining a few organizations can help you network and find like-minded entrepreneurs and resources to help you manage and grow a startup. Several global movements are practicing value-driven business creation, such as the Zebras. Unlike Unicorns that scale meteorically by moving fast and breaking things, Zebras is a founder-driven, grassroots effort grounded in a holistic set of ideals. Zebras are businesses that approach issues from a social impact lens while focused on generating revenue, calling for a more ethical and inclusive movement to counter existing startup culture.

The difference between static planning vs. dynamic planning

Traditional strategic planning looks at long-term history to plan for the long-term future. That may be how things have gotten done in businesses worldwide for generations. Still, in a world where technology moves faster than business, annual planning is becoming archaic. Instead, it's static planning for a dynamic world.

It's time to step away from tradition and into a new way of planning that invests more time in maximizing productivity and flexibility. One that doesn't make you waste time trying to pin down every little detail, only to pin yourself down by a plan without any breathing room. A dynamic plan allows employees to take intelligent risks, pursue unforeseen opportunities, respond swiftly to threats, adopt new technology, and efficiently carry out new ideas.

Business modeling tools

Here we will lean on your mindset. As an entrepreneur and leader, you must lead by example and often into territories where you have little to no expertise. If this is one of those unfamiliar areas for you, fear not. Like the other exploratory work, you've done thus far, here is an opportunity to research before you roll up your sleeves and start entertaining your many options.

You can learn a lot from your competition. First, choose some competitors and map their business models. Take time to do this research before you attempt to make your own. Armed with this information, you'll have deep insight into what customers want and what they are willing to pay for. You'll have a clearer picture of how customers' needs are met across the entire industry, not just your own concept/ company. And you'll uncover vital information about how other businesses, maybe even very successful businesses, have created their own spaces in the market.

Practice activity: How you start using an Environmental and Social Governance Business Model Canvas (ESGBMC)

Building off your research into your competition's business models, you understand better how other businesses work (their economic models). Then, building upon the research you did above, think about how you might approach producing revenue (bringing in the cash!), and you can start to play around with various business models.

You can start using an ESGBMC (Figure 10.3). This maps out the business on a high level: only the most critical aspects of the business model will be asked at this point. As you evolve into the following stages of development and growth, you will need to dive deeper into each bucket of the canvas and layer in the details. Eventually, you'll need to create separate business canvases or sheets for each section that will become necessary over time. All of this will be part of your business's strategic plan that is a live, working blueprint for your unfolding business. In addition, our canvas is sector-agnostic, so there might be a few more questions you'll need to ask yourself that pertain to your sector.

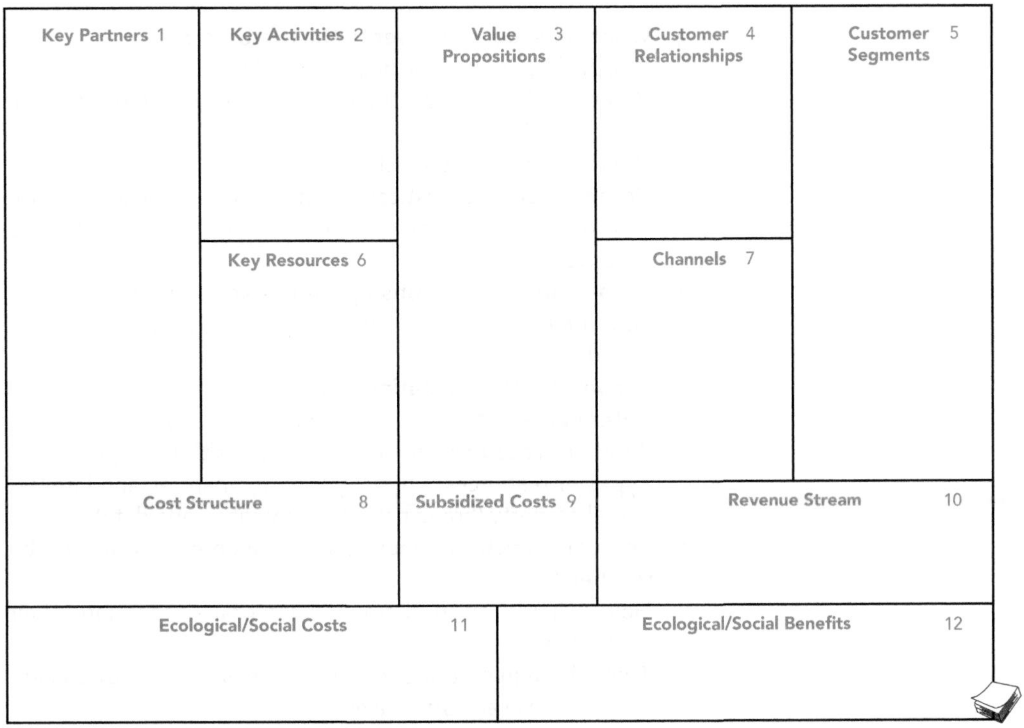

Key Partners 1	Key Activities 2	Value 3 Propositions	Customer 4 Relationships	Customer 5 Segments
	Key Resources 6		Channels 7	
Cost Structure 8		Subsidized Costs 9	Revenue Stream 10	
Ecological/Social Costs 11			Ecological/Social Benefits 12	

Figure 10.3 An environmental and social governance business model canvas.

ESGBMC

This canvas is inspired by the Strategizer canvas but updated with prompts around sustainability and inclusion intended to encourage the entrepreneur to create more responsive and systemic business models.

- Get the right team together.
- Grab a large chunk of wall space or set up a virtual whiteboard.
- Print, draw, or digitize a canvas so you can all work on it together.
- Allow yourself 60 minutes of quiet time to work on it together, reply to the prompts, and keep iterating over time.

1. **Who are your key partners? Crucial suppliers?**
   Possible motivations: Think optimization, reduction of risk and uncertainty, or acquisition of particular resources or activities
2. **What key activities do our value propositions require?**
   Possible categories include: Distribution channels, operational needs, R&D...

3. **What value do we deliver to the customer?**
   Which problems are we helping to solve?
   What bundles of products and services are we offering to each
      segment?
   Which needs are we satisfying?
   Potential characteristics: Newness, performance, custom-
      ization, design, status, price reduction, accessibility, and
      convenience
4. **What types of relationships does each segment expect?**
   How are they integrated with the rest of our business model
      and costs?
5. **For whom are we creating value?**
   Potential possibilities: Mass or niche markets
6. **What key resources do our value propositions require?**
   Types of resources: Physical, human, financial, and intellec-
      tual property (brand patents, copyrights, and data)
7. **Through which channels do our segments want to be
   reached?**
   How will we reach them and integrate them into their
      routines?
   Think through customer evaluation phases—from awareness
      to purchase and after-sales
8. **Cost structure: Which essential resources and activities are
   the most expensive?**
   Models: Lean, low price, expensive with maximum automa-
      tion, or value-driven
9. **What are the subsidized costs within your business?**
   Are there tax subsidies to account for or a 3rd-party funder for
      your venture?
10. **Revenue streams: What are our customers willing to pay
    for?**
    What do they currently pay, and how would they prefer to
       pay? Are there multiple streams?
    Types: Asset sales, subscription or broker fees, licensing,
       usage fees, and renting/leasing
11. **What ecological or social costs is our business model
    causing?**
    Which resources and activities are nonrenewable and
       consumptive?
    Evaluation instruments: Life-cycle assessments or Standard
       Good Matrix
12. **What ecological or social benefits is our business model
    generating?**
    Who benefits, and can you transform it into a value
       proposition?
    Instruments: Social Reporting Standard (SRS)

Connect the dots

Creating a complex adaptive system within existing systems is complicated, so practice stepping back and zooming in and out. First, you'll want to pause to link up the building blocks: every value proposition needs a customer segment and a revenue stream! Then, when everything is on the board, take a step back. Have a short break. Did you miss anything? Forget something?

Always consult others on the team; they will help you to see from different perspectives.

In practice, you'll need to do this from time to time. If you are missing something, go back and get it—like a scientist in a lab, you're methodically testing and logging the changes, refining your concept.

Current state of your model

As hard as this is, try not to get overwhelmed and stay as methodical as you can on the fly while you're testing, mixing, and reflecting. As a design entrepreneur, just like that scientist in the lab, you will need to simultaneously hold (and test) several concepts.

Today and soon, you will have expenses, responsibilities, commitments, and needs. You'll have to take these into consideration while making your business model selections for the near future and distant future when scenario planning. What is feasible today is vastly different after you get funding, right? So, target a *minimum viable product (MVP)/service* goal first, then plan out in phases what might come next in different scenarios.

An MVP is what (product/service) you can bring to market to prove your concept within the means that you have TODAY. Then plan what you might be able to do with a small amount of cash, then with more, and so forth. Your "runway" is the amount of time and money you must prove your idea is viable. Getting funding requires telling your story, and that's why all these diagrams and visuals will come in handy. When you need to illustrate your pitch.

I never lose. I either win or learn.

Nelson Mandela

Milestone to assess and validate plans

Stepping back to check-in, assess your strategy, and plan for your business is an important exercise to build into your practice. When doing this, you make sure costing, margins, and profits are on track to sustain your business, but also consider financing growth. Look to maintain a healthy balance. Tools like the Questions to Assess (Figure 10.4) and Validate Business Plan have helpful prompts and a scale to determine where you are.

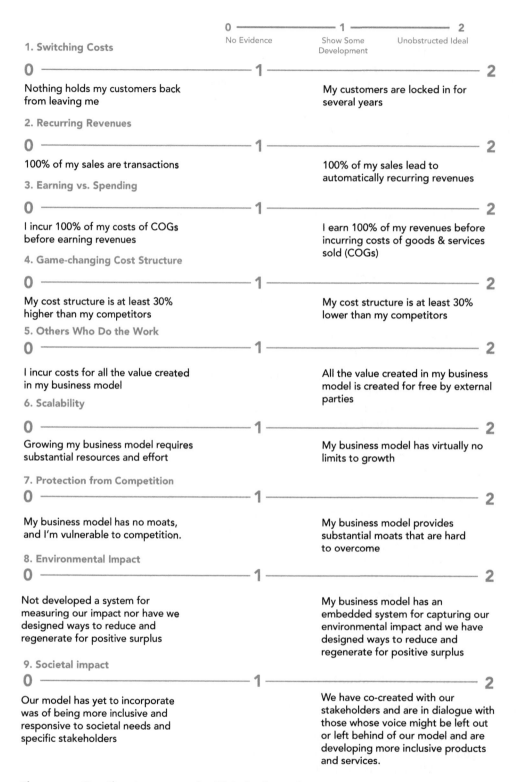

	0	1	2
	No Evidence	Show Some Development	Unobstructed Ideal

1. Switching Costs

0 ———————————————— 1 ———————————————— 2

Nothing holds my customers back from leaving me

My customers are locked in for several years

2. Recurring Revenues

0 ———————————————— 1 ———————————————— 2

100% of my sales are transactions

100% of my sales lead to automatically recurring revenues

3. Earning vs. Spending

0 ———————————————— 1 ———————————————— 2

I incur 100% of my costs of COGs before earning revenues

I earn 100% of my revenues before incurring costs of goods & services sold (COGs)

4. Game-changing Cost Structure

0 ———————————————— 1 ———————————————— 2

My cost structure is at least 30% higher than my competitors

My cost structure is at least 30% lower than my competitors

5. Others Who Do the Work

0 ———————————————— 1 ———————————————— 2

I incur costs for all the value created in my business model

All the value created in my business model is created for free by external parties

6. Scalability

0 ———————————————— 1 ———————————————— 2

Growing my business model requires substantial resources and effort

My business model has virtually no limits to growth

7. Protection from Competition

0 ———————————————— 1 ———————————————— 2

My business model has no moats, and I'm vulnerable to competition.

My business model provides substantial moats that are hard to overcome

8. Environmental Impact

0 ———————————————— 1 ———————————————— 2

Not developed a system for measuring our impact nor have we designed ways to reduce and regenerate for positive surplus

My business model has an embedded system for capturing our environmental impact and we have designed ways to reduce and regenerate for positive surplus

9. Societal impact

0 ———————————————— 1 ———————————————— 2

Our model has yet to incorporate was of being more inclusive and responsive to societal needs and specific stakeholders

We have co-created with our stakeholders and are in dialogue with those whose voice might be left out or left behind of our model and are developing more inclusive products and services.

Figure 10.4 Questions to assess and validate business plan.

> **Assess and Validate Business Plans**
>
> Assessment sheets will help evaluate your business's effectiveness across multiple categories.
>
> 1. Check if every customer segment is linked to a value proposition and a revenue stream.
> 2. Answer the prompts, and then rank your business model's potential performance (**Scale:** 0—no evidence; 1—shows some development of this; 2—mastered embedding this into your model with evidence of positive impact).
>
> *Note: To set up for long-term success, keep up efforts—and stay positive. Remember that your plan doesn't have to be perfect to achieve your goals. Finally, and perhaps most importantly, don't hesitate to ask for help. You risk failing and taking longer to achieve your goals without a plan.*

Empowering financial decision-making best practices

Understanding your business model will help determine the startup costs, initial needs to go to market, and the budget needed to cover growth and sustain over time.

If you don't have funds to invest in your startup, you will need to find outside funding. Luckily, nowadays, there are many options for founders. It is essential to know what you are pitching to investors and understand what types of allocation are offered to which types of businesses. First, let's discuss some regulations and corporate structures in the United States.

Types of U.S. corporations

We'll give you short-form descriptions and references, so you can seek more information from advisors and experts. Also, take advice from a lawyer and accountant. The type of corporation you decide to create will have tax ramifications and limits on what you can do. So give some thought before incorporating it.

We can achieve economic transformation one business at a time if and only if we reimagine our value system and reflect those values in our laws and governance.

Many businesses are reevaluating their value systems and focusing on investment in environmental and social governance (ESG) metrics. Investors and the banking industry are building investment portfolios around social and environmental justice values, creating ratings and benchmarks aligned with the United Nations' sustainable development goals (SDGs). These portfolios of companies outperform the legacy companies that are not moving forward with new practices informed by science and technology, societal needs, and cultural shifts. More must be done, but this is an improvement from where we were.

Benefit corporations are on the rise and offer an alternative to exploit-ative practices other corporate structures allow because of the share-holder expectations to put profits before anything else. This is called shareholder primacy. Alternatively, B Corps offer transparency and accountability where a company's values are baked into the legal entity and filed as such when incorporated. This tends to hold them more accountable to their values, shareholders, partners, and com-munities. Some see this as limiting, while others see it as an ethical decision on how they choose to operate, being transparent with employees and the communities they serve.

The difference between benefit corporations and getting certified from B Lab

A benefit corporation's legal structure is a form of incorporation with the government authorizing you to do business within the designated category with specific restrictions or operating conditions. There are responsibilities to maintain this designation. Many states require B Corps and Benefit LLCs to publish social and environmental perfor-mance reports against a third-party standard to show transparency and performance.

Certified B corporations are businesses that meet the highest stand-ards of verified social and environmental performance, public trans-parency, and legal accountability to balance profit and purpose. B Corps are accelerating a global culture shift to redefine success in business and build a more inclusive and sustainable economy.

B Lab is a nonprofit that certifies B Corps and developed the benefit corporation structure. It offers benefit corporations a free reporting tool to meet their statutory transparency requirements using the B Impact Assessment.

Both designations support a global movement to use business as a force for good. Both meet higher standards of accountability and transparency. Both create the opportunity to unlock our full human potential and creativity to empower business for the higher purpose of helping to solve some of society's most challenging problems.

Cooperatives (Coops) have a governance model where the partici-pants share all aspects of running the company, covering the opera-tions costs, and sharing the profits. Coops are on the rise, becoming a popular form of governance as they are a more equitable way of operating. Platform Cooperativism is a movement giving agency to the workers on gig economy platforms. It arose out of a need from workers to stop the exploitative methods tech platforms were used to scale up and grow fast. Coops have been around for a long time and have proven to be a successful way to govern a business. Although slightly more complex of a structure, worker ownership offers partici-pants agency and control, the opportunity to grow and contribute, and benefit long term from the business's success. In the United States, startups can incorporate as a worker cooperative in Massachusetts, Colorado, and California, or in other states as LLCs (Limited Liability Corporations).

Most worker cooperatives in the United States are small businesses, with between 5 and 50 workers. The largest worker cooperative in the United States is Cooperative Home Care Associates (CHCA), a home care agency with over 2,000 workers based in the Bronx, New York.

Coops offer a model that can be used by any group of people who are interested in creating a democratic decision-making company that benefits all members. It is best to check with your advisors to determine if this is an option.

C and S corporations and LLCs are the most typical for-profit business models created in the United States, but there are many other categories. The formation offers leeway regarding governance (how you choose to operate). These companies often form a traditional hierarchical structure of high earners at the top of the pyramid. There are less requirements for transparency. They are focused on efficiencies to increase profits as their primary goal. They offer equity stakes in the business as shares to investors who have a say in how the company operates and what they spend their energy on. Many investors are interested in extracting as much profit from their investment as possible.

Nonprofit corporations form a legal entity like the above, but their mission is baked into their governance. They follow strict guidelines on organizational structure with a board of governors that oversees how the organization meets its mission, and the corporation's books are made public. Profits earned go back into serving the mission. The tax structure allows them to be exempted from paying some of the typical taxes a for-profit entity might be obligated to pay.

Liability is also a factor in the decision you are making when choosing which entity to incorporate. Although you might not be liable for monies owed by the corporation, you can be personally responsible or sued for your actions.

Tax responsibilities also vary for each model, so it is best to seek guidance from a lawyer and an accountant before proceeding. There are pro bono services through university clinics offering advice in exchange for a real-life learning opportunity for their students. Some professionals offer sliding scales. Then, when businesses earn more income, the fees go up to their current hourly rates. Many platforms and information are available, so spend some time vetting these consultants well and seeking recommendations from trusted sources before venturing forward.

Initial funding options for startups

Equity and ownership are a big topic. We suggest you discuss this with your advisors. Many founders wish to retain ownership, which can hinder your growth and impact your window of opportunity. While giving away too much stake in your business too early can, likewise, affect your personal gains from your work and wealth long-term. Making informed decisions about how and when you seek financing is a critical decision you will need to take on as a founder.

For-profit service businesses

If you're creating a service business, be it an agency or other service provider, your MVP is about finding the first clients to service. Then, you can develop enough potential client relationships to turn them into paying clients to cover your overhead and eventually generate a profit. Overhead includes expenses like rent for office space or a percent of an apartment or home costs, partner salaries + benefits (the lowest possible initially), liability insurance, the initial investment in equipment, other monthly expenses like WIFI, plus extra to grow. Extra will allow investment in software (software as a service, SaaS) packages, new employee salaries, and eventually increasing your own wages.

Before negotiating with your first client, you'll want to work out monthly costs, then break them down hourly, so you have an average hourly rate. This will help you figure out how much to charge when writing your project proposal for the deliverables and estimate the hours it will take, including some extra for incidentals. Include out-of-pocket expenses, travel, or subcontractor costs. It's best to work with a lawyer initially who can customize contracts that you will be able to tweak as needed per client. Using a standard contract from a free web service isn't advised. Always lay the best foundations for your business—this isn't a corner to cut. A good agreement has key performance indicators that are measurable for both parties to evaluate if work was completed and met both parties' expectations. Clients can extend project times, so it is essential to have a clear timeline so that you can manage multiple projects and scale. The more you go over time allotments, the lower your hourly rate, limiting your ability to cover costs and grow.

Getting a first client can be tricky. Therefore, many people in the service industries work for another agency or company first. Then, when they decide to go on their own, they often take their clients with them. Large companies try to protect themselves from client poaching, but it still happens.

We often suggest early-stage agency model startups do case studies, work pro bono to gain experience or trade services for pilot client's services.

Funding a service businesses

Fundamentally, you are your business. Your credit score and ability to get credit are critical parts of this process. They will be taken into consideration when evaluating your company for a loan. Unfortunately, there are very few grant opportunities for for-profit agencies. Still, you should check with your local Small Business Administration (SBA) Office. If you ask your bank or a credit union for a startup loan, they will ask you to back your loan with money in escrow, or if you own a house, perhaps the mortgage as a guarantee. Putting money in escrow to support a bank loan or revolving credit line is often challenging for early-stage founders. Some, therefore, resort to using their personal credit cards at very high rates, which can erode profit margins and compound very quickly to get out of hand.

Be sure to properly budget and plan how you will support yourself while building your client services. This is your runway or the amount of time you give yourself to become self-sustaining.

For-profit product-based businesses

Product businesses can tend to need a lot more upfront capital to startup to buy equipment, materials, and inventory to sell. For example, suppose you can't get a bank loan, revolving credit line, or a loan from friends and family. In that case, using an outside lender called **a Factor** might help. They lend money for a fee, and customers pay them directly. They, in turn, pay you.

This can sound disadvantageous, but if you need quick cash to fund orders or equipment, factors can come in handy. They don't take equity or a stake in your company.

Another option is **crowdfunding** through online platforms. Crowdfunding is the practice of funding a project or venture by raising small amounts of money from many people, typically via the Internet. Crowdfunding is a form of crowdsourcing and an alternative finance option. These platforms can also test your product-market fit and are a terrific way to show future investors' market interest, especially if you exceed your funding goals. These platforms often ask for well-produced videos, do due diligence, and vet before allowing you to post live on their site. So allow time to develop all the materials needed.

Equity crowdfunding—raises capital from online crowds by selling securities (shares, convertible notes, debt, revenue shares, and more) in a private company. If this is of interest, there are many types of crowdfunding platforms.

Stages of funding for scalable companies

If you don't need funding and can grow a little slower but independently, do so! This is the best way to retain ownership and control and reap maximum financial benefits. If you can't do that and want to accelerate your market growth, seeking outside funds is the way. But, of course, everything has trade-offs, so do your homework.

The first phase is generally called seed financing, and some common options are:

Family and friends first for loans, gifts, or convertible notes
An agreement for short-term debt that turns into equity or part ownership in your company; later, when you go for your next round of outside funding, usually called Series A.

Once you have a proven pilot or MVP/Service in operation, you can open to a few series of investments for stock or a percent of your business. But, again, consult your lawyer about equity and ownership—giving away too much too early can be a mistake.

Angel investors or angel groups
An angel investor is a private investor. They are usually high-net-worth individuals who provide financial backing for small startups or entrepreneurs. Like family and friends, they typically invest in exchange for ownership equity in the company.

Credit cards
Some use credit cards but be VERY careful with the interest rates offered. For example, don't use a card with more than a 10% interest rate; the interest alone can tank your business if you're not growing at least double that rate.

Benefits of convertible notes
The debt automatically converts into shares of preferred stock upon closing a Series A round of financing. In other words, investors lend money to a startup as its first round of funding. Then the investors receive shares of preferred stock as part of the startup's initial preferred stock financing, based on the terms of the note. (Preferred stock is stock sold at a discounted rate compared to what you're currently raising at.)

Public venture capital
Public venture capital is a growing opportunity for early-stage (A or B) high-growth companies to raise capital in the $5–100M+ range on the public markets. Usually reserved for large companies, this enables smaller companies to take advantage of the benefits of being a public company and is more flexible and accessible than a traditional listing on large exchanges or additional venture rounds.

Revenue-based financing (RBF)
RBF is an umbrella term for non-dilutive startup financing that relies on revenue-sharing. In return for a fixed investment sum in a company, the RBF investor earns a fixed share of the company's future revenues until a repayment cap is hit. The total amount to be paid is typically viewed as a cash-on-cash multiple of the investment amount. Depending on the RBF investor, the payback time can be just weeks to several years. The RBF investor does not receive shares in return for her investment.

Venture debt
Venture debt is a debt financing loan for equity-backed companies that lack the assets or cash flow for traditional debt financing or

want greater flexibility. A complement to equity financing is typically secured by a company's stock or assets. Overall, venture debt is a "risk capital" form that is less costly than equity.

The benefit of incubators/accelerators

Incubators and accelerators are businesses that offer support to budding entrepreneurs and startup teams. They can provide space, teach you the ropes of starting up, and connect you to strategic networks, service providers, and investors. Some nonprofit incubators are affiliated with universities (like the Elab). They offer stipends and grants, or they can offer their services in exchange for a percent of your business, like a venture capital firm, depending on the university's model.

For-profit incubators and accelerator programs offer funding in exchange for equity. Many are virtual and sector-specific, so do your research before applying to ensure you are a good fit for their portfolio.

Venture capital firms offer similar support through "studios." They incubate several startups within their company, providing support from their infrastructure, administration, network, and investment.

Nonprofit service or agency

Nonprofits are mission-driven and incorporate differently than S or C corporations. Therefore, filing as a nonprofit requires additional restrictions and procedures. You will need a board of directors to oversee the management team and, in the beginning, a fiscal sponsor. A fiscal sponsor helps file taxes by including the startup's revenue and expenses on its books for a fee until it reaches a certain income. Then you will need to file independently and have an outside accounting firm prepare your taxes, and your books are a public record. In theory, this keeps the business honest, where the public can see your salaries, costs, and how much is earned.

Funding for a nonprofit generally comes from grants. Grant writing skills will be needed to keep the revenue coming in. Requests for Proposals (RFPs) are regularly released by foundations, so get on their mailing list. The window to apply is usually limited: it can take months to prepare and hear back. The overall process is long and slow, with a lot of rejection, thus building ample time for this process throughout the year. However, you can be more strategic once you get into a rhythm and understand which funders are interested in your cause. Build those relationships, and network with the right organizations that align with your mission. Many online directories like the Foundation Library help with searches and hold learning sessions to skill up. Many nonprofits work with professional grant writers. The management alone is time-consuming. Be sure to learn how to write a grant and put a proper budget proposal together to ensure you anticipate all the costs necessary. Protect your reputation with annual reports citing your impact to secure more funding and ensure your work is seen and acknowledged.

How to understand pricing for your product or service business to sustain your growth

Now that we've looked at the legal, tax, and the U.S. financial structures, let's drill down to assess your product-market fit by looking at each product or service offered one by one to determine if it is worth keeping. If you can't make a profit margin on an item or service, you need to weigh its value to your overall business. Launching the services and items with the largest margins will prove your concept, bringing in needed revenue to cover labor and costs. Then roll out the other products and services you have in mind. This is called proof of concept.

An early venture's first grip on profit margins and how they financed their growth

Meet Fulya! An Elab fellow, who launched Jaiyou to offer fashionable body braces.

Fulya Turkmenoglu, the founder, started her career in fashion. She sought to disrupt the body brace and prosthetic market by offering fashionable options for people with disabilities or injuries so they could feel their best. She understood that part of the healing process is your mental state. Often, the stigma associated with the look of the braces makes people hesitate to take care of themselves. She developed an early interest in healthcare because of her parents' careers and eventually thought of becoming a doctor.

Flash forward to today. **Jaiyou**, is a medical supply company focused on educating patients and caregivers about their options, quality, and differences in product offerings. She learned early on that there is a vast range in quality and that the regulations are very complex and stringent. Still, many stakeholders do not understand their options.

Figure 10.5 Jaiyou founder Fulya Turkmenoglu workshopping her business.
Photo credit: Elab.

Her approach is educational, encouraging, and unique in the medical supply space that usually targets their wholesale customers (business-to-business). She is working across the entire value chain to change the conversation from the lowest price within the regulations to the value and health of the participants, be it nurses and doctors or the patients themselves.

Starting with body braces, she had her intentions to develop technology-enabled sports braces and prosthetics. She partnered with the Special Olympics as a benefactor of 3–5% of her annual profits. However, when COVID-19 hit, she needed to pivot and dive deep into understanding the personal protective equipment (PPE) that frontline workers required. Putting her plans on hold, she worked with her European suppliers to pivot and make protective gear. While also supporting patients' and consumers' mental health from isolation and the need for exercise. Fulya was astonished to learn the complexities of FDA approval and the material science of some of the braces on the market. She worked with a top European supplier that exceeded European standards and is offering fashionable braces not seen in the U.S. market.

However, when she projected the initial costs of importing, she realized the price points were not competitive with other offshore suppliers. Although the quality of her products was far superior, competing on price was going to be unrealistic.

The financial modeling is the make-or-break moment for young entrepreneurs who get squeezed between the high production costs of pilot orders (initial production runs) and prices at scale. Few manufacturers are willing to take on the risk with you or offer you credit, so many startups are forced to finance their initial production run independently. If she priced her products at the pilot order prices, she would not have any profit margin and would be higher priced than most of her competitors. If she priced the product lower to compete. She would need to either buy in volume or use those costs in her formula, ending up in a deficit until she could grow her sales to surpass the break-even point.

Convincing manufacturers to stop their product run minimums to run a pilot order can be tricky because it means a loss for the producer. Who often must stop their equipment, retool their machines, and waste existing materials. Form a good relationship with your producers and vet them well before partnering. Your suppliers are your business, so choose wisely for all intents and purposes. Offering them a stake in your company could be worth investigating, especially if you can guarantee sales through either pre-orders or client contracts.

Fulya struggled with manufacturers and compromised on her initial product assortment, colors, and styles. The COVID-19 pandemic forced her to pivot multiple times due to shortages and government demands on manufacturers to produce PPE, such as medical-grade masks and hospital protective gear. Instead of seeing this as a hindrance, Fulya quickly pivoted, working side by side with her manufacturers to offer PPE to the U.S. hospitals. She became a certified supplier and learned the strict FDA guidelines. She determined that opening Jaiyou's offerings to overall wellness and health could keep her company afloat while benefiting society by supplying coveted gear.

Testing: More assessment activities

Practicing feedback loops and design-informed business practices for long-term growth and stability are the key objectives of a design-minded entrepreneur.

The activities we share in this section are designed to help you envision your business holistically by testing and assessing key components, then piecing those components back together again.

Break-even point and value chain vis-à-vis sustainability metrics

What is the break-even point for a business?

A business's break-even point is the stage at which the revenues come in equal to all the costs it takes to bring that product or service to market. Once you determine the price of your service or product, test that number by putting it into the break-even formula. Before you do that, you will need to determine your costs to operate the business—some of you will need to estimate. Documenting all your expenses is an important habit to develop, as well as creating budgets to project your future needs. This includes everything from rent to labor costs at a hypothetical salary to materials and other expenses.

Essential questions to ask yourself in these exercises: Are your prices too low or your costs too high to reach your break-even point in a reasonable amount of time? Is your business sustainable? What needs to change to make this viable?

A break-even analysis isn't just useful for startup planning. Here are some ways that businesses can use it in their daily operations and planning:

Materials: Assess if the costs of materials and labor are sustainable. Research how you can maintain your desired level of quality while lowering your costs.

New Products: Before you launch a new product, consider both the new variable or fluctuating costs and your fixed costs, such as design and promotion fees.

Prices: If your analysis shows that your current price is too low to enable you to break even in your desired timeframe, then you might want to raise the item's cost. Check the price of comparable items, though, so you're not setting yourself out of the market.

Planning: When you know exactly how much you need to make, it's easier to set long-term goals. For example, suppose you want to expand your business by hiring more people or move into a larger space with higher rent. In that case, you can then use these numbers to determine how much more you need to sell to cover the potential new fixed costs.

Goals: Knowing how many units you need to sell or how much money you need to make to break even can serve as a powerful motivational tool for you and your sales team.

When determining a break-even point based on sales dollars: Divide the fixed costs by the margin. The margin is determined by subtracting the cost of goods from the price of a product. This amount is then used to cover the fixed costs (usually your overhead, which includes salaries and expenses).

Break-Even Point (sales dollars) = Fixed Costs ÷ Gross Profit Margin

Margin = Price of Product – Cost of goods

To better understand the benefits of this exercise, let's look at what makes up these numbers:

Fixed Costs: These are your overhead costs, which include general business expenses that are not dependent on the number of goods or services produced. They tend to be recurring, such as interest or rent.

Gross Profit Margin: This is the amount of money made after subtracting costs to make the goods, which can often fluctuate. It is important to pad your numbers if you know your material prices will increase. We recommend including a token amount into the costs number in your break-even formula to cover fixed costs, just to play it safe.

Net Profit Margin: This is what is left after subtracting ALL your expenses of running the business and the annual costs determined to support growth.

A break-even analysis allows you to determine your break-even point. Once you crunch the numbers, you might find that you must sell many more products than you realized to break even.

At this point, you'll need to ask yourself whether your current plan is realistic or whether you need to raise prices, find a way to cut costs, or do both to meet the market price. You should also consider whether the products will be successful in the market. Just because the break-even analysis determines the number of products to sell, there's no guarantee they will. So, test your assumptions early on.

See the example below (Figure 10.6) for Jaiyou from a few years back.

Example Jaiyou: **Dated:** Fall Ship't 2021
Surgical gown cost per unit per shipment

This costs includes: product unit cost, freight, customs, product regulation
registrations, warehouse fees, insurance, shipping/handling to warehouse, agency
fees, does not include overhead such as salaries, rent, marketing, misc, etc...

$$\frac{\text{Breakeven}}{\text{Point}} = \frac{\text{Fixed costs}}{\text{Gross margin \%}} \qquad 7 = \frac{\$3.50}{22.22\ \%}$$

Figure 10.6 Break-even formula for a Jaiyou product.

How to Calculate a Break-Even Point Based on Units

Using the formula above, divide fixed costs by the revenue per
unit minus the variable price per unit.

The fixed costs do not change no matter how many units are sold.

The revenue is the selling price of the product minus **the variable
costs**, like labor and materials.

Having a grip on the cost of your products, the sales price the market
will bear, and your margin in between is critical to your business concept's financial sustainability.

Next, we'll look at the testing needed over the next few months before
launch. Finally, we will combine product and business models to hit that
sweet spot where your offering will fit perfectly into the marketplace.
Again, assessing both separately and together will be critical.

Pricing and product/market fit

Developing a business model validation sheet (see Figure 10.7) gives
you a blueprint of your business. It prompts thinking through different
aspects of the company, like the product or service you intend to offer
with the actual market needs, often called the product/market fit.

Financial modeling

Projecting out, modeling, and simulating finances will help plan financial needs to get to market and afford your growth/problem fit/solution
tests. Knowing how much money is needed to finance development,
launch, and beyond will be critical next steps. Many online companies offer business plan development step-by-step, including financial
spreadsheets with preset formulas that integrate into accounting SaaS.
First, do market research to determine which is a fit. Next, use their
spreadsheets to extrapolate from your current operating costs what
your operational budget needs are for each phase of your concept and
business development. Building these financial projections into a narrative to incorporate into your business narrative for investors will be next
on your list and is covered in upcoming chapters.

Problem fit validation	Solution fit validation	Market fit (business model validation)

1 What assumptions do you need to validate?

Top 3 riskiest assumptions	Top 3 riskiest assumptions	Top 3 riskiest assumptions

2 Share your ideas for experimentation. Decide as a group which assumptions are most critical, and how you'll validate them.

Target audience	Target audience	Target audience

Describe the experiment	Describe the experiment	Describe the experiment

Success Indicators	Success Indicators	Success Indicators

After Experiment

3 Write down key learnings. What were the key learnings or insights? Do you consider the assumption (in) validated?

Figure 10.7 Business model and prototype validation plan.

Validating Our Product/Service and Business Model

Whenever you're working from an assumption, test it. Thus, ensuring you're not going down an expensive, time-consuming rabbit hole. It might look great but may not resonate with your community and be quickly adopted.

Start with the Problem Fit validation column, and then move on and answer the same questions for the other two columns.

1. Write down your assumptions about the problem to intend to solve and would like to test.
2. Describe the experiment.
3. Describe what success might look like.

Repeat this for Solution and Market fit columns.

4. Run your experiments and take notes.
5. Step back and assess by writing down your key learnings and conclusions to decide if you have validated or invalidated your assumptions.

Practice assessment: Value chain analysis

Set up partnerships and vendors as you build out products or services. It will be vital to assess your value chain periodically, especially in volatile environments.

Fluctuations and changes are the norms. Suppliers change, costs change, and the price of shipping and raw materials and the supply chains can be disrupted due partly to market demands and climate change. So, keep an eye on the macro view of your "galaxy" within the constellation or your sector. While also watching the trends in other sectors across the economy since you know you are operating within complex systems. Build in the practice of stepping back to look from a bird's eye over the whole system. It will become a routine of a good leader and a cultural activity.

Value chain analysis became famous in 1985 with the book "Competitive Advantage" by Michael Porter, a Harvard Business School professor (Porter 1985). His book outlines how businesses can identify primary and supporting activities that create "value" for their customers. This enables companies to consider whether the value outweighs the production costs, which should inform decision-making. Rather than use this approach to feed current economic models, we updated it to reveal opportunities for increasing shared equity and sustainability. Try making your own and share it with your team to assess where you might be weak. Below we will give an example of a value chain assessment from team Advene, Yijia Wang, and Zi Xuan, fellows from the Elab.

Figure 10.8 Team Advene: Zi Xuan and Yijia Wang.
Photo credit: Youn Jung Kim.

Advene's value chain

In earlier chapters, we met Advene, Elab fellows from the Summer 2020 cohort, while discussing systems and mapping stakeholders, supply chains, and partnerships. Here we'll discuss their value chain. Early on, they had to adapt to the global COVID-19 pandemic conditions disrupting supply chains within a couple of months by pivoting their manufacturing from China to Italy almost overnight. Being agile and adaptable is part of a resilience strategy for any business, but it can be complicated. Volatility causes delays and disruption, impacting your revenue, infrastructure, team, and ambitions. Here we'll learn how founders Yijia Wang and Zi Xuan kept true to their values and vision of maintaining a transparent and ethical value chain. Sharing that this is an integral part of their communications strategy to grow their community by building trust and integrity (brand ethos and North Star).

Advene is a responsibly sourced accessory company that believes that beauty and integrity are one and the same. They have a philosophy of releasing one product at a time, devoted to conscientious craftsmanship, using responsible materials, and designing for minimal impact and longevity.

On their social media and the front page of their website, they boldly diagram their production process, proudly innovating a new playbook. One that thoughtfully selects ethically produced materials with carbon-neutral facilities and LWG-certified tannery to sourcing GOTS-certified Hemp and cotton for their accessories. In addition, they model how they consciously design the construction of their products to minimize the environmental impact. They have deliberately developed a value chain that is growing with the intention of a closed-loop system to reduce harmful environmental effects. This includes designing recycled and recyclable packaging that is still elegant and unique to maintain their brand identity of developing take-back, repair, and repurpose programs. They've deliberately considered all the ways they can grow into their values along the entire chain of custody and developed a sustainable growth strategy that allows for a responsible and adaptable production cycle to remain agile and responsive to the ever-changing world.

See Figure 10.9 to study how they've thought of each step in their supply chain. From the initial research and development stage to the manufacturing and "remanufacturing" plans, to distribution, retail buying and using to final repurposing and repairing to avoid the landfill.

They have future plans of embedding RFID trackers to use blockchain technology to enhance supply chain management. This will optimize their efforts, thus improving customer relations management.

advene
VALUE CHAIN

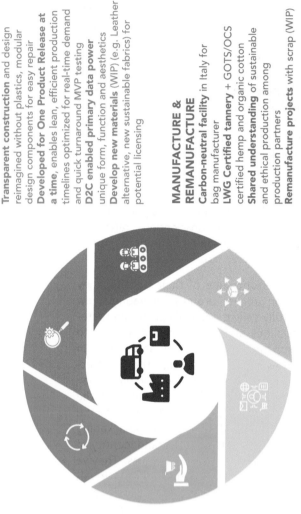

→ RESEARCH & DEVELOPMENT

Traceable, low impact, low maintenance material sourcing and development
Transparent construction and design reimagined without plastics, modular design components for easy repair
Developed for One Product Release at a time, enables lean, efficient production timelines optimized for real-time demand and quick turnaround MVP testing
D2C enabled primary data power unique form, function and aesthetics
Develop new materials (WIP) (e.g. Leather alternative, new sustainable fabrics) for potential licensing

MANUFACTURE & REMANUFACTURE

Carbon-neutral facility in Italy for bag manufacturer
LWG Certified tannery + GOTS/OCS certified hemp and organic cotton
Shared understanding of sustainable and ethical production among production partners
Remanufacture projects with scrap (WIP)

DISTRIBUTION

Lean efficient production 95%+D2C timelines optimized for real-time demand (pre-order averaged 30% of the total orders) and primary customer data, plus accessible pricing for luxury products
Wholesale partnership 5% for publicity

TAKE BACK, REPAIR & REPURPOSE

Easy Repair due to modular construction and design components; (WIP) 1 year warranty and lifetime repair program/tutorial
Reselling and Repurposing from customers old products (WIP)

BUYING & USING

Empowing customers via "last-mile" co-design opportunity with changeable straps (WIP), custom emboss etc.
Quality: product made to stand the test of time, wear, and weather

RETAIL

Develop second-hand platform enabling online sample sale for discounts (WIP) (eg. https://floyd-fullcycle.floorfound.store/)
Carbon-neutral delivery (offset with ecocart)
Recycled/Repurposed, dust bag/cloth from deadstock fabrics, box packaging from unlaminated, FSEco-packaging, minimal packaging incentives with C certified recycled greyboard

(WIP) TOTAL TRANSPARENCY SPANNING THE SUPPLY CHAIN AND CONSUMER EXPERIENCE.

In the midst of integrating RFID and blockchain technology to monitor and optimize our sustainability efforts with our production partners. Beyond ensuring supply chain transparency, the attached NFC-activated chips will create a new channel for enhanced customer relationship management.

Figure 10.9 Advene circular value chain analysis.

The name Advene comes from the word *advenience,* a term coined by Roland Barthes for art that stirs something within. Like many Elab startups, they see themselves building more than a brand. They are joining like-minded producers and consumers in building communities invested in shared values. They invite customers to join a movement changing how to produce value, consume more conscientiously, and contribute to a thriving new economy. One that is built on environmental and social justice is ideal to regenerate societies, cultures, and our planet.

As we wrap up this chapter, know that this is just the beginning of your journey in business modeling and financial projections for your business. This will be one of your most important responsibilities as a founder, leader, and entrepreneur. Know your business's heartbeat and blood flow and know it intuitively. Building confidence around these skills takes practice. As you scale and delegate responsibility, it will ultimately be yours to know and own. To become comfortable with numbers, costs, and projections for funding your business, learn how to make it flourish as passionately as your products or services. The ability to multitask and to have confidence is often the marker of a successful entrepreneur who gets funded, regardless of whether the business ultimately succeeds or not.

Navigational Log + Takeaways

- Test your business model regularly with real customers!
- Embrace dynamic planning to see your biz as a living thing
- Know head-to-toe the regulations + systemic influences to foresee obstacles
- Value chain assessment as a long-game strategy for success
- Always keep the user experience as #1

11

STORYTELL AND LAUNCH

Solution scenarios for a strategic future

Objectives

• Develop preferred futures through narrative
• Storytelling techniques to help shape your story
• Build a brand voice for marketing communications
• Backcasting as an early-stage strategic roadmap and communications tool
• Narrative forms and content for pitching

Developing preferred futures through narrative

In preparation for launch, ask: *What now? Why this?* Your investors will probably ask: *Why you? (And we promise, they do!)* A good entrepreneur will answer these questions with the clarity of a preferred future for the business, rooted in the driving why of our mission, goals, and culture. We call upon the earlier working diving into our mission-driven "whys" in order to shape our story for the world and thus lay the groundwork for our future trajectory.

Seeing and sharing a future with your purpose, mission, and vision can make you into a great entrepreneur. It will give you insights into annual revenue projections, cost of goods (COG), monthly sales, and overhead costs. It will also enable you to foresee the impact and desired goals around social and environmental justice.

Design-driven entrepreneurs can use a tool called the Cone of Plausibility to see what past occurrences shaped the present narrative and the distance between the business vision and the present moment.

Your "probable future" is the one that most likely occurs given your projection of the current trends. It is the place where you believe you can make a difference. Your "preferable future" is a reminder that you have agency over how the future unfolds. It is the place where you see a competitive advantage for opportunities that others may not see. Reference Figure 11.1, the reality apex diagramming future probabilities and memory recall.

DOI: 10.4324/9781003227151-15

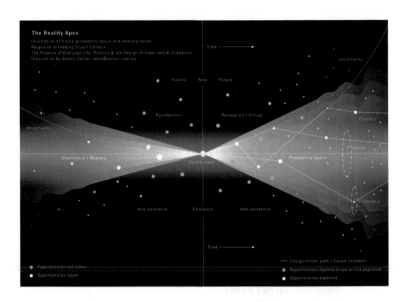

Figure 11.1 The reality apex with permission by Steve Santer, a version of the cone of plausibility.

The Future-Back Cone (Figure 11.2) opens a window onto the number of possible events that could influence your startup, with alternative futures from the probable to the possible, to the preferable, to even the preposterous—which still helps us uncover the multiverse potential of what could be, like the influence of a global pandemic and the need to shift models.

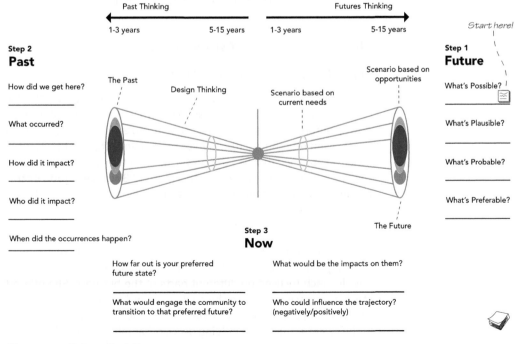

Figure 11.2 Future-Back Cone.

Future-Back Cone Exercise

Understanding what your community went through, has been experiencing, or came from helps you define the present-day and future scenarios where your concept fits.

By sketching out connections between past, present, and future, you will help weave a cohesive narrative that will be later leveraged for pitching your business concept and potential for impact.

1. Start with your desired future state, and consider what might also happen?
   ○ What's Possible?
   ○ What's Plausible?
   ○ What's Probable?
   ○ What's Preferable?
2. Go into the past, asking yourself:
   ○ How did we get here?
   ○ What occurred?
   ○ How did it impact?
   ○ Who did it impact?
   ○ When did the occurrences happen?
3. Come back to the present day (the now) and reflect on:
   ○ How far out is your preferred future state?
   ○ What would engage the community to transition to that preferred future?
   ○ What would be the impacts on them?
   ○ Who could influence the trajectory (negatively/positively)

The science and art of storytelling

Capri Money—Leveraging narrative

In an early startup, your preferred future will change constantly. Nicole launched Capri over the span of two years under COVID lockdown, before launching the website in 2022. She pivoted several times; even rebranding aftermarket testing and pitching to potential investors. She exemplifies the power of reflection and evolution and the art of storytelling. Why does this matter? **Because a good entrepreneur is also a good communicator.** They make the rounds and listen carefully to all perspectives and are sure to take care of each one of their employees, stakeholders, and/or partners.

Her first goal was to build a diverse team with a range of skills to build a strong foundation. The initial team was quite large, with over five people, each focused on different parts of the business. She offered stock as an incentive since she couldn't afford to pay anyone joining the founding team. The equity was a draw and enabled people to put in the sweat equity while holding down other jobs to stay afloat, each with a promise to leave their current positions, should the business grow to offer them full-time positions.

Forming the team was one challenge, and keeping her team motivated during COVID with lockdowns was another. She took a particularly passionate, persuasive, and positive approach. Leveraging isolation, Capri focused their time alone to work remotely on the development, affording them the opportunity to dive deep into the various needs. Nicole refined her message using storytelling techniques, setting the scene, and orienting her personal narrative around financial literacy. She followed up her story of the past with current-day conditions for young women across the country and globe with little access to financial literacy and projected a future scenario with her concept, whereby female-identifying people could gain easy access and support to financial tools to build confidence. As a result, she built trust, empathy, and consensus and was able to bring in a team and early-stage angel investors as a result.

It's not enough to just believe you have a quality product or service; you need to know how to talk about it in a way that differentiates you from the crowd. Like Nicole, at Capri, every entrepreneur needs a clear elevator pitch, one that tells a compelling story that makes the audience care. Telling this narrative *visually* (with a deck) and *verbally* (with your tone and choice of words) is an essential skill for design-driven entrepreneurs. But why do we even need to tell stories with our work? Because stories are human. They help us make emotional connections with our audiences. Knowing how to tell the right story, however, is both a science and an art that takes practice.

Storytelling techniques: Visual and oral

Our brains are wired to understand and unpack stories, taking meaning from their structure, narrative, characters, references, and tone. As well as the talent of the creators and the power of storytelling, our brains play a big role in the success of visual storytelling. We're wired for visual processing! Neuroscientists at MIT found that the brain can identify images seen for as little as 13 milliseconds. The study highlighted our brain's ability to make sense of even briefly presented images, which makes sense when you consider that more than 50% of the cortex is devoted to processing visual information (Potter, *The Economic Times*, 2014). That shows just how many opportunities storytelling provides to add engagement, meaning, and information. Our brains take all that meaning and information in their original compressed form and build connected memorable and complex ideas.

So what makes a story unique? It's the building blocks the author uses, the new ones they create, the old ones they recreate, and how they put all of them together. Even stories with a similar premise can have different executions. It's all a matter of perspective. To communicate our ideas beyond our own teams and show our potential customers the value of our solutions, we need to pull at their heartstrings. This is where storytelling comes into play. See the storytelling canvas, Figure 11.3, for support.

You will need to change your story to fit your audience. So, having an archive with infographics, reports, assessments, shorter and longer

Storytelling Canvas   Be sure to answer: Why you? Why now? Why This?

A prototyping tool for effective storytelling

What	**Why**	**Who**	**How**
What things must be communicated? What us the goal?	Why are you telling this story? Why does it matter?	Who is this story about?	How will this story change the way we think/feel/act?

Who	**Understanding & Beliefs**	**Concerns & Needs**
Who are the individuals you're speaking to?	What do they already know about this topic?	What are the concerns/needs?

Delivery Plan	**Trust**
How will you tell this story? Is it a PowerPoint?	Who should be included in telling of this story?

Set the Seen	**Big Reveal**	**Conclusion**	**Why you?**
What is occurring that needs to change? (explain what is occurring)	What is the Aha (improvement) for the audience?	What is your call to action? (Be sure you covered Why Now?)	Tell a personal story about you that makes you the perfect person or team for this

Figure 11.3 Storytelling canvas.

marketing descriptions, and slide decks will be as important to you as crown jewels. The brand will need to shine through all of these materials in a cohesive, clean way. Distilling the information into minimal words and maximum visuals is an essential part of this task. Graphic images help us communicate our research and ideas to others in a fast and universal way, helping to make complex stories easier to understand, thus delivering a more impactful message.

Great storytelling that stimulates all the senses promotes the release of feel-good brain chemicals like oxytocin and dopamine. These chemicals can prompt us to feel more comfortable, more relaxed, and more motivated. We are more likely to click a button, make a purchase, or follow a readily available call to action. Naturally, the feel-good afterglow of experiencing a great visual story makes viewers want to see another, and another after that. Creating a participatory and immersive experience that allows young learners to enjoy hearing the language in a dynamic, sometimes stylistic, and entertaining way. Participation in using key vocabulary and phrases can create an awareness of rhythm and structure.

How to frame new offerings as opportunities are dependent on the story you tell. Telling the story visually adds an incredibly powerful ingredient, enabling everyone in your ecosystem to empathize with new people/places/situations. It can reveal universal life experiences that help to build a shared representation of a better future for all.

Storytelling Canvas

1. Start at the top and answer the prompts within the Content fields. Tell us your objectives and goals for this narrative.
2. Move on to define your *audience*, then *tell* us the medium you're choosing: will it be through a video, animation, slide presentation, or walk-through experience?
3. Build the story arc by first setting the scene (don't assume your audience knows or has empathy for this subject). Then, be sure you test this narrative on trusted stakeholders and a few people you don't know; to be sure, it is clear and persuasive.

Be sure to answer

Why you? (Meaning, why are you the perfect person or team to respond to this issue?)

Why this? (Why is this endeavor or solution the best one? Use evidence-based research.)

Why now? (Why is now, or in 24–36 months at launch, the right time for this product/service?)

A storytelling script

Developing stories can help us understand the implications of our design and strategy choices. These scenarios are also tangible artifacts that can be used for discussion, debate, advocacy, or planning.

We like to use a storytelling script that starts by visually and verbally painting a scene. By telling your audience where you are and where they are, you pull them into different states, perhaps out of the current broken scenario and into your preferred future. Amp up the drama, to tell the problem story. Problems should also indicate opportunities for making more impact or more meaningful experiences. Do you need something or someone to resolve the problems in your preferred future? Heroes are only as good as the teams they contribute to. Together, they will be able to save the day with a solution that changes the existing situation into a preferred future. When everyone arrives, they will feel the happiness of making a collective difference.

Steps to follow:

Paint the scene: *Where are we?*
There's a problem: *What's the drama?*
We need a hero: *Who will resolve it?*
Save the day: *What's the solution?*
Happy ever after: *What are the emotions?*

Brand stories: Communicate the value of your preferred future

Like superhero films we flock to, good storytelling is even better when the narrative is part of something larger. This is where creating a brand narrative, through a brand voice, can make the difference between a preferred future, and the willingness to co-create a preferred present.

Marketing is a powerful tool for testing your value and how you need to message your brand to support your business. Marketing is the vehicle for the brand story to reach people.

This is where brand storytelling comes into play. Brand storytelling is the cohesive narrative that weaves together the facts and emotions that your brand evokes. In addition to giving your customers reasons to buy a product or service, you need to start sharing the story behind their brand, why it exists, and why this matters, consistently across all communication. This includes everything from the logo and tagline to the color palette, font, and of course narrative of how your concept (product/service) creates value and impacts.

Refining your brand identity and marketing strategy

After you work on your business model, iterating and testing different ways to create value, you will want to revisit prototyping and do more testing around the persona of your brand. Its identity can be intertwined in your own persona or can be a glamorized version of yourself or also completely different. Today, founders are brands in and of themselves, with a large social media following that can be leveraged for testing and feedback. Social media is an inexpensive way to test out concepts, products, and brand identity, and even drum up presales with followers. The interconnectedness of the system you are building, and how it then interconnects to the systems it inhabits, are all integration projects that require strategic planning and focus. The complexity today of developing a business is easier than ever before and yet, far more complex than in the past.

Tips to make sure your stories grab people's attention include:

1. Be sure to have your goal in mind.
2. Stop telling a story and start visual storytelling.
3. Be clear about your message with a goal in mind.
4. Make it personal.
5. Don't always tell a story from beginning to end. Get creative and approach the narrative from new angles.
6. Less is more.

Finding brand voice and value to build narrative

The Dimensions of Value and the Customer Value Story templates (Figures 11.4 and 11.5, respectively) help you develop and articulate your value for customers, enabling the development of your brand voice and

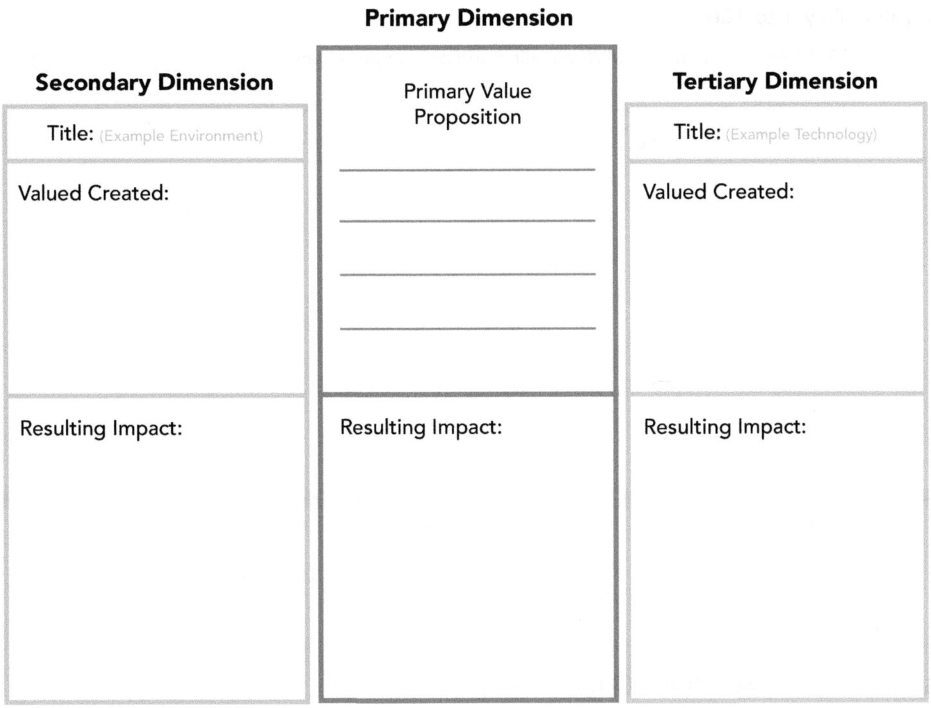

Primary Dimension

Secondary Dimension	Primary Value Proposition	**Tertiary Dimension**
Title: (Example Environment)	_____ _____ _____ _____	**Title:** (Example Technology)
Valued Created:		Valued Created:
Resulting Impact:	Resulting Impact:	Resulting Impact:

Figure 11.4 Charting dimensions of value and value impact.

Charting Dimensions of Value

This template offers the team an opportunity to determine the value and impact of the product-service mix across distinct dimensions—or industries. This can help you shape your voice or messaging of the brand and also consider: who might we be impacting that's part of our system, yet isn't a direct consumer?

1. **Name Your Context:** Start with jotting your primary value proposition in the center top box, and select three distinct "dimensions"—or industries, areas of operation, that you play in, as a business. Examples include Technology.
2. **Complete the First Dimension:** In the first dimension, likely your most relevant, articulate with bullet points the specific value points that you give and provide in this sphere of business. Next, you'll reflect on the *resulting impact* of that value. Consider the value as the input and the impact derived as the aftereffects of the value received by businesses or consumers in that space.
3. **Secondary + Tertiary Dimensions:** Do the same for the next two sections, naming the value points that you shape + provide within these industries or areas, and again, the resulting impact. *An example might be: strengthening a culture of refill by using glass bottles, fewer plastic bottles purchased by consumers.*

Consumer Value: Day 1 to 100

Consider alongside TAM/SAM/SOM and for MVP planning and prototype testing

Figure 11.5 Customer value storytelling (Day 1 to 100).

a resilient, thorough picture of your company. Once you have those components fleshed out, creating a marketing strategy and a marketing plan won't be far off. Although we don't go into detail explaining how to develop a brand or how to market, the tools we are sharing are foundational for this development.

Alongside the Minimal Viable Product (MVP), which is the bare minimum version of your product/service you can go to market with you should have an idea of the size of your Serviceable Obtainable Market (SOM) from your market research conducted earlier in order to be able to fully create your narrative around the product/market fit. When we think about our Obtainable Market, we're considering the story of our value to our very first users, first subscribers, and the first buyers. How many of this audience are there? Where do we find them, and what value do we provide them?

We build data points using tools like the Dimensions of Value and the Customer Value Story to help develop and articulate your value in sentence formation (concise!) which will form content to create a brand narrative, pitch deck, website, and marketing content.

Customer Value Story

The Minimal Viable Product (MVP) is the bare minimum you feel you can go to market with to gain traction and show investors and stakeholders the product/market fit is correct. Alongside this, you should have an idea of the size of your addressable market from your market research conducted earlier. Use your exploratory research to shape your psychographic elements of who your audience is and shape your story with these. What are their behaviors? What does it look like to solve their problem? With a strong offering, we want retention of customers. We map this projected value narrative from Day 1 through Day 100 (and on!).

1. **On Day 1:** In a short-story format, tell us what the value proposition is on the day when your company launches through the eyes of the consumer.
2. **On Day 10:** Now, tell us in sentence form what the value proposition looks like for a consumer ten days down the line. Has the value to them increased? What does your company look like integrated into a routine? What's different on Day 10 from Day 1?
3. **On Day 100:** What is the vision 3–4 months out? Are there new features they're interacting with? What does that future state possibly look like from a service/product standpoint? Give us a snapshot of what the value looks like for consumers over time. If a one-time purchase, what's the lifecycle? How might you extend it?

The goal here is to verbalize, in clear persuasive sentences, what the next few months look like in narrative form both from your point of view in development and also the hopeful value increase over time of what you're providing consumers and users.

Using backcasting as an early-stage strategic roadmap and business narrative for change

Developing future scenarios helps us develop a roadmap to our preferred future and then communicate it. It also helps us stay resilient, plan for a rainy day, or react to other forces out of our control like climate change or pandemics.

Backcasting (or reverse engineering) was first outlined by John Robinson from the University of Waterloo in 1990. Here's how it works. First, chart a potential occurrence sometime in the future, then help your team walk backward to today. Chart the steps your organization might take if certain situations were to play out. The type of events your team comes up with should be on the spectrum from advantageous to catastrophic, from events based on reality to the supernatural, to help push divergent ideas and solutions that could be adapted to other scenarios. Reference the backcasting worksheet in Figure 11.6 on following page and activity box below.

Backcasting from Potential Future Scenarios

Imagine a roadmap to transformational change based on potential ideal states. Work backward to your current state, by planning out and imagining the actions you would need to take to get there.

This is good to do before and after your financial modeling.

1. Start with the "Ideal State" boxes: Think about future scenarios of the world today, to create your ideal state. There are a few ways of using this tool to model or project out:
   ○ Project or model out what your business would look like, internally, and externally, in an "ideal or not so ideal but possible" scenario or state of the businesses growth to prepare your business for the volatility of the market or the launch of a new product or service you are thinking about.
   ○ Project or model out what your communities and people impacted by your product/service might look like (good or bad).
   ○ Project or model out what external scenarios (good or bad) might impact your business to prepare for the volatility of the world and global impacts with more environmental extremes, market volatility, wars, and pandemic.
2. Assumptions: Moving right to left, start to fill in the assumptions one would need to make if living under those conditions. We created four but you may have more or fewer.
3. Actions: Moving right to left, start to fill in the actions one would need to make if living under those conditions.
4. Fill in the current state of your business (you might need to write in a few more details to address each scenario).
5. Step back and assess with your team: How do you all feel about these conditions of transformation, and what choices would you need to make to create these ideal scenarios? How can you prepare for possible volatility you won't be able to control?

The goal of thinking future-back is to help you chart a course to your preferred future, communicate it to stakeholders, prepare and strategize for the unknown, and bring about positive change within a VUCA world.

Backcasting is not only about designing a roadmap to transition toward a preferred future but also about preparation for the challenges of changing any existing situation. Embracing the social aspects of change is what makes designing in a multiverse special. A design-driven entrepreneur designs something not to be an end-unto-itself, a final solution to a problem, but to open opportunities. Any design must solve some problems, but the point is to always also ask what new options are generated by the conditions that successful design generates. Strategic Designers ask, "... and so ... and then ..." For example, designing a digital service system that enables people to ride-share creates new habits and expectations. Design-driven

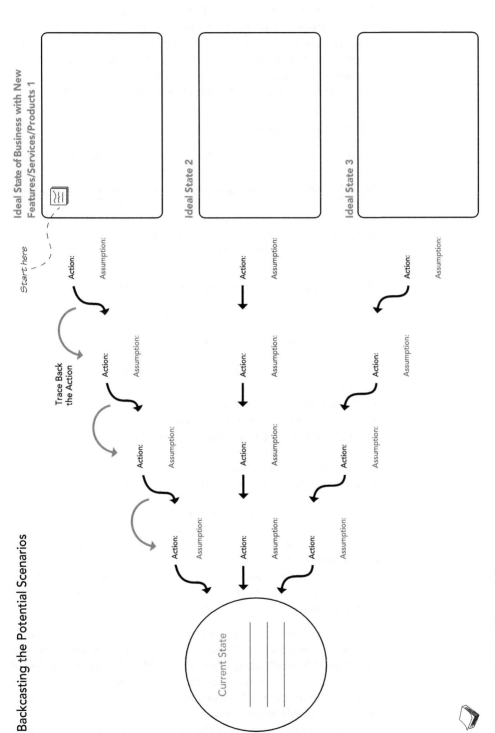

Figure 11.6 Backcasting worksheet.

entrepreneurs seek to take these new behaviors even further, to scale them into other ways of living and working that create larger organizational, economic, and cultural change.

Though long-term thinking is inherent to Design, these practices are unlike strategic planning. The multiple stages mean that after each accomplishment, the way forward needs to be re-evaluated because unforeseen consequences will have arisen. Strategic Designers in this way seek to see around corners, moving in one direction, not to reach the endpoint, but instead to discern other change possibilities.

Communicate your resiliency

Resiliency is the capacity to recover quickly from challenges, your ability to adapt quickly to new conditions and thrive, and the courage to be our authentic selves moving beyond the constructs that are assigned to us. Entrepreneurs who enact design-driven transformation will be able to create more resilient and inclusive startups. The choices of how to coordinate, with clarity on the transformation journey, will make or break any intentions for better futures.

Personalize your pitch and infuse it with stories

Pitching is an exciting part of being an entrepreneur and starting up. At a certain stage, it is something you will do daily. There are a few types of pitches you need to be familiar with.

- Pitching to investors and equity funding stakeholders
- Pitching to banks
- Submission for an incubator
- Informal elevator pitches when your audience is known
- Informal social pitches when you're not familiar with who's in the room
- Pitching to partner organizations
- Pitching to potential team members or soon-to-hires

Knowing your audience determines how you pitch, what content to use, the language, the tone, and the narrative format that goes with it. Each of the circumstances might include different materials, with a different focus. It's not easy to pull these materials together, and it will take many iterations over time. Because your business is constantly growing and changing, the materials will need to be updated constantly.

You'll also commonly submit and record videos of yourself. Startups also make videos and post them to digital funding platforms. You'll be accustomed to sending out videos along with a pitch deck, or in lieu of one, depending on the audience. You can use platforms like DocSend that help you track your funding process and monitor who's viewing content or simple shared drives. Even if you're not seeking external funding in this way, you'll still need to be prepared to properly communicate to foundations, or to your audience, in ways that are concise and captivating. A good orator is memorable because of their tone, pacing, and clarity of message.

Start by pitching to friends and family before you do it officially. Be sure to ask people what stood out, and what were the top three things they remembered from the presentation, to help you edit and focus.

In addition to making your presentation deck visual, using infographics, photos, or video content, we advise you to take 30–90 seconds to make part of your pitch personal. Answer the question, *why you?* Telling the audience about a pivotal moment in your personal journey, and showing your passion and expertise around the topic, will help build trust in you and your team. Be it a financial investor, potential partner, onboarding team member, bank, or potential partner organization, most people want to know your level of commitment and expertise to guide the ship; 30–90 seconds might not seem long, but when you're given under 10 minutes to pitch, that can be a lot of time to dedicate. Your story needs to be memorable and memorized. As we mentioned above, our brains are hardwired for stories. Adding this little narrative, within the greater business narrative, makes it more memorable for the audience, especially if they are listening to 10–20 pitches daily. You'll need to stand out in more ways than one. Ultimately, it's all about trust because relationships are built on trust.

All the design methods, tools, and templates we've introduced to you help make perfect data visualizations for your slide decks. Using an ecosystem or stakeholder map, a systems diagram, or a persona, can help you convey lots of data in a short amount of time, and convey your depth of understanding and research. Including a customer, the journey story is very helpful to audiences who might not have empathy for the sector or community you intend to serve. Humanizing the problem space is an important part of your pitch beyond the business model, potential market size, unique value proposition, and KPIs. It is important to end with an ask, meaning: what is it you need from them? Articulate "what's next," either with a roadmap laid over a calendar, or a description of what the next 6–24 months look like. Nothing is complete, especially at the beginning of a startup's journey. Audiences don't expect you to be perfect, but they do expect you to be prepared to answer fundamental questions about your attainable market size, business plans, model, social and environmental impact, amount of cash on hand, profit margins, profitability over time, ability to meet market demand, and your resilience plans for financial longevity.

Navigational Log + Takeaways

- Understand the building blocks for preferred futures
- Lead with narrative techniques for better communication
- Leverage design tools and methods for communicating your value
- Develop pitches with the right content for diverse audiences

Dimension D

Multiplicity

Designing to strengthen and scale our collective futures

How might our company remain resilient on the journey across space and time? As founders and team members, how do we prepare for a shared future? Here we demonstrate how to leverage futures-thinking and show how founding leaders can inspire collective action. We build upon design-driven entrepreneurial mindsets to engage a broader community with a shared vision for organizational development. We take new mental models from Mind, a clear vision and stable ethos from Mission, and an iterative process from Methods for a resilient company launch and future.

DOI: 10.4324/9781003227151-16

12

CHARTING A (RE)GENERATIVE FUTURE

Maintaining resiliency with strategic foresight

Increasing clarity on the future

Over the past 40 years, we have created new forms of currency, new ways to augment our intelligence, and even seen new galaxies. This has helped to interconnect global societies, economies, and environments. Our multiverse is where what happens on one side of the earth reverberates on the other. Perhaps innovations will not impact your startup today. However, they may open opportunities that wouldn't have existed if you didn't spend time learning about them.

Not everything is positive. With industrialization, we have seen many negative environmental impacts. Man-made wars, exploitation, and extraction have also negatively impacted the environment, leading to depletion of the Ozone layer, overuse of fossil fuels, leading to temperature increases, causing extreme weather patterns. All these factors will now be on your radar as a business owner. How will the next storm, pandemic, or election affect your business?

These are good reasons why founders need to spend time researching the complexity of their world and preparing to be resilient because changing anything in a multiverse isn't easy.

DOI: 10.4324/9781003227151-17

Developing resiliency to be future-ready

Resiliency is the ability to recover quickly from setbacks. Resilience planning starts with financial resilience. How many reserves are needed? What type of bank loan to get?

Just as important is one's ability to adapt rapidly to new conditions and thrive is an essential capability. One will need the courage to be our authentic selves, to resist the constructs assigned to us.

The critical areas of focus for immediate goals and the actions to take to get there (planning for what will happen if disaster strikes) are crucial to your survival. See Figure 12.1, a planetary metaphor, for layers of resilience.

Resilience planning is threaded through this entire guide because it's a potent way to prepare for any future. To prepare for any scenario, building resiliency into your strategy and plan will be vital to whatever the future may bring. To prepare for this, ask yourself:

1. What are the possible impacts of this future scenario?
2. Where is the business most vulnerable?
3. What is your capacity to adapt, be it your business model, place of business, people, or technology?

A resilient startup with a resilient leader and team is not developed overnight. In a resilient organization, everyone contributes. Like any other skill, anyone can develop resilience, but it's a consistent effort, every day and over the years. The payoff is empowered people who are resilient at work and in life.

Forecasting futures

Strategic Foresight is a practice that builds resiliency. The good news is that it has been gaining popularity in response to the uncertainties of our volatile, uncertain, complex, and ambiguous (VUCA) world.

Strategic foresight builds on the practice of backcasting. The difference is that it adds a futures mindset. The result can result in a startup concept with a compelling narrative of a better future.

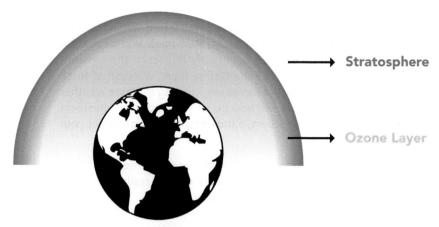

Figure 12.1 Metaphor for the layers of resilience needed to protect your business.

Strategic foresight prompts you to look at the signals and trends in your sector or adjacent to it. Then, team members can envision a better world using foresight, insight, and action.

As illustrated in Figure 12.2, First we look for signals, these are new products or services, technologies, or policies with the potential to create change and then look for drivers that might accelerate them.

Signals are helpful for people trying to anticipate a highly uncertain future. They are phenomena that we can see, touch, and feel but are unfamiliar with. Unlike trends, they turn our attention to possible innovations before they become apparent. Unlike indicators, they often focus our attention on the margins of society rather than the core. In this way, they are more likely to reveal disruptions and innovations. They signal a change in the larger population when innovation moves beyond the lead user stage and begins to diffuse much more rapidly.

Drivers, on the other hand, are likely to accelerate change. Also known as trends, they are forces accelerating change in today's world include climate change, the aging of the world's population, and the rise of disinformation/decrease in trust in government. We use the STEEP tool to collect and categorize drivers. Although drivers of change can move at different scales and speeds, they often overlap because no single driver operates in a vacuum. For this reason, drivers work across multiple industries and topics, as their impact will inevitably be felt in many different contexts. As a result, drivers provide critical context for analyzing signals, allowing practitioners to understand how a signal came to be and the implications it might have for the future.

Many organizations focus on futures and foresight, like the Futures Centre, an open, participatory futures community tracking signals and drivers of change to empower practitioners to create a more just and regenerative futures.

Strategic foresight uses signals and trends to describe the world to come. In 1979 and then 2002, the director of the U. Hawaii foresight Ph.D. program Jim Dator proposed a recurring group of images and stories that influence social change (Dator 2002). As illustrated in

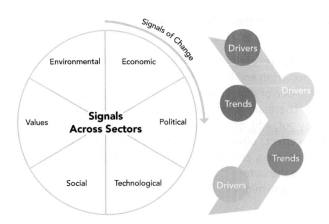

Figure 12.2
Scanning for signals
and drivers.

Figure 12.3 by Steve Santer, Dator proposed categorizing all futures narratives into four stories describing the trajectory of change:

1. Continuation (business, as usual, more of the status quo growth)
2. Limits and Discipline (behaviors to adapt to growing internal or environmental limits)
3. Decline and Collapse (system degradation or failure modes as crisis emerges)
4. Transformation (new technology, business, or social factors that change the game)

Figure 12.3
Scenario compass, with permissions by Steve Santer.

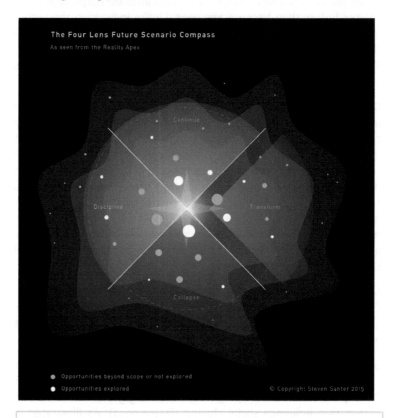

Futures Wheel

Once envisioned and the potential impacts unearthed, one can better articulate them as a leader.

1. Start at the center of the diagram and list the prospective event or trend occurring and how it might play out.
2. The first order of consequences often happens internally for a startup. There are boxes to describe various scenarios that might play out, add, or subtract as needed.
3. Secondary effects often are reserved for external stakeholders such as customers and perhaps broader community impacts. List those in the outer layer.
4. Discuss how you might build upon these scenarios and prepare for them.

More recent models of alternative futures draw inspiration from science fiction. Fergnani and Song propose six scenario archetypes systematic investigation of based on science fiction films, that encourage design-driven entrepreneurs to create provocative, bold, and surprising scenarios: Growth & Decay, Threats & New Hopes, Wasteworlds, The Powers That Be, Disarray, and Inversion (Fergnani and Song 2020)

Scenarios stretch our strategic options. They can create a conceptual wind tunnel where we can test how well our strategies will "fly" under various conditions. They can also help us break out of our habitual thinking to inspire innovation and help build resilience.

With signals, trends, and scenarios, design-driven entrepreneurs can think and act like futurists—developing multiple competing forecasts that describe different versions of the future. The advantage is to have clarity—not certainty—for future possibilities. Futurist, Jane McGonigal reminds us, to have strong opinions about the future but hold them lightly. In other words, don't be too convinced your future will happen but believe it will!

Once you have a plausible and provocative future scenario, you will want to evaluate the impacts—on your business and the world you want to enter. To generate insights into the impacts, we recommend the Futures Wheel Figure 12.4. First developed by Jerome

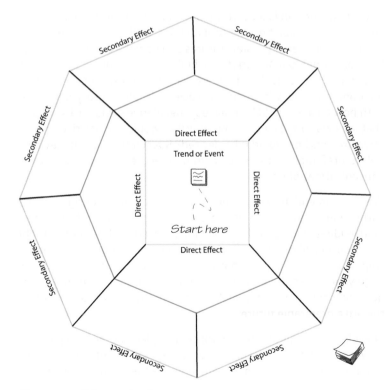

Figure 12.4 Futures wheel.

Glenn in 1972, the Futures Wheel is a diagram modeling how a (hypothetical) change is likely to directly affect your startup and sector. It moves on to a secondary and even tertiary level of indirect consequences.

Designing futures: Variations of speculative design

Designers have practices to help startups and incumbent firms better prepare and innovate, using various methods and graphic tools that complement the spreadsheets. These exercises are best when completed by transdisciplinary teams working together to approach from different perspectives. Remember that many stakeholders may not be on the same page or see the world similarly. As a leader, one is a part salesperson and part storyteller to build a consensus on the direction without resistance or misinterpretation.

Speculative design, sometimes called critical design or design fiction, zooms out beyond user-centered design to ask what effects our designs could have on future societies. Instrumental in bringing speculative design into design practice Anthony Dunne and Fiona Raby explain why this practice is critical: "Design today is concerned primarily with commercial and marketing activities, but it could operate on a more intellectual level. For example, it could place new technological developments within imaginary but believable everyday situations, allowing us to debate the implications of different technological futures before they happen."

Speculative design is a powerful precursor to prototyping. It's concerned with possibilities, not probabilities, pushing to consider preferences over a set of possible futures and how the objects we design help or hinder our attempts to build those futures. Speculative design helps us articulate how we want to interact with our future environment and within future society. While prototyping deals with how an idea could be realized, speculative design asks, what if that idea was prevalent in society? What would the positive or negative impacts be? Would it be desired? Speculative design may help define preferable futures for communities, economies, and even concentrations of power.

We recommend making time for future-oriented design sprints within your organization as the best way to transform these speculative ideas into something tangible. Questions like "What might nutrition look like in the future?" "How might we understand 'friendship' in the future?" or "What could the concept of money be like in 50 years?" can drive "speculative design sprints" that may spark new ideas for unique partnerships or form the basis of a movement toward a preferable future.

Speculative design practices inform your planning and preparation for whatever future may come. It encourages different points of view to enter the company mindset and educate the team and leadership

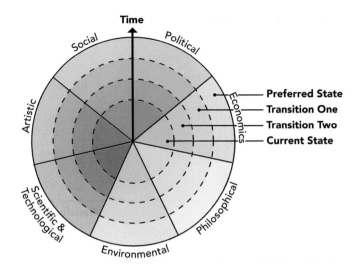

Time

Social

Political

Artistic

Economics

Scientific & Technological

Philosophical

Environmental

— Preferred State

— Transition One

— Transition Two

— Current State

Figure 12.5
Seven foundations of
worldbuilding, with
permissions by Leah
Zaidi.

about cultural shifts or changes occurring. Related tools and frame-works, like backcasting, can help plot a tactical road map to get to imaginary scenarios. For example, they might help innovate and create new business opportunities or help take precautions and stay alert to signals.

Worldbuilding: Designing stories of alternative futures

Worldbuilding is a metaphor we've been using throughout this book to convey with optimism the limitless possibilities to create a business that will be resilient and positively impact all.

Engaging in worldbuilding means imagining alternative futures with a diverse group of stakeholders, illustrated in Figure 12.5.

As designers in business, we imagine by asking "What if?" We do this across cultures, politics, weather, and more. Because we live in a global world, we must understand how situations can affect business in the near and far future to anticipate and protect stakeholders, the community, and the planet. It is also needed to innovate and anticipate upcoming shifts and changes, stay relevant, be prepared and forecast production needs several years out.

Often the design teams work in tandem with the business team in planning. Both disciplines involve a lot of imagination and extrapolation techniques to help organizations meet the needs of their communities and plan (Figure 12.6).

Once the team has gathered information, having periodic intel sessions baked into the culture and calendar as part of KPIs to display the value and importance of this work to your team and organization. When you gather for these workshops, leverage the power of visualization techniques, and draw connections out as a team exercise to help achieve results.

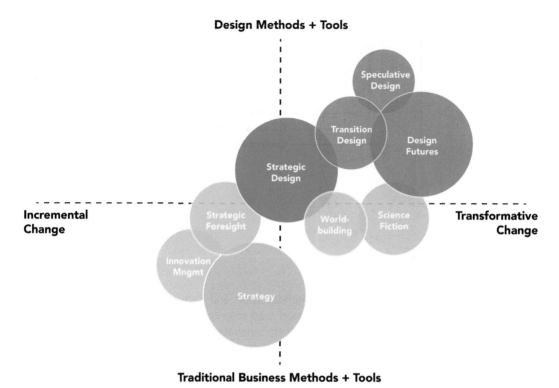

Figure 12.6 Spectrum of change-making practices for design-driven entrepreneurism.

Our preferred world: Circular and (re)generative

As design-driven entrepreneurs, we create businesses that are restorative by intention; we rely on renewable energy and eradicate waste. We go beyond the mechanics of producing and consuming goods and services to take insight and inspiration from living systems to optimize systems rather than the individual components. (See *Figure 12.7 Spheres of concern for the design-driven entrepreneur.*)

We seek to establish Environmental and Societal Governance (ESG) metrics that make headway to ensure our existence beyond the middle of the century. We know that we can't keep creating businesses with the same extractive playbook; we must do it more (re)generatively.

Our preferred world is circular and (re)generative. A regenerative economy differs from the prevailing linear model, based on the assumption that resources are abundant, disposable, and cheap. In this economic model, biological materials should always reenter the biosphere safely.

In contrast, technological materials should circulate without entering the biosphere at all.

Inspired by the earth and its many atmospheric layers that protect us, future businesses will have similar layers.

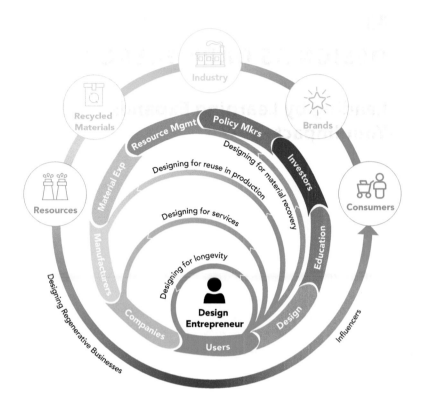

Figure 12.7
Spheres of concern for the design-driven entrepreneur.

Maintaining a multidimentional perspective

After each accomplishment, the way forward needs to be reevaluated because unanticipated consequences will have arisen. Strategic Designers lean into better futures, the goal is not to get to the endpoint but to discern the possibilities afforded by having shifted current conditions by inserting new designs or designed activities.

Navigational Log + Takeaways

- Embed strategic foresight methods into your culture to maintain resilience
- As a leader, practice an innovation mindset by developing a habit of surveying trends, drivers, and signals
- Practice speculative design for innovation and team agility
- As a regenerative design-driven entrepreneur, practice assessing the spheres of concern

13

DESIGN AS DARK ENERGY

Leading by Learning Expands Your Impact

Objectives

* Contextualize design to build your product *and* your leadership
* Demonstrate the value your learning culture brings for sustained employment + sense of purpose
* Discover why committing to a learning persona represents the design studio
* Be encouraged to create a living document to spearhead your culture

Expand your impact with mind and matter

By now, we hope we've demystified design-driven strategies for entrepreneurship. The message should be clear—design as a method and mindset should be incorporated into everything you do to unlock your full potential. It should be integrated into the business's core strategy, culture, mission, and vision. When this happens, you will lead your business to more transparent, open communications and reflection, delighted customers, engaged employees, sustainable communities, and greater profit with purpose. Mindset for maintaining a strategic design + innovation culture.

As we've seen throughout this book, innovation does not just happen. Ideas are the easy part. For companies to stay ahead of the curve and remain fresh, innovation must continually expand, tackling new problems and touching more people.

Design can expand the impact of your innovation like dark energy expands the universe (Figure 13.1).

Only 5% of our universe is visible. About 20% is made up of dark matter, the mass that keeps the universe in order by exerting a "gravitational pull" on everything. The remaining substance, dark energy, accounts for almost 70% of the universe. We can't see dark energy, we don't understand it, but we know it's out there. It pushes everything away from everything else at an ever-increasing speed. Dark energy is believed to be the source of the expansion of the universe.

DOI: 10.4324/9781003227151-18

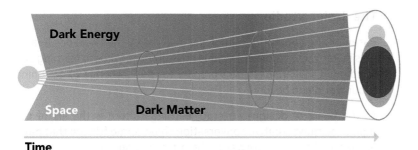

Figure 13.1 Dark matter and dark energy powers the entrepreneur's multiverse.

As part of a new generation of entrepreneurs, you will need to bring others toward you and simultaneously continue to expand your world by embracing others. Design as your dark energy can reframe your notion of the universe—from scarcity to abundance.

This is where the design studio comes into play because it is a well-spring of creative and cultural renewal, a crucible for individual and collective regeneration.

Whether as formed as a business plan or more abstract like a user experience storyboard, design entrepreneurs need to shift their mindset to cultivating regenerative ecosystems that create a shared value culture.(Figure 13.2).

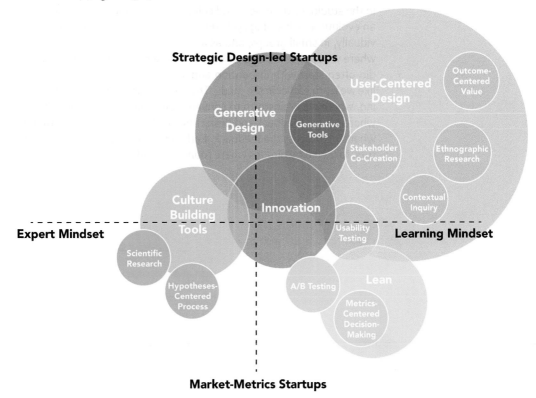

Figure 13.2 Mindset choices for maintaining a strategic design + innovation culture.

The design studio

Based on the apprentice model and inspired by the École des Beaux-Arts in Paris, the studio is a unique environment for both learning and bonding. It's where designers prepare for the challenge of designing in our world and beyond.

At the heart of design-centered learning-culture is the art of critique. The most creative conversations have some friction that must be resolved to move forward. The art of critique is honed through practice with others who also want to learn. In the studio, designers learn what Roberto Verganti describes as the power of critique to pivot on the path of innovation (Verganti 2016, 18–26). Critique helps bring new insights and breaks down old patterns of thinking.

The resolution of critique is all about converging on the thing you are trying to create, in this case: our businesses. Convergence doesn't mean compromise when designing with others (which is the distinctive feature of design vs. art). Instead, it means learning and adapting together. This give-and-take is being able to listen, see, acknowledge, and propose while holding strong opinions lightly. Critiquing and convergence result in a better product, service/experience, and a shared understanding with your team—and perhaps even a strengthened meaning of why you are pursuing your innovation.

In the studio, environment and culture are fostered through practicing an evolutionary learning cycle (Figure 13.3) where designers work individually, in small groups, and as a cohort through a series of activities where we apply the design methods. The sequential actions in the studio often start with inspiration and inquiry: where research happens, like we learn earlier in the guide. The next phase is imagining and creating, where we brainstorm to converge on an idea. Share and iterating: where we get feedback and desk crits. Lastly, reflecting and reframing: where we process the feedback. Early on, desk crits happen with mentors, followed by pin-ups where rounds of feedback occur.

Prepare to transition to the next evolutionary cycle

Inquire & Inspire
Step 1: Ignite the process by inquiring into your design world, and spark inspiration to build possible and preferred new worlds

Imagine & Create
Step 2: Imagine opportunities then co-create representations with your mentor to explore potential solutions

Share & Iterate
Step 3: Share your representations with peers or external reviewers to iterate the potential solutions

Reflect & Reframe
Step 4: Reflect on what you have learned about your design world, and reframe your perspectives (and yourself) to prepare for the next cycles of evolution

Figure 13.3 The design studio pedagogy An evolutionary learning cycle.

The final iteration is presented to the public for review and a final round of feedback. This is the culmination of the constant productive friction (Hagel and Brown 2005) and collaborative reflection and action is the centrifuge of a powerful educational experience. Participants gradually understand one another through the representations circumscribing their creative conversations.

At the core of the design studio is learning. Learning is the catalyst for renewing the individual mindset of the leader, the team, and your community, both internally and externally. Like a human nervous system, Figure 13.4 cultivating a social synapse, can shape your startup's culture to be prepared to reinvent itself on every level (individual and system-wide). You will need this because, most likely, the product or service offered today will not be the same in five or ten years.

Managing a learning culture with a systems approach isn't easy. As illustrated in Figure 13.2, the gravitational pull of expertise and metrics will pull you away from learning. However, develop it from the beginning rather than try to superimpose it after other behaviors set in. You will be more likely to evolve with the times, stay relevant, and grow at scale. Learning must be everywhere, and we believe there is no other world where learning permeates better than the Design Studio.

The design studio is a microcosm of the multiverse. Design researcher Donald A. Schön defined the studio as "a reflective practicum in designing" (1988, 4). Similar to Eli Blevis et al., who describe the architectural studio as "… creative, collaborative, and most of all highly material" (2007, 2821). In the Studio, Schön observed that design is not about problem-solving but "a reflective conversation with the materials of the situation" (1988, 4).

For Schön, design is to discover a framework of meaning in an indeterminate situation through practical operations in the case. This is the basis for practitioners who "reflect-in-action."

The studio environment exposes designers to what John Seely Brown and John Hagel describe as "productive friction"—in the form of continuous peer and customer feedback—provoking iterations on our solution delivery. Combined with reflection-in-action, each round of prototyping powers subsequent iterations, building innovation as the collaboration cycle continues. As a natural part of the collaboration, these behaviors trigger the neurological rewiring required for innovative thought and action. The innovator's need to communicate ideas to collaborators encourages experimentation and risk-taking. Their need to integrate different perspectives and iterate new versions ensures collaborators synchronize toward a common objective.

Lovesac: Culture built by design—Not by default

We know by now that design amplifies the entrepreneur's potential—but what does that look like over time and throughout a company's growth?

Lovesac is a direct-to-consumer eCommerce-led furniture brand with more than 100 "Lovesac" retail showrooms supporting its unique delivery model. Shawn Nelson, whom we met in an earlier chapter and the founder, started Lovesac over ten years before returning to school for his master's degree in Strategic Design and Management. Armed with a designerly mindset and design-driven methods, he created a unique strategy infused with living his values openly, building his secret sauce for maintaining an innovation culture. In addition, he leverages design methods to evolve a set of principles to align his team as he scales. He continues to support a strong, vibrant corporate culture that feels like a startup while publicly traded on NASDAQ.

Historically, we're used to seeing companies try to "center design" or prioritize design in culture. However, objectifying design as an entity or a concrete Lego block of your organization misses the point. It won't achieve the design-driven culture many organizations intend to do in the first place.

Why? Design is the fluid of the system and interconnects its pieces, and the studio is our real-world application to receive friction and feedback. We hear "systems design" and think of mechanical engineering or information architecture. Design is the holistic picture of what's going on across the nodes and the relationships informing the goal. Treating the design process in this book like a Lego block for your

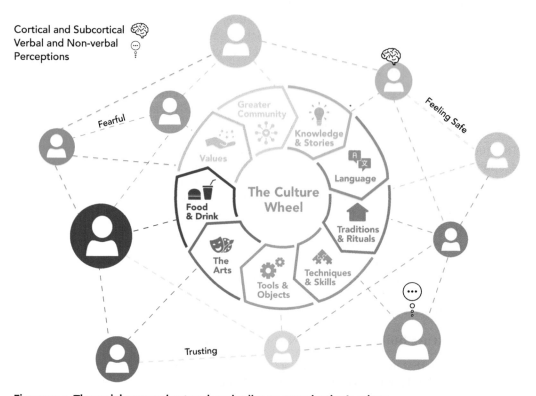

Figure 13.4 The social neuronal network embodies an organization's culture.

Figure 13.5
Shawn Nelson, founder
of Lovesac, meeting
with team members.
Photo credit:
Lovesac.

company is a start. Still, the depth and integration of design will arise from an understanding that design **is** your company. Your culture is a living, breathing design to bring life to your mission and vision.

Rather than dissecting an organization into moving process pieces, **Shawn is an example of what it looks like to center a design-driven life into an organization.** As a result, this provides him with the cultural resilience to sustain innovation, change, and adaptation.

Leadership in the studio: The design mentor

Being a design mentor is an ongoing practice as everyday co-creation. As a founder, you're both the recipient of design advice (and driver of iteration) and a design-led mentor for your organization. As a design mentor, your job is to recognize what a culture of innovation looks like and to reinvent business models. As practitioners of corporate innovation and entrepreneurship, we know from experience how hard it is to change organizations.

Companies structurally organized around a successful (pre-existing) business model find it more difficult to evolve. In an article for the Financial Times, the Undercover Economist notes that successful companies are more likely to struggle when innovations require them to change their organizational structures (Harford, *Financial Times*, 2018). As a design mentor, consider your business strategy as a hypothesis: a constantly updated proposition to test, rather than a static document you rigidly follow. The speed at which your overarching strategy can be deployed, and understood, in your teams— the more agility you can lead with. Let's call this rating your strategy velocity—how fast strategy permeates throughout your organization.

Imagine an organization that moves in perfect sync, with every member aligned toward a shared vision of the future. It's possible.

Sensing as a leader: A persona to build culture

"Upon reflection, that was the moment that really defined me as an entrepreneur, and I would only reflect on that 20 years later, not just having an idea but doing it now." Shawn's journey is the epitome of flowing between learning and practice, idea and execution that captures the essence of the studio. At the center of Lovesac's success as a thoroughly design-infused company is Shawn's commitment not only to the company but also to a deep and authentic understanding that the company is only as strong as his ability to weave culture: create a functional, flowing system in which the life and purpose of each player are acknowledged, independent, and yet executing the same goal with the same ethos on all touchpoints.

When Shawn talks about leadership, he acknowledges his winding path and the degree to which his company has evolved in and out of success. We introduced the persona tool in the Method Dimension. A persona functions beyond serving as a psychographic user; in Shawn's case, he also uses this to guide his leadership. While it may sound counterintuitive or manipulative to craft a leadership persona, it's a method and honest acknowledgment that leaders, like customer segments, have attributes that define their character. We require learning (and tools) as leaders as much as teams utilize tools in the workflow.

Shawn's commitment to learning is unparalleled and a great example of what it looks like to lead in a design-driven way: using design knowledge to inform leadership practice. He behaves like a design mentor or coach to his community. Designing a culture lays the road to company success while running the company. So co-create it with the community; this is part of what distinguishes a design-led culture from other models. If a persona represents a human psychographic profile, Shawn's persona is captured by strengths, gaps, and sensing to embody Lovesac's ethos.

- **Owned strengths:** Use these traits to inform what context to create, where to step up, and ways to maintain the character and ethos of the company.
- **Known gaps:** Use this assessment technique as part of your culture to inform what tactical knowledge to learn, what books to read, when to re-educate, and whom to hire. Having book clubs and participatory discussions on integrating new thinking into the company helps foster agency, ownership, and dedication to a learning culture within the community. Co-creating knowledge sessions and feedback loops are integral to identifying gaps, understanding what the pulse feels like, and utilizing the leader's strengths to respond to it.

- **Sensing:** Use this awareness to understand the ebb and flow of your internal organization by creating feedback loops for leadership and integrating strengths/gaps learning into your culture sensing. The sensing is like the pulse of blood flowing fluidly between strengths and gaps. Here we transition between "knowing" and "observing" and between "learning" and "sensing."

Startup energy: Building a living system

Getting employees to participate energetically in company culture and vision is key to maintaining a healthy sustained innovation culture at scale. This takes an agile stewardship mentality that implements strategic design methods, internally and externally.

Design is inherently perception and iteration within leadership, not just the work process. It can be applied to constructing our organization and not just developing our product or service. Design research as a sensing method within the organization can be implemented by co-creating meetings and registering feedback loops to inform what works and what doesn't. Instead of siloed teams, integrate small, agile cross-disciplinary teams of different members from different groups to help inform the larger organism.

Documenting the living system that works for you

For culture building, Shawn has a strategic guide to how Lovesac answers questions like, Why do we exist? What do we believe? This company is a living system. Shawn drives that ideal forward and has for nearly 20 years, breathing life into their mission and methods of sharing their vision. Over time, Shawn developed a 12-W's Framework as part of their manifesto, that has heuristically shaped their culture and evolution. This living document reflects, maps, and channels his living system. The framework guides him as a leader to carve the company's path through things like "why we do what we do," and defining the vision and mission. It also contains a set of processes determining the "how" they achieve their goals.

None of the questions in his framework are questions that require process explicitly. Still, he has built the evaluation and evolution of their answers into specific reviews and meetings periodically throughout the year.

More than just a framework, designing his roadmap to reference, as a personified leader, is used for both macro and micro: for guidance on the high-level strategic vision, and day-to-day tactical to center cultural behaviors. Shawn has designed this document to serve the persona he embodies as a leader, while also integrating it into monthly company-wide meetings around performance goals and values. In addition, he revisits and constantly edits to keep it fresh and to meet the demands of a rapidly evolving socio-political-environmental economy.

A design-centered culture implies bringing in the creative studio mindset that fosters exploration instead of efficiency. There is a time and place for efficiency. When appropriate, encourage and appreciate an embedded understanding in your culture that explores new methods or practices, such as software. A culture that values experimentation and active reflection is key to maintaining an innovation culture. Like being in a classroom, this means that leadership, like a teacher, needs to go out of its way to commend, positively point out, and foster these behaviors in their team members. Whether the team is successful is less the point because the encouragement of stepping up is to try something new.

Leading by learning

Creating a design-centered learning culture requires more than treating employees well, offering work-life balance options, or allowing experimentation and failure. It's first and foremost about building a culture around trust; this is no easy feat. Creating environments where individuals can be vulnerable, learn and grow needs a community that values and encourages self-awareness, self-actualization, and education. On the macro level, centering learning at the core of a business allows flexibility to pivot as needed, cultivating a mentoring, caring community based on knowledge, science, and wisdom. Individually, it will enable the team members to feel nurtured, heard, and envision their long-term career building and development. Finally, it creates positive feedback loops, encouraging each other instead of competing with or criticizing one another.

As a leader, take time to understand what each team member aspires to be or do in your organization, then help your employees set those plans in motion. Connecting staff with leadership training, cross-training, and continuing education fosters a work culture where people can reach their professional goals.

If you want them to stay, don't let talented people stagnate at your firm. Instead, build a culture that emphasizes continuous learning and provides on-the-job development opportunities. As you add team members and partner organizations who have common goals, think of this essential team-building exercise as building a community. Think about the critical enablers, skills, and characteristics needed to reach your North Star, bring your mission and vision to life, and live your values daily.

You might still be at the early stage with only a founding team, but growth can happen fast. So be strategic and plan for what your mission, vision, and culture look like when you've hired two, three, five, and then ten more people. Before long, the team will be co-creating, building out, and iterating on the initial vision.

Make work meaningful

Talented people want to be in jobs that make the best use of their abilities and give them a sense of accomplishment. Employees must understand how their work impacts the firm's purpose and bottom line or triple bottom line. Help them see the connection between what they do, the company's core mission, and broader business goals. The traditional human resource (HR) processes of staff meetings, performance reviews, and regular check-ins provide opportunities for established companies to explain how employee contributions benefit the business.

While the new generation of entrepreneurs expects a different social contract: continual dialogue, open conversations, and constant feedback enabled by technologies. These are the actions of a farmer tilling the soil, fertilizing the ground, planting, and harvesting an abundance of commitment to a shared purpose. Engaging people to co-create something new is never easy. Still, with deliberate actions and a compelling purpose, one can help those in the ecosystem make something more meaningful than if everyone continued to operate alone. Once designerly mindsets are embedded, daily life should be filled with a higher purpose and many meaningful moments. But to grow a company means to develop its culture.

Leading beyond agility

The dynamic disruptions of our current economy dictate organizations' need to be nimble. Yet humans need homeostasis, a balanced ecosystem, and harmony within discord. We need a paradigm that balances opposite and equal conditions at the same time. It is a paradox, but good organizations can master this. They consciously design their ecosystem to be dynamic and responsive, enabling capacities to adapt quickly to new challenges and opportunities.

These practices and mindsets necessitate leaders to go beyond agility. Therefore, we recommend leaders seek to lead beyond skill and internal feedback loops to a broader holistic point of view and interaction. At the Elab, (Figure 13.6) we see these as fundamentally

Figure 13.6
Parsons Elab studio workshop, mentor, and designers collaborating.
Photo credit: Elab.

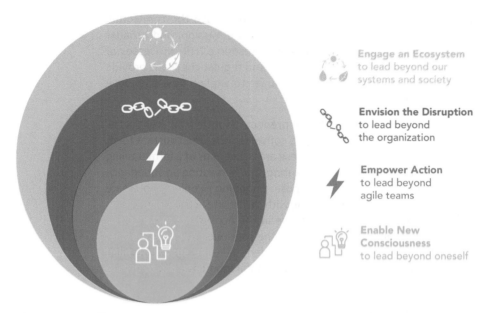

Engage an Ecosystem
to lead beyond our
systems and society

Envision the Disruption
to lead beyond
the organization

Empower Action
to lead beyond
agile teams

Enable New
Consciousness
to lead beyond oneself

Figure 13.7 Leading beyond agility: Holistic leadership.

different ways leaders can shape organizations to prepare for the new ways of working required in an uncertain world.

A leader should begin by finding a resonant purpose that offers an opportunity to change the systems and constraints we function within. In the face of wicked problems, such as sustainability, education, and health, leaders should engage an ecosystem to lead beyond our current systems and society. A movement seeking transformative change can bring new meaning to our working methods. The leaders who attract people around a common goal will be the ones who bring society together for collective impact. Holistic leadership transcends traditional boundaries that prevent systemic collaboration. Empowered actions enabled by information transparency democratize ways of working, flooding the dated dependencies of hierarchy with openness and trust.

Leaders can envision leading beyond the organization with a resonant purpose to confront disruption (Figure 13.7). Spanning the boundaries of an increasingly complex and uncertain world is necessary to cultivate communities with a shared purpose that can collectively solve the new challenges facing customers. We know that teams whose members can span boundaries and get to know one another more deeply perform better. Fundamental to enabling boundary spanning is information transparency.

With an engaged team seeking purpose with profit, holistic leaders can empower action within the group to lead beyond internal agility, find partners and connect within the greater system. However, in our experience, having better conversations every day is more important. An improved dialogue, characterized by critique and candor, changes the conversation, which influences the culture of the ecosystem. Heightened presence and persistent resilience are essential in an ever-complex, ever-evolving ecosystem. We have observed that leaders who can raise cognitive and spiritual awareness will be better prepared for the fluidity of work in the digital era. Seeking biases will increase a leader's agility in learning, unlearning, and relearning. As leaders reach higher levels of consciousness, the emergence of shared consciousness—characterized by a common language, heightened empathy, and constant resilience—moves the collective to synchronized action.

Documenting the living system

To bring the culture building together, Shawn has a strategic guide to how Lovesac answers questions like, Why do we exist? What do we believe? This company is a living system. Shawn drives that ideal forward and has for nearly 20 years, breathing life into their mission and methods of sharing their vision. Over time, Shawn developed a 12-W's Framework as part of their manifesto, that has heuristically shaped their culture and evolution. This living document reflects, maps, and channels his living system. The framework guides him as a leader to carve the com- pany's path through things like "why we do what we do," and defining the vision and mission. It also contains a set of processes determining the "how" they achieve their goals.

None of the questions in his framework are questions that require process explicitly. Still, he has built the evaluation and evolution of their answers into specific reviews and meetings periodically throughout the year.

More than just a framework, designing his roadmap to reference, as a personified leader, is used for both macro and micro: for guidance on the high-level strategic vision, and day-to-day tactical to center cultural behaviors. Shawn has designed this document to serve the persona he embodies as a leader, while also integrating it into monthly com- pany-wide meetings around performance goals and values. In addi- tion, he revisits and constantly edits to keep it fresh and to meet the demands of a rapidly evolving socio-political-environmental economy.

The precedent of collective, iterative alignment can be drawn together with tools, like Shawn built for himself, with a Team Alignment Map. This can kick off the dialogue and facilitate alignment—much like we see in our early-stage process chapters to align around mission. The repeated cycle of iteration reoccurs to generate momentum forward, incrementally supporting change + alignment.

A team alignment document

Creating an alignment document helps gain calibration across teams, and even individual relationships. Expect to give more time for more people. Consider the future of this document: could this serve as a template for your company? For this type of relationship?

First steps:

1. Establish the relationship on the table.
2. Jointly agree on the purpose: what is your shared objective?
3. Determine how often you will meet: what synchronous time is necessary?
4. Determine the nature of accountability: what do I owe you and you owe me?
5. Set up clear lines of communication: when can we expect to hear from each other?
6. Clarify the level of confidentiality: who can we invite into this process?
7. Agree upon lengths of time: what is our timeline?
8. Occasionally, evaluate process, effectiveness, inclusion, sustainability, and ethics: what are our governing metrics of success?
9. Calculate expectations for the current situation: what's our deliverable?
10. Bring closure to the relationship: what threshold signifies a need to revisit this document?

This can also be done in a workshop with your teams and include more detail:

- Goals: Define what the objectives are: what does success look like?
- Liabilities: What are the inherent risks? What could stop us?
- What are the responsibilities and joint commitments?
- What are the skills and resources required?

Reinvent yourself by cultivating a future-forward team

Designing in the multiverse depends on your ability to evolve while not succumbing to the entrapment of evolution, your ability to grow while avoiding the excesses of a growth economy. Cognitive capabilities like clear communication, decision-making, curiosity, and compassion are essential but insufficient to ensure your ability to navigate the multiverse. Instead, we recommend thinking and acting across spectrums—balancing the extremes confronting every entrepreneur. Profit vs. purpose, sufficient vs. perfect, now vs. the future, and independence vs. interdependence. The list of contradictions in the multiverse is endless. Your ability to span the spectrums is essential when designing generative businesses in the complexities of our world today.

Neurologically speaking, you may even see your mind as a multiverse. Each world can reveal new insights, but colliding worlds will bring even more. Learning at its core is all about breaking the boundaries

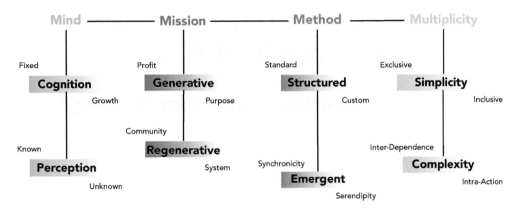

Figure 13.8 The spectrums of choices for the next generation of design-driven entrepreneurs.

of current understanding. If this becomes part of your North Star, you set a trajectory to go beyond where you are and, more importantly, who you are.

Spanning spectrums requires continually redefining and reinventing yourself (Figure 13.8). The real power of diversity is when you continually question who you are, what motivates you, and why is the impact you seek more significant than yourself. When you jump the dimensions of the multiverse, you can only go as far as your mind can see.

Navigational Log + Takeaways

- Be familiar with the design studio and its influence in/on design practice
- Strive to be iterative as a leader
- Understand mentorship as central to your role
- Center learning for a meaningful, agile culture
- Get in the practice of utilizing team alignment documents

Conclusion

BEGIN AGAIN, CULTIVATE A CULTURE OF RENEWAL

Mobilizing a movement, by design

Are you ready to (re)generate? Then go beyond sustainability

According to the U.N. report, Our Common Future (Brundtland 1987), more than half of humanity's total historical fossil fuel emissions (since records began in 1751) had already occurred since 1987. This was the year the concept of sustainability was launched into the mainstream.

In the last 50 years, we have lost a significant portion of the world's flora and fauna, crucial to our planetary ecosystem's function and food production. But, as Katrin Kaufer and Otto Scharmer depict in Figure 14.1, this is only the tip of one iceberg. The ecological divide is adjacent to a social and spiritual divide. These divides, or cracks in our multiverse, are inflated by bubbles of bloated mental frames—that we need more growth, wealth, technology, consumption, and ownership. They propose becoming more aware of our current ego-centric mindset and transitioning to an eco-centric mindset.

This book to inspire a new generation of entrepreneurs to adopt design approaches that contribute to regenerating our broken systems and creating shared value. The Elab and author team hopes it will open pathways that amplify the global shift toward a more regenerative world by working together to design purpose-driven systemic solutions. The responsibilities of a new generation of entrepreneurs will have to push further than sustainable design into the birth of new models that understand impact on systems before building. We call on *generative design* as our preliminary pathway forward. It creates new opportunities for an ever-expanding ecosystem of entrepreneurs, change-makers, and people with purpose as their passion. Be it reforming how healthcare or social welfare is delivered, changing supply chain production methods, or designing with inclusive voices, we hope they inspire you to join us on a positive pathway to a new, more just, and verdant economy, one startup at a time. We can accelerate the next step to innovate the biosystems of the planet and all

DOI: 10.4324/9781003227151-19

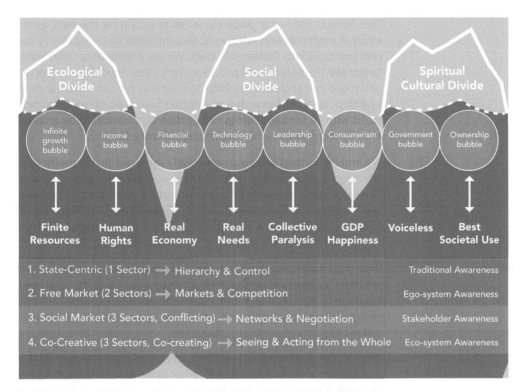

1. State-Centric (1 Sector) ➡ Hierarchy & Control	Traditional Awareness
2. Free Market (2 Sectors) ➡ Markets & Competition	Ego-system Awareness
3. Social Market (3 Sectors, Conflicting) ➡ Networks & Negotiation	Stakeholder Awareness
4. Co-Creative (3 Sectors, Co-creating) ➡ Seeing & Acting from the Whole	Eco-system Awareness

Figure 14.1
Leading from the emerging future.
From Ego-System to Eco-System Economies, by Katrin Kaufer and Otto Scharmer.

its inhabitants. We need to go beyond sustainability because the long-term impact of such practices is dependent on regenerative cultures—models that we, still yet, are conceiving.

Navigating spaceship earth through a multiverse

Buckminster Fuller's 1969 classic *Operating Manual For Spaceship Earth* is our inspirational metaphor for entrepreneurs who seek to innovate in a multiverse. The book relates Earth to a spaceship flying through space: noting the lack of any user manual to help Earthlings steward this ship, Fuller offers guidance to understand, manage, preserve, and sustain our spaceship, which has a finite amount of resources and cannot be resupplied. As Fuller writes, "The designed omission of the instruction book on how to operate and maintain spaceship earth and its complex life-supporting and regenerating systems has forced the man to discover retrospectively just what his most important forward capabilities are" (Fuller 2008, 62). While we've provided you a handbook with human-centered tools, we can't give you a manual—your mission, purpose, and drive will write your instructions.

Designing in the multiverse requires *knowing who we are and what we want*. Navigating our ship toward creating a preferred future, including purpose with profit, requires clarity of intention. A future of regenerative worlds that thrive across all boundaries despite all communities' challenges involves resilience.

This book is not just a guide but a call to action for the next generation of entrepreneurs who want to contribute to transitioning current practices into sustainable ones. We are a generation who wants to remake the policies and processes to nurture equitable enterprises and more just societies. By helping humans, we can inspire a more symbiotic relationship with Gaia (Mother Earth), which seeks homeostasis with all sentient beings rather than dominance. To be empowered by technology rather than being controlled by it.

We amplify human and environmentally centered design methods of building your company in order to shape your trajectory using generative value: the production of value not just for your users, but for your stakeholders and their own objectives. Generating a rippling effect of beneficial, positive, and impact-forward effects will catapult us closer toward the agency + intention required to *re*-generate.

With this handbook, should you be inspired with increased agency to maintain a planetary perspective, provoke what-could-be, and yes—continue to iterate, adapt and adjust! You are now equipped to drive re-generative value with sustainable solutions by being systematically engaged and spiritually connected.

With a post-Anthropocene era as a preferred future in mind, what could our role be, and specifically, what dimensions can we influence to spark a movement? Not only to enable our survival but also to cultivate the conditions to live and thrive in abundance. **Designing a movement is 3-Dimensional: passionately pursuing sustainable design-led solutions and systemic approaches, and spiritual connection to design's dark energy.**

Sustainable, design-led solutions: Embedded in all our missions should be to design sustainable solutions across all sectors, with a consideration of what sustainable means to our company, and our business. One inspiring example of systemic and sustainable solutions is architect Stefano Boeri's Bosco Verticale (vertical forests) residential buildings (Boeri 2022). One high-rise building developed

A regenerative design-driven entrepreneur.

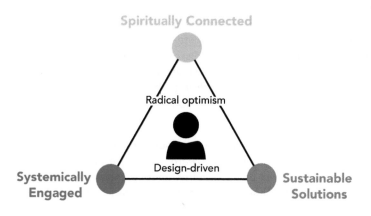

in Eindhoven has over 900 trees, is self-sufficient, uses renewable energy from solar panels, and filters wastewater to sustain the facilities and plant life. This is a compelling example of the architectural design community creating circular and sustainable solutions. It reduces carbon footprint, contributing to shifting our professions toward more sustainable ways of being. Sustainable solutions are ones that consider their implications of use, resources required, and can sustain value over time.

Systemically engaged: If we are to design a movement to accelerate the transition to a post-Anthropocene era, we will need to create new systems of interaction. This requires designing new economic, educational, legal, governance, and social systems. Sooner rather than later, we will need to create new political systems that maintain the core tenets of democracy, but incorporate technologies that empower citizens to converge on preferred futures. To be systematically engaged is to not just consider the dynamic elements and goals of our system, but to incorporate them as we consider what we're building and why.

Spiritually connected: Creating transcendence drives internal motivations and purpose of being, like the wisdom of forests, which according to Suzanne Simard, a Professor of Forest Ecology, operate as a single organism wired for care (Simard 2022). The future is about being able to engage people to overcome the neurological biases that we all carry. This way, we create a new system that goes through the spheres of awareness to help us develop a collective consciousness. One characterized by belonging and rational compassion, embracing diversity, and helping create ecosystems that embrace earth in a way that encourages acceptance, grows the commons, and produces abundance for all.

To make the world's pie bigger and awaken an awareness that this doesn't need to be a different kind of competition. Instead, we redesign the fundamental concepts of wealth, equality, competition, community, opportunities, availability, and business models. Only the next generation can spark a movement to use design to build a better future.

Be a future-maker—Write a personal manifesto

Manifestos are decrees that inspire and rally people around a mission and articulate your driving purpose. We encourage your final activity to co-create a manifesto. What will the world look back on your mission fulfilling? How powerfully might you chart your trajectory forward?

- What do you believe in?
- What are you passionate about?
- What are you committed to, and why?
- How will you achieve this?
- What are your principles?

These dimensions are what R. Buckminster Fuller encouraged us to do over 50 years ago. He had the foresight to see where unbridled innovation would take us and the mindset to forecast how building boundaries between disciplines would hinder collective action.

Today, we call on neuroscientists, social activists, designers, economists, entrepreneurs, citizens, and community leaders to make decisions and take actions that set us out on pathways toward preferred futures. Design should ensure that the solutions we create are meaningful for humanity. But we cannot stop there. We can use design to cultivate the shared leadership needed to mobilize people for the great transition to a more holistic, inclusive, and regenerative world.

Join the movement to make our future!

References

Introduction

deGrasse Tyson, Neil. "What is Dark Matter? What is Dark Energy?" YouTube. Accessed June 10, 2022. https://youtu.be/uBbxXNhZ78c

Figueres, Christiana, and Tom Rivett-Carnac. *The Future We Choose: The Stubborn Optimist's Guide to the Climate Crisis*. London: Manilla Press, 2021.

Fuller, R. Buckminster, and Jaime Snyder. Operating Manual for Spaceship Earth. Zurich: Lars Müller Publishers, 1969 & reprinted 2008.

Fullerton, John. "8 Principles for a Regenerative Civilization." Films For Action. Accessed June 10, 2022. https://www.filmsforaction.org/articles/regenerative-economies-for-a-regenerative-civilization/

Giovannetti, Manuela, Luciano Avio, Paola Fortuna, Elisa Pellegrino, Cristiana Sbrana, and Patrizia Strani. At the root of the wood wide web: Self recognition and non-self incompatibility in mycorrhizal networks. *Plant Signaling and Behavior*, 1(1), pp. 1–5, 2006.

Mazzucato, Mariana. *Mission Economy: A Moonshot Guide to Changing Capitalism*. New York, NY: Harper Business, an imprint of HarperCollins Publishers, 2021.

Rittel, Horst, and Melvin M. Webber. Dilemmas in a general theory of planning. *Policy Sciences*, 4(2), pp. 155–169, 277, 1973.

Ward, Barbara. *Spaceship Earth*. New York, NY: Columbia University Press, 1966.

Chapter 1

Alexander, Jones, Mysore. *Managing Vulnerability and Uncertainty: Building designerly ways of doing within non-designer teams*. Co-Authors: Rhea Alexander, Sarah Jones and Vinay Kumar Mysore Publication Number: ISSN 2632004-5 (online), (2019, 1552).

Buchanan, Richard. Wicked problems in design thinking. *Design Issues*, 8(2), pp. 5–21, 1992.

Schön, Donald A., and Martin Rein. *Frame Reflection: Toward the Resolution of Intractable Policy Controversies*. New York, NY: Basic Books, 1994.

Swart, Tara. *The Source: The Secrets of the Universe and the Science of the Brain*. New York, NY: HarperCollins Publishers, 2019.

Chapter 2

Avery, Dan. "Google Combines 225 Million Images to Create the Most Detailed 3D Map Ever of the Human Brain." Daily Mail Online. Associated Newspapers, June 7, 2021. https://www.dailymail.co.uk/sciencetech/article-9660835/Google-combines-225-million-images-create-detailed-3D-map-human-brain.html

Dweck, Carol S. *Mindset: The New Psychology of Success*. New York, NY: Ballantine Books, 2016.

Greenberg, Sarah S. *Creative Acts for Curious People: How to Think, Create, and Lead in Unconventional Ways*. Berkeley, CA: Ten Speed Press, 2021.

Norton, Michael, Daniel Mochon, and Dan Ariely. "*The IKEA Effect: When Labor Leads to Love.*" *Journal of Consumer Psychology*, 22, pp. 453–460, 2011.

O'Connor, Elizabeth. *Search for Silence*. Waco, TX: Word Books, 1972.

Papanek, Victor J. *Design for the Real World: Human Ecology and Social Change*. New York, NY: Random House, Inc., 1971

Riel, Jennifer, and Roger L. Martin. *Creating Great Choices: A Leader's Guide to Integrative Thinking*. Boston, MA: Harvard Business Review Press, 2017.

Schön, Donald A. *Educating the Reflective Practitioner*. San Francisco, CA: Jossey-Bass, 1995.

Senge, Peter M. *The Fifth Discipline: The Art and Practice of the Learning Organization*. London: Random House Business, 2006.

Chapter 3

Covey, Stephen R. *The 7 Habits of Highly Effective People*. Provo, UT: Franklin Covey, 1998.

Kaufman, Scott B. "Sailboat Metaphor." N.d. Accessed June 10, 2022. https://scottbarrykaufman.com/sailboat-metaphor/

Maslow, Abraham H. A theory of human motivation. *Psychological Review, 50*(4), pp. 370–396, 1943. Accessed June 10, 2022. https://doi.org/10.1037/h0054346

Mazzucato, Mariana. *Mission Economy: A Moonshot Guide to Changing Capitalism*. New York, NY: Harper Business, an imprint of HarperCollins Publishers, 2021.

Nieto-Rodriguez, Antonio. *How to prioritize your company's projects*. Harvard Business Review, 2016. Accessed June 10, 2022. https://hbr.org/2016/12/how-to-prioritize-your-companys-projects

Porter, Michael. Creating shared value. *Harvard Business Review*, 2011. Accessed June 10, 2022. https://hbr.org/2011/01/the-big-idea-creating-shared-value

Chapter 4

Schnall, Marianne. *Forbes, How to Bounce Back*. November 14, 2018. https://www.forbes.com/sites/marianneschnall/2018/11/14/billie-jean-king-on-leadership-and-making-a-difference/?sh=57d9fbb445a2

U.S. Bureau of Labor Statistics. "Survival of Private Sector Establishments by Opening Year." 2022. Accessed June 10, 2022. https://www.bls.gov/bdm/us_age_naics_00_table7.txt

Wahl, Daniel Christian. *Designing Regenerative Cultures*. Axminster: Triarchy Press, 2016.

Chapter 5

Holmes, Kat, and John Maeda. *Mismatch: How Inclusion Shapes Design*. Cambridge: The MIT Press, 2018.

SHRM. "Shaping an Ethical Workplace Culture." SHRM Foundation's Effective Practice Guidelines Series, 2022. Accessed June 16, 2022. https://www.shrm.org/hr-today/trends-and-forecasting/special-reports-and-expert-views/Documents/Ethical-Workplace-Culture.pdf

Swart, Tara. *The Source: The Secrets of the Universe, the Science of the Brain*. New York, NY: Harper One, an imprint of HarperCollins Publishers, 2020.

Chapter 6

Kluser, Stéphane UNEP Emerging Issues: Global Honey Bee Colony Disorder and Other Threats to Insect Pollinators, 2010. https://www.unep.org/resources/report/unep-emerging-issues-global-honey-bee-colony-disorder-and-other-threats-insect

Chapter 7

Brown, Tim. *Change by Design: How Design Thinking Transforms Organizations and Inspires Innovation*. New York, NY: Harper Collins, 2009.
Clear, James. *Atomic Habits: An Easy & Proven Way to Build Good Habits & Break Bad Ones*. New York, NY: Penguin Random House, 2018.
IDEO. "Design Thinking Defined," 2022. Accessed June 10, 2022. https://designthinking.ideo.com/
Nelson, Harold G., and Erik Stolterman. *The Design Way Second Edition: Intentional Change in an Unpredictable World*. Cambridge: MIT Press, 2012.

Chapter 8

Tufte, Edward. *Envisioning Information*. Cheshire, CT: Graphic Press, 76, 1990.

Chapter 9

Alexander, Rhea A., and Darcy Keester. Experience. *The Six Dimensions of Online Learning Experiences*. Germany: Konigshausen & Neumann, 138–140. CC-BY-SA 4.0, 2021.
Stolterman, Erik, and Harold G. Nelson. *The Design Way Second Edition: Intentional Change in an Unpredictable World*. Cambridge: MIT Press, 2012.

Chapter 10

Porter, Michael E. *Competitive Advantage: Creating and Sustaining Superior Performance*. New York, NY: The Free Press, 1985.
Raworth, Kate. *Doughnut Economics: Seven Ways to Think Like a 21st Century Economist*. London: Penguin Random House, 2017.

Chapter 11

Potter, Mary. "Brain Can 'See' in the Blink of an Eye: Study." *The Economic Times*, 2014. https://economictimes.indiatimes.com/brain-can-see-in-the-blink-of-an-eye-study/articleshow/28953796.cms?from=mdr

Chapter 12

Dator, James Allen. *Advancing Futures: Futures Studies in Higher Education*. Westport, CT: Praeger, 2002.
Fergnani, Alessandro, and Zhaoli Song. The six scenario archetypes framework: A systematic investigation of science fiction films set in the future." *Futures*, 124(2020): 102645, 2020. https://doi.org/10.1016/j.futures.2020.102645

Chapter 13

Blevis, Eli, Youn-kyung Lim, Erik Stolterman, Tracee Vetting Wolf, and Keichi Sato. "Supporting Design Studio Culture in HCI." *CHI '07 Extended Abstracts on Human Factors in Computing Systems*, 2007. https://doi.org/10.1145/1240866.1241086

Hagel, John, and Brown, John Seely Productive friction: How difficult business partnerships can accelerate innovation." *Harvard Business Review*, February 2005. https://hbr.org/2005/02/productive-friction-how-difficult-business-partnerships-can-accelerate-innovation

Harford, Tim. "Why Big Companies Squander Good Ideas." *Financial Times*, September 6, 2018. https://www.ft.com/content/3c1ab748-b09b-11e8-8d14-6f049d06439c

Schön, Donald A. Designing: Rules, types and worlds. *Design Studies*, 9(3), pp. 181–190, 1988. https://doi.org/10.1016/0142-694x(88)90047-6

Verganti, Roberto. The innovative power of criticism. *Harvard Business Review*, 94, pp. 18–26, 2016.

Conclusion

Brundtland, Gro Harlem. *Report of the World Commission on Environment and Development: "Our Common Future."* New York, NY: United Nations, 1987.

Fuller, R. Buckminster, and Jaime Snyder. *Operating Manual for Spaceship Earth*. Zurich: Lars Müller Publishers, 1969 & reprinted 2008.

"Trudo Vertical Forest." Stefano Boeri Architetti, June 20, 2022. https://www.stefanoboeriarchitetti.net/en/project/trudo-vertical-forest/

Simard, Suzanne. *Finding the Mother Tree: Discovering the Wisdom of the Forest*. New York, NY: Vintage Books, a division of Penguin Random House, LLC, 2022.

Index

Note: Page numbers in *italics* refer to figures.